MONEY
TALKS

Psychoanalysis in a New Key Book Series
Volume 13

PSYCHOANALYSIS IN A NEW KEY BOOK SERIES

DONNEL STERN

Series Editor

When music is played in a new key, the melody does not change, but the notes that make up the composition do: change in the context of continuity, continuity that perseveres through change. "Psychoanalysis in a New Key" publishes books that share the aims psychoanalysts have always had, but that approach them differently. The books in the series are not expected to advance any particular theoretical agenda, although to this date most have been written by analysts from the Interpersonal and Relational orientations.

The most important contribution of a psychoanalytic book is the communication of something that nudges the reader's grasp of clinical theory and practice in an unexpected direction. "Psychoanalysis in a New Key" creates a deliberate focus on innovative and unsettling clinical thinking. Because that kind of thinking is encouraged by exploration of the sometimes-surprising contributions to psychoanalysis of ideas and findings from other fields, "Psychoanalysis in a New Key" particularly encourages interdisciplinary studies. Books in the series have married psychoanalysis with dissociation, trauma theory, sociology, and criminology. The series is open to the consideration of studies examining the relationship between psychoanalysis and any other field—for instance, biology, literary and art criticism, philosophy, systems theory, anthropology, and political theory.

But innovation also takes place within the boundaries of psychoanalysis, and "Psychoanalysis in a New Key" therefore also presents work that reformulates thought and practice without leaving the precincts of the field. Books in the series focus, for example, on the significance of personal values in psychoanalytic practice, on the complex interrelationship between the analyst's clinical work and personal life, on the consequences for the clinical situation when patient and analyst are from different cultures, and on the need for psychoanalysts to accept the degree to which they knowingly satisfy their own wishes during treatment hours, often to the patient's detriment.

MONEY
TALKS

in therapy, society, and life

Edited by
BRENDA BERGER
STEPHANIE NEWMAN

Routledge
Taylor & Francis Group
New York   London

Routledge   Routledge
Taylor & Francis Group   Taylor & Francis Group
711 Third Avenue   27 Church Road
New York, NY 10017   Hove, East Sussex BN3 2FA

© 2012 by Taylor and Francis Group, LLC
Routledge is an imprint of Taylor & Francis Group, an Informa business

Printed in the United States of America on acid-free paper
10 9 8 7 6 5 4 3 2 1

International Standard Book Number: 978-0-415-89170-7 (Hardback) 978-0-415-89171-4 (Paperback)

Library of Congress Cataloging-in-Publication Data

Money talks : in therapy, society, and life / edited by Brenda Berger, Stephanie
  Newman. -- 1st ed.
      p. cm. -- (Psychoanalysis in a new key ; 13)
  Includes bibliographical references and index.
  ISBN 978-0-415-89170-7 (hardcover : alk. paper) -- ISBN 978-0-415-89171-4
  (pbk. : alk. paper) -- ISBN 978-0-203-81911-1 (e-book)
  1. Money--Psychological aspects. 2. Finance, Personal. I. Berger, Brenda. II.
  Newman, Stephanie, 1964-

  HG222.3.M667 2011
  150.19'5--dc22   2011006860

Visit the Taylor & Francis Web site at
http://www.taylorandfrancis.com

and the Routledge Web site at
http://www.routledgementalhealth.com

Contents

Acknowledgments

We would like to express our deep appreciation to our series editor, Donnel Stern, for his encouragement, support, and expert guidance throughout the development of this collection, from discussing our early ideas to the final birth of the book. Many thanks also to Irwin Hirsch for leading us to Donnel. Kristopher Spring at Routledge has been a gracious delight to work with and has made everything we have asked for somehow easier. Judith Simon, our project editor, has also been very helpful and kind.

The authors who talk so directly and openly in the chapters of this book have truly educated us, both clinically and theoretically. Many thanks to all of you for being such fine and stimulating teachers. Thanks also for your honesty, elegant thinking and writing, enthusiasm, and the professional way in which you worked.

Our thanks go to Dr. Jean Petrucelli, director of the Eating Disorders, Compulsions and Addictions Service at The William Alanson White Institute, for her conference "Money Matters: The Collapse of Consciousness." It was there in 2010 that we heard presentations of a few of our authors, Drs. Dimen and Hirsch, and Dan Grech. Thank you, Bruce Giarraffa, for your technical help around this conference.

We also express our appreciation to Routledge for their permission to reprint Dr. Muriel Dimen's paper and to *Contemporary Psychoanalysis*, journal of the William Alanson White Psychoanalytic Society and William Alanson White Institute, New York, for allowing us to include Kachina Myers's paper in this collection.

To our friends, colleagues, and family who talked through concepts or offered helpful editing advice: To Drs. Shelley Orgel, Paul and Anna Ornstein, Alon Gratch, Michele Sacks, and Ivor Shapiro, we express our warm thanks for being so responsive to our work. To Wednesday Martin, who made many helpful suggestions about proposal writing and book publishing, we express our appreciation. Thank you so much Stephen Kling for your generous gift of our beautifully designed cover.

Stephanie Newman would like to acknowledge Sheila and Joel Newman for their help and support along the way, and Arianne and Peyton Levine who provide a daily source of awe and inspiration to her. Brenda Berger warmly thanks her daughter Annie for her editorial savvy and steady love.

Finally, and importantly, we are grateful to our husbands, Joe Berger and Michael Levine, for all the support they gave us: emotional, creative, technical. We especially want to acknowledge Joe's generous reading and wise counsel and Michael's silver tongue—without it we might still be searching for a proper title for the collection. We deeply appreciate their special care and steadfast engagement all along the way.

Brenda Berger, PhD
Stephanie Newman, PhD

Contributors

Brenda Berger, PhD (coeditor), is a clinical psychologist and psychoanalyst and practices in New York City and Larchmont. She is a clinical assistant professor of medical psychology in psychiatry at Columbia University and on the faculty at the Columbia University Center for Psychoanalytic Training and Research, where she serves as senior associate director for psychology and directs the Psychology Externship training program. Dr. Berger is an author of the Parent Development Interview and of several articles. She received a Woodrow Wilson Fellowship and the Lionel Ovesey Award of the Columbia University Center for Psychoanalytic Training and Research for developing a psychodynamic teaching program.

Harold Blum, MD, is a training and supervising analyst at the Institute for Psychoanalytic Education affiliated with the New York University (NYU) School of Medicine, a clinical professor in the Department of Psychiatry at NYU Medical Center, a Distinguished Fellow of the American Psychiatric Association, and an executive director of the Sigmund Freud Archives. He is a past editor in chief of the *Journal of the American Psychoanalytic Association* and a past vice president of the International Psychoanalytic Association. He is the author of 150 psychoanalytic papers and several books and is a recipient of numerous professional awards and prizes. Dr. Blum delivered the plenary address to the American Psychoanalytic Association on two occasions.

Muriel Dimen, PhD, is adjunct clinical professor of psychology, NYU Postdoctoral Program in Psychotherapy and Psychoanalysis, and professor of anthropology, emerita, Lehman College (City University of New York, CUNY). On the faculties of the Massachusetts Institute for Psychoanalysis, Psychoanalytic Institute of Northern California, the Stephen A. Mitchell Center for Relational Psychoanalysis, and other institutes, she is editor of *Studies in Gender and Sexuality*, is an associate editor of *Psychoanalytic Dialogues*, and is a founding board member and former treasurer of the International Association for Psychoanalysis and Psychotherapy. Her most recent book, *Sexuality, Intimacy, Power* (Analytic Press, 2003), received the Goethe Award from the Canadian Psychological Association for the Best Book of Psychoanalytic Scholarship published in 2003. Dr. Dimen is the author of numerous other books on gender and culture. She is a Fellow at the New York Institute for the Humanities at NYU and practices in New York City.

Robert Alan Glick, MD, is a professor of clinical psychiatry, Columbia University, and a training and supervising analyst and former director of the Columbia University Center for Psychoanalytic Training and Research. He is the associate editor for education of the *Journal of the American Psychoanalytic Association*. Dr. Glick received the Teacher of the Year Award, Psychiatric Residency, New York State Psychiatric Institute, and the George S. Goldman Award of the Columbia University Center for Psychoanalytic Training and Research for Special Achievements and Excellence in Clinical Psychoanalysis and Psychoanalytic Education. He is the editor of five books and author of over 40 chapters and journal articles on diverse topics in psychoanalysis and psychiatry.

Dan Grech was correspondent for "Your Mind and Your Money," a year-long series on behavioral finance and neuroeconomics that aired on *Nightly Business Report* on PBS in 2009 and 2010. He is the radio news director of the WLRN *Miami Herald News*, a daily newscast serving South Florida, and is a creator, host, and senior producer of *Under the Sun*, a public radio show airing on 91.3 FM WLRN, South Florida's NPR affiliate. He has taught journalism at several institutions, including Princeton and Columbia Universities.

Irwin Hirsch, PhD, is distinguished visiting faculty at the William Alanson White Institute. He is a faculty member, supervisor, and former director at the Manhattan Institute for Psychoanalysis and is adjunct clinical professor of psychology and supervisor, Postdoctoral Program in Psychotherapy and Psychoanalysis, New York University. He is coeditor, arts and culture, *Contemporary Psychoanalysis* and is on the editorial boards of *Psychoanalytic Dialogues*, *Psychoanalytic Perspectives*, and *Ricerca Psicoanalitica*. Dr. Hirsch has authored more than 70 psychoanalytic articles, chapters, and reviews, and the Goethe Award–winning book, *Coasting in the Countertransference: Conflicts of Self-Interest Between Analyst and Patient* (Routledge, 2008).

Theodore Jacobs, MD, is a training and supervising analyst at the New York Psychoanalytic Institute and Society and the Institute for Psychoanalytic Education affiliated with the NYU School of Medicine. He is a child supervising analyst at the institute affiliated with NYU Medical Center, as well as a geographic supervisor for the Florida and Minnesota Psychoanalytic Institutes. He is also a clinical professor of psychiatry at the NYU School of Medicine. Dr. Jacobs has served on the editorial boards of the *Psychoanalytic Quarterly*, *Journal of the American Psychoanalytic Association*, and the *International Journal of Psychoanalysis*. He is the author of several books and over 50 papers on a variety of psychoanalytic topics.

Janice S. Lieberman, PhD, a psychoanalyst with a private practice in New York City, is a training and supervising analyst at the Institute for Psychoanalytic Training and Research (IPTAR) in New York. Dr. Lieberman serves on the editorial board of the *Journal of the American Psychoanalytic Association*. She is the author of *Body Talk: Looking and Being Looked at in Psychotherapy* (Aronson, 2000) and coauthor of *The Many Faces of Deceit: Omissions, Lies and Disguise in Psychotherapy* (Aronson, 1996). She has published and presented numerous articles and book reviews on gender, body image, psychoanalysis and art, and deception.

Pamela Meersand, PhD, is assistant professor of psychology at Columbia University, as well as training and supervising analyst and associate director of the Child Division at Columbia University Center for Psychoanalytic Training and Research. She is the author of several papers on the subjects of psychological testing and child treatment. She maintains a private practice in New York City.

Kachina Myers, LCSW, ACSW, is a member of the faculty and a supervisor at the Institute for Contemporary Psychotherapy. She is a cofounder and supervisor of the Association of Lesbian-and-Gay-Affirmative Psychotherapists (ALGAP). She has presented widely on the topic of money for clinicians and maintains a clinical and supervisory practice in New York City with a specialization in the area of money.

Stephanie Newman, PhD (coeditor), a clinical psychologist and psychoanalyst with a private practice in New York City, is a member of the faculty of the Institute for Psychoanalytic Education affiliated with the NYU School of Medicine. She has presented numerous times on diverse topics in psychoanalysis at the scientific meetings of the American Psychoanalytic Association, as well as at the American Psychological Association, and APA Division 39 (Psychoanalysis). Dr. Newman is a regular contributor to the online edition of *Psychology Today* and the author of *Mad Men on The Couch*, which is to be published in 2012 by St. Martin's Press.

Shelley Orgel, MD, is a former director of the NYU Psychoanalytic Institute and former chair of the Board of Professional Standards of the American Psychoanalytic Association. He is an associate editor of the

Psychoanalytic Quarterly. His published papers include psychoanalytic studies on Iago, Henry Adams, Anton Chekhov, and Sylvia Plath; several papers on psychoanalytic education; on Freud's "Repudiation of the Feminine" (a P.A.N.Y. Freud Anniversary Lecture); and on "Letting Go: Some Thoughts on Termination" (a plenary address to the America Psychoanalytic Association); as well as retrospective critiques of classical papers by Karen Horney and Kurt Eissler.

Arielle Farber Shanok, PhD, is the assistant director of Student Counseling Services at the Wellness Center at the Graduate Center, CUNY, and maintains a private practice in New York City. She has published a number of articles in peer-reviewed journals, has presented at multiple conferences, and was awarded the New Researcher in Services Intervention Award from the National Institutes of Health. She recently served as adjunct assistant professor at Barnard College, Columbia University, and visiting assistant professor at CUNY.

Preface

Money talks

Brenda Berger and Stephanie Newman

In our training to become therapists and psychoanalysts, money, like sex, is absorbed into our bones as a clinically meaningful and important issue to address in our patients. We become familiar with the multiple ways in which money talks and is often used in fantasy and reality to express early oral, anal, narcissistic, and oedipal meanings.

But paradoxically, in our practices, we seem to end up too often not actually talking about it, certainly not openly and concretely. For various and complicated reasons richly elucidated by the authors in this volume, money has remained the last taboo (Krueger, 1986). In fact, as analysts we routinely remark to each other that our patients will talk more to us about their sex lives than they will about their money. And, we ourselves know that as a group, we also seldom talk to each other or to our patients about the financial business we are in daily. We are comfortable in our healing identities. Dare we say, we are even a tad superior in those cloaks. But, we are less easy when it comes to being honest about the fact that what we do as clinicians is not only because we love healing, but also because we actually need our work to make a living.

Enter the subprime real estate market crash of 2008. The grandiose housing bubble burst, a pair of powerful investment banks collapsed, and the Great Recession was born. Since then, the financial and economic landscapes have never been the same. Nine million people have lost jobs. Millions of homes have been foreclosed. Automobile manufacturers have ceased to manufacture several long-established brands of cars. With the stock market contracting, Americans have seen their retirement funds and nest eggs shrink.

For the past several years, we have been struck, even astonished, by how often and how deeply our patients have been talking about money, about the effects of the Great Recession—on livelihood, on family relationships, and on their personal psychologies. They have revealed to us more than ever about their fears around money, about just how intensely the financial collapse has rocked their worlds. Money as "an ever-flowing breast" (Chapter 8, this volume) has dried up. At every turn are money matters.

And it is not only the patients who are talking about and preoccupied with money. As clinicians, we have felt the earthquake professionally and personally. Along with the rest of the country, we have lost college and retirement funds even as we have also lost some patients, or have lowered fees for others who have lost their jobs.

It seemed to us that perhaps, with so many hurt, their financial vulnerability more exposed, this could be a moment in psychological history when money could become less of a taboo subject of discussion. In conceiving of this collection, we wanted that conversation to happen from both sides of the couch. So, we invited psychoanalysts to talk about themselves as well as their patients and to focus on different aspects of money matters. They listened to us well when we described the tone we wanted for their chapters. We asked that they model being direct, personal, and open to bring money more out of the dark and into the daylight.

It is our hope that their reflections, along with our own, will encourage increased talking and teaching about money. And, we wanted to broaden our book to include perspectives outside psychoanalytic theory, to hear other views that expand our thinking, so we invited the ideas of a behavioral economist, Dan Grech, and Dr. Muriel Dimen, who in addition to being a psychoanalyst is a cultural anthropologist.

In mulling this national and international trauma, we wondered if we could learn from the consulting rooms and the excellent minds of our authors something that might help us all better understand the crisis that happened recently in our society. This is a book that attempts to probe the micro ordinary fantasies, wishes, and fears of real people around money. By doing so at a particularly trying time in economic history, we hope our volume provides a deeper understanding of some of the larger dynamics and complexities at play when money talks in the big picture of our world.

Our book holds central an idea showcased in a bold and provocative essay we have included by Dr. Janice Lieberman. She points out that "greed and envy are on the short list of 'the Seven Deadly Sins.'" She says that "in this age of the 'narcissistic man' and of a widespread affluence, we observe a lack of guilt over greed and envy, little apology for hurting others." The "outgrowth of the 'age of narcissism' is an 'age of entitlement,'" she declares.

In our view, Dr. Lieberman calls it like it is. In planning this collection, we were captured by how rampant in recent years the drive for increasing amounts of money has become. It has become so uncontrollable that, through grandiose, entitled behavior, it managed to bring down on our heads the hugely destructive subprime real estate market crash of 2008.

A seasoned giant in our field, Dr. Harold Blum offers us an engaging discussion of Dr. Lieberman's chapter. It provides one of two rich minidialogues that we are fortunate to offer in this collection. The other is an indepth discussion by Dr. Shelley Orgel of our own two chapters; his chapter includes his additional fine insights about money. These he gleaned over the course of his long and distinguished career as a psychoanalyst.

Other senior psychoanalysts, Drs. Jacobs, Glick, Hirsch, and Berger, provide chapters in which they offer reflections based on decades of practice and consideration of money matters in their work. Dr. Theodore Jacobs discusses the impact of the analyst's unanalyzed countertransference around money, which, if left out of awareness, can and does threaten treatments and training situations. Dr. Irwin Hirsch deals with the analyst's own powerful feelings of greed and shame in conducting long-term, lucrative treatments. He boldly discusses the potential conflicted interests that can become a challenge because analysts need both to heal patients and to make a living.

Dr. Robert Glick discusses particularly interesting and different dynamic issues that arise in the transference and countertransference during the course of treating wealthy patients. Dr. Brenda Berger tackles the role of money in marital relationships. Through two contrasting clinical vignettes, she describes how, during the economic downturn, one couple who lost money grew together, while another who gained millions did more poorly in their relationship.

Drs. Stephanie Newman and Arielle Shanok are in earlier phases of their clinical practices. They reflect on the impact of fees in the building and maintenance of practice and in the training situation overall. Dr. Shanok describes fees and money at the institutional level and discusses gender differences as they pertain to therapists' feelings about their work and incomes. Dr. Newman shows how she has used money, fees, and unpaid balances as tools to further both the analyst's and her patients' understanding of the clinical process.

Dan Grech, a radio and TV financial journalist, focuses on cognitive decision-making biases and their role in bubbles and investing. Dr. Muriel Dimen reflects in a rich, textured way through different theoretical lenses on psychocultural contradictions between money and love.

From Dr. Pamela Meersand, a child psychoanalyst, we can view a particularly interesting perspective on money. We hear about how it is understood by children at different levels of development and how some parents use money to influence child treatments. Kachina Myers warns us through two contrasting vignettes about the clinical value of confronting money dynamics as they appear in a treatment, and about how much can be lost when the clinician hides from the topic and keeps money taboo.

Through different angles, then, this book conveys the editors' view that many people might indeed want to talk about money but need help and company with the many primitive, difficult emotions that often link with money. It is tough to be alone feeling anxious, hungry, ashamed, smug, greedy, withholding, stingy, envious, angry, or rigid. It is our hope that more money talk will move readers toward remembering their complicated childhood feelings around wanting and getting and not getting, about having and not having, or giving and not giving, and sharing and not wanting to share at all. Through *Money Talks*, we hope to diminish the kind of repeating we have all endured during the economic collapse, the destructive entitled financial enactments that recently brought much pain to so many.

We hope that patients and therapists alike will benefit from what they learn here. Through reading these papers, perhaps our audience will discover that even the most seasoned and senior psychoanalysts struggle with money in their own practices and in their lives. Although we clinicians have begun the journey, we still have a way to go before fully embracing the path that Freud (1913) laid out for us nearly a hundred years ago: "It seems more respectable and ethically less objectionable to acknowledge one's actual claims and needs rather than, as is still the practice among physicians, to act the part of the disinterested philanthropist." (p. 131)

REFERENCES

Freud, S. (1913). On beginning the treatment. In J. Strachey (Ed. & Trans.). *The standard edition of the complete psychological works of Sigmund Freud* (Vol. 12, pp. 121–144). London: Hogarth Press.
Krueger, D. (Ed.)(1986). *The last taboo: Money as symbol and reality in psychotherapy and pschoanalysis*. New York: Brunner Mazel.

Chapter 1

Money

Some reflections on its impact on psychoanalytic education and psychoanalytic practice

Theodore Jacobs

A student in a continuous case seminar at an analytic institute is presenting the initial sessions in his analytic treatment of a young man. The student paints a vivid picture of his new patient and a detailed account of their first contact. With impressive openness, he recounts his reaction to the patient, including the mixture of feelings aroused in him by this individual as well as his fantasies about what it will be like to work with him. The candidate is also quite explicit in describing the way that he introduced the idea of analysis, the patient's response to it, and the discussions that followed. He also described the practical arrangements that they made for the treatment. His account of the exchanges and, ultimately, the negotiations that took place were complete with one notable exception: There was no mention of the fee.

Initially, none of the other students in the class asked about the fee. When, finally, one member of the group, shyly, raised that issue, the analyst responded in a vague and general way. The patient, he said, had some resources from his family, and the fee had been negotiated in a satisfactory way. No specific figure was mentioned, and none of the candidates asked for that information. It was clear that they had gotten the message: The analyst did not want to disclose the amount of the fee, and the group respected his wish for privacy in this matter.

This is a scene that could have, and no doubt has been, repeated in various institutes throughout the country. It illustrates the secrecy concerning fees, and money in general, that exists throughout the analytic world, a phenomenon that pertains not only to students but also to analysts at all levels of experience.

Fees that analysts charge—or pay for treatment of their own—are rarely discussed openly even among close colleagues. It is as though there is something embarrassing about our interest in money. It is not a matter to be talked about. Many analysts are self-conscious about what they charge, whether it is more than the going rate, in which case they fear the criticism or envy of their peers, or lower than that, about which they might possibly feel ashamed. In the latter case, the analyst often fears appearing foolish, naïve, or lacking in self-confidence. Comparisons with others are regularly made, and in many cases, the judgment of one's colleagues becomes a major source of anxiety.

It is also striking that despite years of personal analysis, many analysts still harbor considerable anxiety about money—a fact that contributes to the silence that surrounds this issue. Why these colleagues have not better resolved their neurotic anxieties over financial matters is an open question. One would have thought that the exploration of these problems would have constituted an important focus in the analysts' own personal analyses. Perhaps this particular issue, having its roots very early in life and relating to many different aspects of the personality, proved particularly resistant to change. Or, maybe the same guardedness concerning money that colleagues often display outside the analytic setting has existed within it as well, making access to this important, but highly protected, area difficult.

It is entirely possible, however, that the issue of money, avoided in social relationships, is not sufficiently engaged in the analytic work, including the training analyses. If that is the case, it may be that an unconscious collusion between patient and analyst not infrequently takes place, one aimed at excluding the uncomfortable topic of money from the analytic discourse. For not a few individuals, being open and forthright about money is more difficult than talking about sexual matters. Money has been termed the last taboo (Krueger, 1986), and in a very real sense, it has become just that, not only for patients but also for analysts.

For the young analyst, problems concerning money begin from the outset of training. There is no doubt that psychoanalytic education is one of the more expensive postgraduate programs that a student can undertake. The overall cost to the candidate varies from one institute to another, but the combination of the personal analysis, tuition, and supervisory fees creates a formidable financial hurdle for all but those few candidates who have substantial means.

The high cost of training, coming at a time when many candidates are young parents who are trying to meet rising expenses and to maintain a satisfactory standard of living, puts enormous pressure on them to earn a substantial income from their private practices. The amount of time, however, that the average candidate can devote to private practice is limited by several factors. Those female candidates who have children are obliged to ration their practice time to be available for their youngsters. In addition, many feel free to practice only during the school hours. Those with preschool children are often reluctant to leave them with caretakers for more than several hours at a time. Thus, in both of these situations the candidate is limited to a part-time practice.

Many of the single women and a majority of male candidates hold down hospital or clinic jobs on a half- to three-quarter time basis to have a steady income. Only gradually, over time, as their practices increase, is it possible for them to relinquish these paying positions. Such employment clearly restricts practice to several hours a day, thus increasing the pressure that many candidates feel to use those hours to maximum financial advantage.

This goal, however, is made difficult by the fact that as a requirement of their training, candidates are obligated to treat three analytic patients under supervision. In my own training in the 1960s, at least one, and usually two, of these patients were clinic referrals whose fees went directly to the institute. Thus, most of us gave 10 hours of practice time plus 2 hours of supervision to the training program without financial compensation of any kind.

The financial stress was great, and as partial compensation, we expected the clinic to send us good analytic patients, that is, patients who could utilize the analytic method and who could benefit from this kind of treatment.

When this did not happen—in my case, the two referrals from the clinic turned out to be troubled individuals for whom psychoanalysis was only marginally helpful—the resentment that I felt toward the institute, partially displaced onto my patients, created a countertransference problem that immediately complicated the treatment. This kind of situation is not unusual. Negative feelings toward the institute on which many candidates are dependent for the analytic patients that they treat at greatly reduced fees are often a source of this kind of troublesome indirect countertransference, one that Racker (1968) spoke about in his seminal book on this subject.

Today, the situation for candidates is somewhat improved but still requires much financial sacrifice. Most candidates treat at least two analytic patients at fees that not unusually are in the range of $10–$40 a session. And in many institutes, the candidate is expected to pay substantial supervisory fees.

It is inevitable, then, that the difficult financial situation that many candidates must contend with in the course of their training will increase their potential for acting out around monetary issues. In fact, enactments that have their roots in conflicts over money are among the problems most commonly encountered—and least talked about—in analytic training.

An issue of importance that can have profound implications for a young analyst's career concerns his or her acceptance of analytic patients. Because of their perceived financial needs, not a few candidates are reluctant to accept more than two patients at reduced fees. Taking the view that they have done their share of low-fee work, such candidates hold out for a full-fee, or near-full-fee, patient for their third and subsequent analytic cases. Since they are required to treat three patients during their training and full-fee analytic patients are extremely hard to come by in the present economic climate, the progress and graduation of such candidates are often delayed for several years. In fact, a number of such candidates never graduate, as they become discouraged at not being able to find a suitable patient and, ultimately, withdraw from training. Those who do manage to graduate often encounter another problem linked to financial issues, as will be elaborated.

For a young analyst to develop a largely analytic practice, a step that is necessary both for continued growth as a psychoanalyst and, ultimately, for advancement in the field, he or she must be open to accepting analytic patients at reduced fees. Senior analysts frequently see patients in consultation who would benefit from analysis but who are unable to afford a full fee. These consultants regularly seek to place these patients with younger colleagues at reduced fees. Those young analysts who are willing to accept these patients gain a reputation as individuals who are dedicated to doing psychoanalysis and to developing their skills. These are the graduates who tend to advance at institutes, are given roles of responsibility, and, eventually, are referred higher-fee patients. Those who decline to accept reduced-fee patients, or accept them for psychotherapy rather than analysis in order to charge higher fees, are not looked on with favor. As a consequence, they find it much more difficult to develop an analytic practice. In fact, these graduates have few analytic patients, a situation that not infrequently leads to discouragement about their careers and to disillusionment about the field of psychoanalysis. Such individuals often give up doing psychoanalysis to focus on other modalities of treatment, and not a few of them turn against their institutes and the American Psychoanalytic Association, demanding changes in rules and procedures that, in part, are motivated by personal frustration and disappointment.

A student whom I was working with was extremely slow in picking up a second analytic case. The problem, he maintained, was money. Due to difficult family circumstances, he explained, he had to help support a number of dependents and simply could not afford to take on another low-fee case.

This student waited for months for a patient who would afford his regular fee, and as a result of not having a second case, he could not move ahead at his institute. All of his classmates managed to find cases and to progress to the next year, but this student was unable to do so. Feeling very much excluded, he became depressed and stopped looking actively for a case. Instead, he filled his practice with psychotherapy patients, and when a suitable case finally came along, he did not have the hours available to accept the patient. It took some months for the candidate to clear his schedule, and in the interim he was unable to continue his matriculation at the institute. Discouraged by this state of affairs, the student's interest in analytic training declined, and he began to experiment with other modes of therapy. Eventually, he dropped out of the institute and became antagonistic to psychoanalysis.

Although the financial pressure on this student was great and there was a realistic need for him to earn a substantial income from his practice, it became clear that this was not the only factor that contributed to his behavior around money and fees. In fact, the student unconsciously made use of his realistic financial problems to screen out other issues that contributed in major ways to his reluctance to take on a second low-fee analytic patient.

The candidate's father was a powerful and well-to-do industrialist who had risen through the ranks to become a top executive in his company. A hard-driving, self-made man, he measured success quite exclusively in monetary terms. He had devoted his life to the accumulation of wealth, and he had little use for those who did not share his values. In addition, he had little sympathy for the poor who, he maintained, squandered their money on gambling and drink and did not know the meaning of thrift. As a consequence, he was reluctant to give money to charities that helped those in financial straits.

The student had a strong wish to please his father as well as a fear of falling out of favor with him. This need to remain in his father's good graces propelled him to want to prove to this parent that he had a financially successful practice and was doing everything possible to maximize his income. This attitude precluded his taking on another low-fee patient. He believed that if he did so, and suffered a loss of income, his father would regard him as a fool. Thus, this student's need to maintain a particular image in the eyes of his father contributed in no small measure to his procrastination in taking a second analytic case. In other words, his focus on money as his central problem concealed factors in himself that he did not wish to examine.

Also important was this student's ambivalence about psychoanalysis. He had doubts about the effectiveness of his own analysis and, in fact, harbored many negative feelings toward his analyst. Not having experienced many gains in his own treatment, he had difficulty believing that psychoanalysis could be an effective therapy.

Added to this problem was the fact that this candidate found it difficult to conduct an analysis in the way that he was being taught. An extremely active person, he was unable to tolerate the degree of passivity necessary to listen quietly for substantial periods of time. His impulse was to do something, to confront patients directly with their defenses and their underlying dynamics. He also found it anxiety provoking not to have answers to the dilemmas posed by his patients and to have to wait for lengthy periods of time before being able to understand a patient sufficiently well to be of help to that individual.

All of these factors played a role in influencing the student's behavior and determining the pathway that he took. This is often the case when students cite money as the sole obstacle to their taking on analytic patients. As was true in this case, it is important for educators both to acknowledge the reality of a student's financial situation and to look beyond it. For, often, it is other factors, ones concealed behind the issue of finances and acted out unconsciously, that prove to be as important as the manifest financial problem.

It is true, of course, that the financial hardships faced by many young analysts and the sacrifices they have to make to obtain training are realities that contribute in no small measure to the unwillingness of some analysts to take on additional patients at reduced fees. Other factors, too, as we have seen—often less-conscious ones—may influence this decision. Important in this regard is the issue of self-esteem and its relation to money.

For many analysts, as with much of the population, their personal sense of worth is closely linked to financial success. This connection, which often is only loosely tied to reality considerations, begins early in life with the unconscious association of money with bodily products, particularly feces. In the child's mind, these bodily products are linked with objects of value and often offered as gifts. To this association, in time, is added unconscious identifications with parental attitudes toward money and its use as a vehicle of personal security and self-esteem, as well as an object of envy. Important, too, is the parents' attitude toward the productivity of their offspring, an attitude often linked to financial success, which is internalized by the child, and in later life not infrequently becomes a goal that is pursued without recognition of its roots in a wish to win the love of parents by living out their aspirations.

In the case of analysts, this multidetermined self-esteem issue often lies behind, and is concealed by, their focus on the reality of their financial situation. In fact, their insistent focus on the reality aspect of their financial circumstances is often utilized defensively to avoid recognition of the deeper and more pervasive issues. In the best-case scenario, these underlying problems can be understood and the unconscious link to childhood anxieties and parental attitudes worked through in the analyst's own analysis. The analyst will then be free to pursue his or her analytic career without excessive concern about financial matters. However, as I have noted, such an outcome is achieved less often than one might wish. More commonly, one encounters candidates and young analysts whose ongoing conflicts over money are expressed in countertransference enactments that may create much difficulty for both patient and analyst.

Because of such unresolved problems, certain analysts are unable to make a sound assessment of a patient's financial situation and arrive at a fair fee. Not infrequently, they will set a fee that is higher than the patient can reasonably afford. In one such situation, when the patient, a young man striving to become independent of his family, stated that the proposed fee was beyond his means, the analyst strongly suggested that he ask his parents to finance the treatment. And when the patient protested that this request would undermine his goal of gaining independence and removing his treatment from the influence and interference of his parents, the analyst interpreted this objection as a resistance against undertaking the analytic work.

In fact, the analyst was an able candidate who, under other circumstances, would clearly have appreciated the importance of the patient's paying for his treatment himself. But, under the sway of his wish for a substantial fee, a fee that, in his eyes, would add to his stature and help confirm his self-worth, he was unable to make an objective clinical assessment of the situation.

Another problem that arises with some frequency concerns the question of terminating analyses of clinic or low-fee patients (McRae, 1980). These are the patients who the analyst has taken into treatment as candidates to gain experience and to satisfy the requirements of his or her training program. In most cases, the analyst has been willing to accept the financial sacrifice involved in exchange for the benefits of having an analytic case.

Once the analyst has graduated, however, and may need only to have a terminated case for purpose of certification by the American Psychoanalytic Association, this situation has changed psychologically for a young analyst. At that point, the not-infrequent wish to bring the low-fee case to an end, both to obtain a better-paying patient and to achieve the goal of terminating a case, may be quite strong. Most often, this wish is not conscious, but the analyst finds him- or herself thinking in terms of ending the treatment and may, without being aware of it, subtly suggest to the patient either that the patient is ready to end or that the analysis has progressed as far as it can go. The patient gets the unspoken message that the analyst wants to terminate the analysis and, usually sooner rather than later, the treatment comes to a close. I have seen a number of patients who have been in that situation. Looking back on what happened in their analyses, these patients had a distinct feeling of having been pushed out of treatment—and shortchanged—by an analyst who, once graduated, was no longer invested in working with them.

At the other end of the spectrum is the practice of holding on to patients who pay a substantial fee for unduly long periods of time. This situation, an increasingly common one in today's climate, in which analytic patients are hard to come by, involves graduate analysts far more than it does candidates.

Most analysts are dependent on their patients for their living, and when referrals are scarce, as has been the case in recent years, the temptation to hold on to patients, often well rationalized by the need for lengthy treatment, is considerable. As in the case of the young analyst who wishes to terminate the low-fee patient, the more senior analyst's need to hold on to patients is often not conscious. It is played out, rather, in a prolonged enactment that extends from one year to the next without conscious recognition on the part of the analyst of the enactment that has taken place. It is not rare for an analyst to treat certain patients for 20 or more years without the case being discussed or reviewed by anyone. In fact, once an analyst has graduated, the analyst is free to practice without supervision of any kind.

While it is true that the best young analysts regularly seek consultation with senior colleagues and participate in study groups of their peers, there are quite a few analysts who work alone and whose practices are never monitored in any way. The tendency for such practitioners to develop their own style and idiosyncratic way of functioning is considerable. This poses a genuine problem for psychoanalysis, as such analysts may engage in practices involving fees as well as other matters that are questionably ethical.

An analyst of my acquaintance has at least four patients who have been in continuous analytic treatment with him for over 15 years. In none of these patients has the question of termination been raised by patient or analyst. Both act as though there is nothing wrong with analysis continuing indefinitely, their behavior rationalized by their belief that as long as progress is being made, there is no reason to think about ending the treatment. Thus, a collusion has developed between patient and analyst, one that reflects their joint denial of the reality that treatment is a time-limited endeavor that must come to an end, and that termination is an integral—and essential—part of the analytic process. Patients and analysts who do not accept this reality distort the treatment and, in the process, avoid facing not only the pain of separation but also often the unconscious association of termination with the end of life itself.

In the situation just cited, financial considerations play an important role in the analyst's reluctance to end treatment. He or she receives substantial fees for this work, fees that the analyst has come to rely on as the mainstay of his or her income. An individual who has limited contact with colleagues, the analyst gets few referrals and fears that as patients leave treatment he or she will not be able to replace them. Thus, this colleague's practice of holding on to patients is motivated to a considerable extent by anxiety over money.

While this anxiety is a common one, especially among analysts who are solely dependent on private practice for their income, the extent to which such anxiety influences practice varies a great deal. In the aforementioned case, that influence was strong, and it reflected the analyst's long-standing concern about money, which was rooted in his childhood. This colleague comes from a poor immigrant family that struggled financially for many years. Often, there was not enough money to pay the rent and to put food on the table. Although he has done well over the years and lives comfortably, he has never fully overcome his fear of becoming impoverished. Therefore, it is of overriding importance to him to maintain his income. And to a considerable extent, this anxiety dictates the way he practices. Over time, his referrals have decreased, and correspondingly, his fear of not being able to replace patients who leave treatment has increased. This change has led him to hold on to patients for many years and to rationalize what is, essentially, a problem of his that has not been resolved.

While perhaps this is an extreme case, it is true that concerns about money and fears of losing income play an ongoing role in the questions of how and when treatment is terminated. No analyst is totally immune to this anxiety, and it is necessary at all times for us to reflect on this issue in ourselves and to assess its influence on our way of practicing. And, it is also important to keep in mind that, important as they are, concerns about money are often used unconsciously to keep at bay other anxieties, especially those concerns over separation and loss that are always with us and that are often acted out unconsciously around issues of termination.

Another issue of importance concerns the increasing of patients' fees during treatment. While it is perfectly legitimate for an analyst to increase a patient's fee from time to time to keep up with the cost of living or because the patient's financial circumstances have improved, some analysts raise their fees whenever there is any increase whatsoever in the patient's income, regardless of any other considerations, and others do so yearly, whether or not there is any improvement in the patient's financial situation.

When patients' needs are disregarded in this manner, they soon sense that the analyst is more interested in the fee than the patient, and the treatment is undermined by what, essentially, is the analyst's acquisitive need to increase income.

With some frequency, we also encounter the opposite kind of problem: that of candidates or young graduates who are unable to charge adequate fees. Such individuals consistently undercharge patients and have great difficulty raising fees even if the patient is in a position to afford more. This problem usually stems from feelings of inadequacy and a negative perception of oneself and one's self-worth. These are long-standing problems that require sustained analysis, but doubts about the validity and effectiveness of psychoanalysis can contribute a great deal to the difficulty.

Analysts who struggle with this problem may become vulnerable to manipulation by patients who sense the analyst's self-doubts and, consciously or not, take advantage of the situation to press for concessions in the fee and for alterations of the frame. Out of anxiety and a lack of confidence, the analyst may find him- or herself yielding to the pressure from the patient. Although initially gratified by their ability to get the analyst to comply with their wishes, patients ultimately do not benefit from what, essentially, is an acting out of a personal problem of the analyst. The message that is transmitted is that the analyst has little confidence in the patient's ability to meet the challenge of a higher fee, and that the analyst views the patient as weak and in need of special help. Such a message will undermine, rather than augment, the patient's sense of self.

Supervisors can play an important role in helping the candidate set an appropriate fee and hold the line against the patient's efforts to bend the frame. And by means of tactful interventions, they can help the candidate recognize and seek help for the problem in him- or herself that is acting as a handicap in analytic work.

In general, supervisors, teachers, and the training analyst play central roles in helping to shape the candidate's attitude toward, and handling of, money as an important constituent of the analytic process (Rocher, 1968).

The candidate's most important teacher of technique and his or her model for how an analyst thinks is, of course, his or her own analyst. In issues concerning billing procedures, one's policy regarding missed sessions, and one's method of determining the patient's financial situation and setting the fees, most young analysts follow the example of their own training analyst and utilize the same approach. This piece of identification is a powerful one, and it is not rare for a candidate to apply the approach that his or her analyst has used in an automatic way. This can create a serious problem in treatment, and it is the job of the supervisor to help the student take an independent view of the patient's financial circumstances and to set an appropriate fee.

Because of the enduring nature of the young analyst's identification with his or her training analyst, it is particularly important for the latter to be straightforward, fair, and open in all dealings with the candidate. A training analyst who is rigid, dogmatic, or acquisitive is likely to affect a candidate in treatment with him or her in such a way that the latter will identify with the manner in which he or she has been treated and in turn will display some of these self-serving attitudes in personal behavior.

Supervisors also can exert strong influence on the candidate's attitude toward and way of dealing with financial matters. Candidates often feel compelled to comply with the supervisor's own practices in this regard. In one such situation, Dr. L, a bright and able candidate, was working with a young man who had very little money and deep-seated anxiety over the prospect of having to declare bankruptcy. The candidate felt, under the circumstances, that it was appropriate to have a flexible policy with regard to the timing of the patient's payments and the requirement that the patient pay for all scheduled sessions. For a number of reasons, including the arbitrary manner in which the patient was raised, the analyst felt that it was important for the patient to have some vacation time without being charged for his hours during this period. The supervisor, on the other hand, insisted that the rule concerning payment for missed sessions be strictly enforced. He viewed the analyst's position as a piece of acting out and stated that he could not continue to supervise the candidate if he did not follow the supervisor's recommendation. Against his better judgment, the candidate complied. The patient objected vigorously to his analyst's stance, which he found arbitrary and unempathic. As a result, the analyst's alliance with the patient was damaged, and the patient broke off the treatment. In this case, it was the rigidity of the supervisor who insisted that the candidate implement the policy that he used with his own patients that led to this unfortunate outcome.

Many of the descriptions in this chapter are, in essence, serious difficulties—in some cases actual abuses—involving money that often go unrecognized and uncorrected. Part of this problem stems from the failure of our field to confront the issue of money forthrightly in our educational programs, in the training analysis, in supervision, and in the postgraduate years. As long as analysts continue to participate in what, essentially, is a collusion to avoid dealing more actively with money and its complex psychological meanings for analysts, as well as our patients, the kinds of enactments that I have described—ones that affect our patients and ourselves in deleterious ways—will continue to exist as one of the most important, and neglected, problems facing psychoanalysis today.

REFERENCES

Fuqua, P. (1986). Classical psychoanalytic views of money. In D. Krueger (Ed.), *The last taboo*. New York: Brunner/Mazel, 17–23.

Jacobs, D. (1986). On negotiating fees with psychotherapy and psychoanalytic patients. In D. Krueger (Ed.), *The last taboo*. New York: Brunner/Mazel, 121–131.

Krueger, D. (Ed.) (1986). *The last taboo*. New York: Brunner/Mazel.

McRae, J. F. (1980). The influence of fee assessment on premature therapy termination. *Administration in Mental Health*, 7(4), 282–291.

Racker, H. (1968). *Transference and countertransference*. New York: International Universities Press.

Chapter 2

It was a great month: None of my patients left*

Irwin Hirsch

In this chapter, I will attempt to expose my psychoanalytic profession and myself as simply human when it comes to money and to greed. I believe that an analyst's awareness and acceptance of his own disquieting characteristics are likely to lead to more productive use of these feelings in our everyday analytic work. When we analysts deny our shameful or personally discordant feelings and strivings around money and project them into patients, we lose touch with them and are at risk for doing harm in our work.

A number of years ago, shortly after I left my hospital job and began full-time independent practice, I ran into a former supervisor of mine who I had not seen for some time. She was with her lawyer husband, and after she congratulated me for making the bold move into private practice, something she had been reluctant to initiate, her husband asked me bluntly how I dealt with the conflict between my patients getting better and leaving and the loss of income that followed. He implied quite clearly that his psychologist wife, senior to me and more qualified, had chosen the professional high ground by continuing to see her patients on a hospital salary basis. His commentary was not only pithy, but also profound and jarring. It was a distinct departure from the normal congratulatory, well-wishing responses to which I had grown accustomed. I had no intelligent answer to his question, and I recall mumbling something about recognizing that this was a problem, and that I hoped my successfully discharged patients would be satisfied consumers and refer others to me.

I had a similar encounter some 30 years later while I was in Germany for a conference. At a dinner with a few German colleagues I had just met, I learned that national insurance paid 100% of psychotherapy and multiple times per week psychoanalytic fees for prolonged periods of time. I was further told that because of this coverage, virtually every analyst had a

* This is a revised version of Chapter 7 from *Coasting in the Countertransference: Conflicts of Self-Interest Between Analyst and Patient* (Routledge, 2008). Reprinted with permission.

full practice and a waiting list for new patients. My envy was palpable, although tempered by their lament that the fees that I and other American analysts were charging were roughly two to three times what they received. Parenthetically, the issue of fees and busyness of practice is a primary subject of discussion whenever I travel, as soon as a drink or two loosens tongues.

One of my German colleagues, when learning from me that the practices of the vast majority of American analysts were not full, and that the competition for patients in the marketplace of supply and demand was often considerable, asked the same question put to me 30 years earlier. He wondered how I could try to help patients when an ultimate positive outcome would lead to my losing income. This time I was more prepared and had a better answer. I had already coauthored an article identifying economic conflict as the single greatest problem in our profession (Aron & Hirsch, 1992), and I was in the planning stages for a book dealing with issues such as these (Hirsch, 2008). I essentially told this man that I believed his system created far better conditions for productive analytic work, and that despite my enjoying much higher fees, that I thought I personally would be both less anxious and a more useful analyst in their system.

Economic anxieties plague all but a very few analysts I know, especially in large American urban areas like New York City where the supply of trained analysts is voluminous, and the relative number of potential patients who can afford preferred analytic fees creates considerable competition among analysts. Most colleagues are elated when a new referral comes and depressed when a patient leaves prematurely. Sadly, even after a successful analytic experience, it is often difficult to feel satisfaction and pride only, without this being tempered by anxiety and regret in relation to lost income. This is best captured by an interchange I had with a colleague. "How's it going?" I asked him when I ran into him one day in the street. "It's been a great month—none of my patients left," he responded.

The degree to which we are dependent on our patients both to exercise our skills and to create economic security is powerful, and although this is preoccupying, it is rarely addressed in the literature or as part of formal panels and conferences. Analysts' economic dependence on patients leads to an inherent and profound conflict between self-interest and patient interest, and this conflict always has the potential to severely compromise analytic work. Indeed, I believe that analysts' financial concerns reflect the most vivid example of this conflict, and I believe that our anxiety about income is the single greatest contributor to compromised analyses.

There are many and often major consequences of this worrying about money. Perhaps the most common one is the problem of keeping patients in treatment for too long and the excessive mutual dependency that inevitably arises. I have no actual research data to support this, but my own anecdotal observation is that many patients remain these days in analysis for a staggering number of years. This appears to be more common than it was in previous generations. Modern patients (many of whom are analysts themselves) seem to remain in analytic treatment for 10, 15, 20, or even 25 years, with the same analyst.

A related effect of analysts' economic interests emerges in the number of times per week that patients are seen. With most analysts, I also believe that at least three sessions per week is optimal for good analytic work. But analysts' motives for seeing patients multiple times each week are sometimes unrelated to this analytic ideal. Some patients who are seen frequently are not necessarily being treated in an analytic context with analytic aims. That is, some analysts do supportive or maintenance-oriented work with patients who can afford this, and they behave as if they were conducting an analysis that actually requires the frequent sessions. Similarly, many patients who can afford high fees will be seen multiple times per week for many, many years, long after analytic goals still prevail. One colleague has said to me, without shame, that a couple of his patients are so troubled that he anticipates that they will be "patients for life." Another well-respected one proclaimed at a clinical meeting that she and all of her colleagues have what she called their "lifers," patients who allegedly "need" to be in analysis for literally their entire lives. Shockingly, this statement was not challenged by others at the meeting.

In these situations, "analysis" has become a vehicle for the creation of mutual attachment and dependent ties, and the rationale for this centers around biased assessments of patients' psychopathology. The very idea of adhering to the patients' original analytic goals or aims is forgotten too often. Maintenance of the analytic relationship can, and frequently does, become an end in itself.

Another compromise precipitated by analysts' anxiety about money occurs when the analyst strives to be liked by his or her patients so that they remain in treatment. This takes the form of analysts being overly supportive and complimentary or striving to be helpful in ways that do not correspond to the analytic aim of facilitating autonomy. They may avoid challenging patients when this would be potentially useful, or they may duck uncomfortable transference themes, particularly those related to anger and disappointment. Analysts may be too tentative so patients' anxiety, even productive anxiety, is kept to a minimum. They may use deliberate self-disclosure to gratify patients' wishes.

I also believe that certain theoretical points of view are sometimes embraced more because they are gratifying than because they are likely to effect ultimate separation and autonomy. Both analytic reserve and analytic challenge can be eschewed for fear that these attitudes may provoke patients to quit, while measures that are more traditionally associated with supportive psychotherapy serve to maintain patients in prolonged attachments.

It is my view that analysts will be more likely to conduct briefer analyses, and analyses that foster independence, when they are more willing to let patients leave and bear the loss of income. Unfortunately, this does not occur enough in our current analytic culture. When it does, it may be a function of an analyst's practice being full, the analyst having new patients waiting, or the patient's fee being so low that the analyst does not wish to prolong this commitment at such a reduced fee. I am not suggesting that the willingness to see patients leave is always good. This also can easily be misguidedly based on wishes for higher fees or to see someone new or perhaps more interesting. Keeping patients for many years and seeing them frequently can of course be appropriately based on what is genuinely best for patients or be evidence of a strong and ultimately fruitful attachment. However, analysts' financial needs carry much weight in the myriad judgments and choices we make daily in our clinical work. These choices are often quite conscious on our part.

There are several other money-driven practices that have become somewhat common even among the most ethical and respectable among us. They concern the ways in which the modality of psychoanalysis is often compromised and other treatment modalities are collapsed into each other in confusing and potentially damaging ways. For example, when an appealing patient who is highly motivated (someone with whom an analyst wishes to work) can afford to pay only a demarcated amount of money, the analyst often opts for a higher fee to see this individual once or twice weekly. This is selected over dividing the dollar amount by three or more sessions per week or referring the patient to someone whose fees are lower, an analyst who could provide a more optimal psychoanalytic experience. Another example of this occurs when it is difficult for a patient in analysis three or more times weekly to commute to an analyst's office. Such a patient might be offered a double session at double the fee, thereby defeating some of the original aim of psychoanalytic frame that occurs multiple times per week. This coconstructed "deal" between analyst and patient maintains for the analyst the advantage of receiving payment for an ideal number of sessions.

More recently, telephone sessions have also attacked the analytic frame. They have become a way to reduce inconvenience for busy patients while maintaining the patient's consistent willingness to stay in therapy. An analyst may cooperate with this to maintain the patient in therapy or to secure optimal income. Finally, although it has long been recognized as poor practice, analysts might accept referrals from patients who are either close friends or family members of their patients. They may also see a patient while regularly doing couples therapy with that same person and the person's significant other.

It is clear to me from all that I have struggled with personally and seen practiced in my field that we psychoanalysts are no more noble as a group when it comes to financial greed than are our counterparts in the financial sector, the "business world," law, and medicine. In denying to ourselves our own financial ambitions, psychoanalysts often have little to offer by way of understanding to people in other fields who make headlines for their so-called disregulated affect or compulsive irrationality.

Fundamentally, I do not believe that these criticisms veiled as semidiagnostic designations are warranted. I think that the wish to earn maximum money and to be recognized as successful or powerful is but a variant on normative ambition. Any human quality, like ambition, that can be seen as productive for individuals and for society at large can also in extremis cause harm. The desire for recognition, power, and status is normal across disparate cultures, and the degree to which any individual possesses these qualities lies on a bell-shaped curve. Because many psychoanalysts and others in the helping professions deny having such personal needs to any significant degree, strong ambition and greed are often projected onto those "bad" others in different professions. These "others" then become demonized in the best way that psychoanalysts do this—the designation of diagnostic labels that conveniently lead to a "good me and bad them" binary.

In private conversations, at committee meetings, in published articles, and in the context of clinical presentations of patients, those others outside our profession are often discussed as living on a moral low ground in comparison with the prototypical psychoanalyst, allegedly in aggregate embracing higher moral standards with respect to money and other forms of ambition. Because psychoanalysts belong to a helping profession for which fees and income may on average be lower that those of other professionals mentioned, and because most psychoanalysts, at least in large urban centers in America, lean leftward in their political beliefs, analysts may readily deceive themselves and deny that ambition for status and money plays a role in their aims. This superior moral attitude, indeed, often disguises what is actually a sense of weakness and inferiority toward those who earn appreciably bigger incomes or have more social power and stature, including many of the patients whom psychoanalysts treat.

There exists a clear irony in the fact that psychoanalysts invariably prefer to see patients who can afford what we call a "full fee" (the analysts' maximum fee), and that this fee, often barely or not at all covered by insurance, is more than the vast majority of people can afford. Without considerable income, family money, or rarely available terrific health insurance coverage, only a very small percentage of people can engage in a psychoanalytic process once weekly. Once-weekly treatment, however, is only one third to one fifth of what psychoanalysts desire. And, as is well known, these sessions one to five times weekly often last for many years. It is rare that an analytic patient who is productively engaged in treatment and who can afford to keep coming will spend less than 5 years "on the couch." Of course, 10 to 20 or more years are not at all uncommon. Although many analysts may reduce their fee from their full fee to a lower one to accommodate analyses multiple times per week, the total income accrued from such therapy is likely quite significant. And yet, with all the education and years of study and personal analysis, analysts' income is often less than counterparts in other professions like medicine and law. It is especially less when compared to those earning in the world of finance, banking, and private business.

I see great hypocrisy in analysts' distinct preference for patients who are wealthy enough to help support them and simultaneous denigration of those patients with their colleagues for their greed, mercenary values, and economic ambitions. Most contemporary analysts have integrated Harry Stack Sullivan's now-famous phrase, "We are all more simply human than otherwise," (Sullivan, 1940, p. 16) and have embraced the value that Racker articulated so well: "The first distortion of truth in the analytic situation is that analysis is an interaction between a sick person and a healthy one." (Racker, 1968, p. 132). The best analysts are those who readily acknowledge their subjectivity and their personal flaws, and view themselves as neither objective observers of specimen patients nor inherently more psychically healthy because of being in the role of healer. The term *wounded healer* has been widely embraced by modern analysts, who largely have been increasingly free to speak and to write publicly of their most intimate feelings and foibles.

Although economic greed is a shortcoming analysts share with many others, I have observed, paradoxically, that this remains one area wherein analysts commonly differentiate themselves from their patients and in their remarks about public personalities. That is, I have observed that when speaking or writing about them, analysts often split off and deny their own financial and power-related ambitions, while emphasizing, in a condemning and a pathologizing way, these qualities in others.

I do not have many speculations regarding why this happens. I previously suggested that analysts often feel inadequate in comparison with patients whose ambition has led to far greater material success and comfort than that available to the purportedly stronger person in the analytic dyad—the analyst. An analyst's ambition for, or envy of, wealth and power may be quite painful in this context, so these uncomfortable emotions may be attributed to belonging to the patient only and then be regarded as bad or pathological characteristics. Such attribution not only pathologizes a patient (or a public person), but also pumps up the analyst so that he or she may then feel more like a powerful healer. In the analyst's eyes, he or she is now in a position to cure the allegedly sick patient of the latter's pathological greed and ambition—moral and personal failings, allegedly inferior to the qualities of the allegedly healthy analyst. Here, the analyst positions him- or herself not only as more powerful by virtue of heartier mental health but also as stronger through an attribution of moral superiority. This positioning, clearly not useful to patients, is supported often by left-leaning political beliefs shared by a majority of psychoanalysts, beliefs that often encourage a suspicion of dishonesty toward almost anyone whose ambitions have led to an accumulation of wealth and power.

It is my view that those analysts who are most successful in achieving either relatively high income or public professional recognition have ambitions quite parallel to others outside this profession. I further argue that many analysts who do not feel successful along these dimensions are soothed in their disappointments by denying their thwarted ambitions and attending to the ambitions of others only as pathologically excessive.

For example, the term *mania* is often used in our field to describe people who work long and hard and with much energy to reach very high aims or reap strong economic rewards. Other designations, such as *type A personality* or *workaholic*, are also common. Mania comes from the colloquial *maniac* or, more respectfully, from the severe psychiatric diagnosis, manic-depressive. The connotation of these terms is most negative, although I believe personally that when harvested productively, a fair touch of mania is often highly productive both for the individual and for what the results of this mania may produce for society. I have long believed that many people who have contributed greatly to the human race have been driven in ways that could be called manic. This designation could be viewed as either "healthy" or pathologic depending on the eye of the beholder and his or her motives, conscious or unconscious. Leaders and pioneers in the arts, the sciences, philosophy, business, politics—and yes, even psychoanalysis—have been motivated by ambition for recognition, power, and sometimes wealth. They could be called workaholic, manic, or both in either the productive or the pathological sense of the words.

In conclusion, the economic realities of psychoanalytic practice in America create choices that I believe very few of us would make were we working for a salary at a clinic or under the German national insurance system. Some analysts opt for therapeutic configurations that constitute, or come close to constituting, unethical conduct. I believe that almost every analyst makes some decisions about the basic physical structure of the analytic relationship that reflects compromise that falls short of analytic ideals. Such decisions can only be controlled when they are acknowledged and made without self-deception. However, even in full consciousness, I suspect that most analysts will make some basic frame decisions that are affected by financial self-interest. The more that these realities are embraced, the less they will be projected onto ambitious or wealthy patients such that these patients become demonized or pathologized for qualities that we analysts share with them.

REFERENCE

Aron L. and Hirsch I (1992) Money Matters in Psychoanalysis. In *Relational perspectives in psychoanalysis*. M. Skolnick & S. Warshaw (Eds), Hillsdale, NJ: The Analytic Press, 239–256.

Hirsch, I. (2008). *Coasting in the countertransference: Conflicts of self interest between analyst and patient*. New York: Routledge.

Racker, H. (1968). *Transference and countertransference*. New York: International Universities Press.

Sullivan, H.S. (1940). *Conceptions of modern psychiatry*. New York: Norton.

Chapter 3

The rich are different
Issues of wealth in analytic treatments

Robert Alan Glick

In 1925, F. Scott Fitzgerald wrote (1926/2006):

> Let me tell you about the very rich. They are different from you and me.
> They possess and enjoy early, and it does something to them, makes
> them soft where we are hard, and cynical where we are trustful, in
> a way that, unless you were born rich, it is very difficult to under-
> stand. They think, deep in their hearts, that they are better than we
> are because we had to discover the compensations and refuges of life
> for ourselves. Even when they enter deep into our world or sink below
> us, they still think that they are better than we are. They are different.
> (p. 5)

While I may not share Fitzgerald's bitter and envious character-
ization of the rich, the question of how wealth shapes character and
makes people different is of more than passing analytic interest. Money
carries the meanings of desire, security, sex, gender, and freedom. Freud
(1905) was far from immune to concerns about money, and he folded
money into his theory of infantile psychosexuality as a fixation at the
anal stage. But, Fenichel (1938) unpacked the idea and posited oral,
anal, and the narcissistic elements in the drive to amass wealth. Wealth
does confer power, the power to turn desire into fact, to make wish into
reality.

Psychoanalysis is concerned with the expression of hidden wishes and
fears. Freud taught us that our lives are molded by our struggles with our
infantile sexual wishes and fears, and that in adulthood, our unconscious
sexual conflicts can and do make us suffer. Money, like sex, can actualize
unconscious fantasy, and make inner hidden psychic reality come to life
in the external world. The meaning of wealth joins the meaning of sex
as a lens into the unconscious life of patient and analyst. In the clinical

situation, wealth can "raise the heat" for the analyst, creating tensions about our personal sense of freedom, values, strengths, and meaningfulness in life.

As analysts, we often find ourselves haunted by envy and struggling with our own wishes for liberation, easy gratification, and superiority. Much as I might wish to believe otherwise, my experience suggests that Fitzgerald was correct in ways that we analysts need to take seriously. He insisted that in life, and therefore in analysis, we are consequently drawn into our sense of difference—strong and weak, good and bad, real and imagined, past and present—that defines us to ourselves.

Psychoanalysis inevitably becomes a conversation about values. The analytic process is a lens through which patient and analyst explore those implicit values that underlie the patient's suffering, his character defenses, and his approach to life. Analysts also have values that we hope will shape the process, allow for the patient's freedom from neurotic distress, and result in growth and change. They are elements in the therapeutic action and goals of analysis: Candor, flexibility of mind, self-reflection, and satisfaction in life are positive values. We view negatively forms of denial, avoidance, rigidity, self-delusion, and self-injury. Analysts believe in the value of self-knowledge, adaptive tolerance of ambiguity and uncertainty, healthy narcissism, and empathy.

However, other more subtle and personal values of the analyst can influence the process. When we do not recognize and acknowledge their influence on us, we are at risk for insidiously imposing particular values on our patients, secretly suggesting that they should share our notions of the importance of deep and abiding relationships, of achievement over status and possessions, of altruism and ethics over self-centeredness and exploitation, of certain forms of gratification over others.

In the context of treating the wealthy, we may run up against our own unconscious conflicts over money and values that can touch our narcissistic vulnerabilities and evoke envy and defensive moralism.

In this chapter, I deal with issues facing the analyst working with wealthy patients. I examine some of the ways in which the wealthy may be "different from you and me" and how wealth may be represented consciously and unconsciously in the minds of both the patient and analyst. Transferences to wealth can be complex, and their forms can pose significant and at times insidious challenges in analytic treatments (Olsen, 1986).

A caveat: My impressions about wealth as a dynamic force in clinical work are offered for their heuristic value, to suggest questions for exploration. They do not reflect judgments about the fact of wealth. All my clinical examples are illustrative composites and not specific individuals.

WEALTH IN THE MIND OF THE PATIENT

The facts of life

All families teach their children about the world and their place in it, and wealthy families transmit their versions of norms, values, traditions that shape identifications and character structure. Wealth is an essential dynamic developmental force and becomes the stuff of transference. As children grow, how their parents educate them about money and its meanings and effects shape their sense of themselves and their internalized object relationships. Wealth can carry a sense of superiority, privilege, access, power, and responsibility. It can define one's place, or class, in the social hierarchy, and with a challenging sense of difference from others. For some, feeling different is often a burden (e.g., like being tall or short, thin or fat, straight or gay). The intergenerational transmission of the meanings of wealth can be a powerful force for independence and maturity or for crippling narcissistic vulnerability. Reality about wealth matters. How much there is, who made it and how it was made, and who controls it are all defining features of wealth. Because of their unconscious, transferential power, these questions can dominate an individual's life and treatment.

In two families, grandfathers had created dynastic wealth, and their families became "special." In one, the next generation learned the values and challenges of wealth in ways that fostered independence of mind, social responsibility, and an intense need to have a positive impact in the lives of others. A member of the subsequent generation came for treatment for depression, which ran in the family. She had been taught the facts and responsibilities of her family's wealth early and well and managed her money effectively. Her depression, however, was related to an academic failure. Academic success had been a bulwark against her sense of herself as simply being "an inheritor," "a trust funder." This was tied to a profound but an unconscious pathological identification with one of her parents. When she failed, she experienced a severe narcissistic injury, which brought with it a profound depression and feelings of worthlessness and failure. She experienced paralyzing shame and guilt about her wealth and entitlement. "All I am is a great deal of money!" When her depression was treated with analytic therapy and medication, she regained her sense of independence and responsibility. She understood how her vulnerabilities about unconscious identification had plagued her, and she came to see that neither her wealth nor her academic success need completely define her.

In another family, the self-made patriarch left a legacy of narcissistic trauma. Being his heir indeed made one rich and privileged, but with an unshakable sense that one could never accomplish what he had. His gift to his family became both grandeur and emptiness, and no amount of material indulgence could resolve this. Such was the dilemma of a grandchild who came to treatment after college, torn between overwhelming expectations and paralysis. He grew up with a feeling of specialness but was subjected to contradictions about the realities of money woven out of secrets about how much there was, who controlled it, and how one received it. He never felt secure or capable of self-reliance. Over the course of his treatment, he learned how money had been used to tie him to his mother as she had been masochistically enslaved by her own father. With pain and bitterness, he saw how she was doing with him a version of what had been done to her. Money had given license for subjugation and humiliation. These lessons allowed him to see his wealth more realistically, as conferring both adult freedom and adult responsibility. This enabled him to break out of a narcissistic enslavement and passivity that had dominated his development. He took on new challenges that tested him as an adult man in the world.

Being impolite

While the realities of wealth matter, it is rude to talk about money; so we are all taught, and the wealthy even more so. Acknowledging and revealing the truths about money and wealth are matters of establishing trust. Only trusted advisors can know the facts. The building of therapeutic safety and trust involves more than tact and timing. The experience of the telling and the meanings of the told dominate all treatments. However, I have found that the taboos against revealing one's financial self can be more intense than revealing one's sexual self. It may be easier to ask and get answers about sexuality than about money; patients assume that you need to know about their sexuality, but ask about money and you may get "Why do you need to know that?" All patients want to trust their analysts. Wealthy patients can fear (and at other times wish) that their analyst become blinded by their money. Experience teaches to be cautious and discreet lest others envy them and want to exploit them.

The source of wealth

It is not just the sheer fact of the wealth, but its source and its history that have enormous meaning to the wealthy patient and therefore for the analysis. Where the money came from, who made it, and how it was acquired are defining features of the lives of wealthy families. There is a world of difference between self-made wealth and inherited wealth. As analysts, we should be attentive to this distinction and not be blinded simply by the wealth itself.

Inherited wealth can be quite different from self-created wealth. Individuals with "old money," several generations of established wealth, tend to develop normative adaptation to their circumstances. They may seem reserved and aloof to others and appear modest in taste and style. This is not necessarily neurotic inhibition but a cultural-familial adaptive trait. Showing off with money can be as "rude" as talking about money. Growing up very wealthy can create a needed insularity that reflects a concern that others only see the money and not the person. The wealthy can fear exploitation. If well schooled in the family about the opportunities and responsibilities of wealth, a person does become cautious and guarded in assessing how others are relating to them. The wealthy are a minority, and as such, live with some of the suspiciousness of all minorities. Adaptively, or not, growing up wealthy brings with it a vigilance about the envy of others. Efforts to make the money "disappear into the background," to "pass" quietly in the general human population, can be protective and strategic in assessing and adapting to others when outside their protective environments.

Freedom

One of the challenges of inherited wealth is the absence of the need to work for a living. Relieved of that near-universal burden (for which almost everyone, including this analyst, must find a means to survive materially and sustain themselves and those who depend on them), such freedom can paradoxically bring a sense of powerlessness and emptiness. One can feel useless, without daily meaning to one's life. As noted, simply being an inheritor, a trust funder, "a playboy or socialite" can continually erode a mature and realistic sense of self-esteem. Questions like, "Who am I? And what am I supposed to do with myself?" can create despair and paralysis.

Financial freedom can engender a need to have a positive, creative, generative impact in the world. For some, only the most impossible, unreachable goals can repair the sense of damage. They come to treatment shameful and paralyzed in the face of any choice or action. At times, alcohol and drug abuse, reckless and impulsive behaviors propel them to seek help. The analytic work aims to uncover how the unconscious fantasies of grandiosity and immortality serve to protect against the narcissistic injury that follows from acknowledgment of realistic limitation and real-world accomplishment.

Narcissistic rage and devaluation are often defensively expressed in sadomasochistic transference reactions that seek to destroy the treatment and the analyst. A fragile young woman with a trust fund came to treatment in despair after many failed attempts to study and work at various places around the world: "I don't know what to do with myself." She denied that she felt lonely or needed anyone, feeling superior. Over time, as she became more attached to her analyst, the threat of dependence prompted her to react with contempt for the analyst and the analysis. She impulsively quit when in a rageful storm, insisting that the analyst wanted to tie her down, force her into a mediocre life, like the analyst's.

Oedipus and wealthy sons and daughters

Wealth can have a troubling impact on Oedipal struggles. The sons and daughters of the wealthy bear complex burdens when struggling with their competitive aggression, rage, problematic identifications, and feared loss of attachments. These conflicts can be expressed in painful and crippling feelings of inadequacy, bitterness, and inhibition.

Consider one man whose father created a family fortune. This son grew up in showy opulence, enjoying material advantage but feeling self-conscious, intimidated, and oppressed by his bombastic father. In adulthood, he worked and "did well," but the luxury and ease with which his family lived rested on the father's success, not his own. He came to treatment because of painful feelings of low self-esteem, inhibition, and chronic dissatisfaction. He saw himself as stunted and felt little pleasure in his career and his marriage. Only his children made him happy because he knew he was a good father, unlike his own. The roots of his dilemma were explored and much was worked through. As he recognized the unrelenting power of his fearful conflict with his internal representation of his father, he came to feel much better about himself and his life. However, when the father catastrophically lost virtually all of the family fortune, the shock and challenge unleashed an unexpected sense of liberation and repair of damaged manliness. The patient was surprised by his own bitter satisfaction in the father's failure and the newfound pride that came with the lost life of luxury. It was as if an enormous and crippling weight had been lifted, and he could stand up like a man (in several ways). He took control of the family crisis, navigated successfully through difficult financial challenges, brought some stability and security to the family, and found a new sense of satisfaction in his life. Money had given him means but not a sense of his own efficacy. Losing it allowed him to find his inner power and value.

Another man grew up in the shadow of a legendary self-made financial giant. By contrast, he grew up with a sense of himself constantly battling with his father and then with surrogate giants. He was a rebel, energetic, creative, and unconventional. He lived in fear of being crushed but thrived on the struggle—a David and Goliath myth dominated his life. Problems in his marriage brought him to treatment, but the need for true success plagued him. As the treatment deepened, his desire for recognition, to be "a giant" revealed certain inhibitions and constraints in his creative work. When he recognized how his continuing need to fight involved hidden and powerful fear and guilt that compromised his freedom and creativity, he felt empowered and emancipated. He left his failed marriage, established truly gratifying relationships, and discovered a new dimension in his creativity that led to genuine success (and wealth) in his field. One of the side effects of this working through was a surprising and humbling feeling of age, a loss of "eternal youth," and narcissistic omnipotentiality. He gained a fuller and more empathic picture of his father.

Daughters of wealth do not escape Oedipal struggles. Wealth can intensify gendered stereotypes. Daughters can feel like they are either supposed to be "sons" and defeat their mothers or other siblings or they must be passive, admiring, and never compete. One woman came to treatment after the early death of her mother because she felt frightened by the opportunities, both sexual and professional, that now confronted her. Until her mother died, she had not been aware of how much she had inhibited herself so she did not compete with her mother for her father's admiration. As her analytic treatment deepened, she recognized how her fear of antagonizing her female analyst had led her to avoid appropriate temptations.

Another woman came to treatment after her parent's divorce, complaining of feeling "surprisingly lost." In her early 40s, happily married with children, she was aware that growing up as an only child in the comfort of her mother's family wealth had provided security but a quiet sense of inhibition and inadequacy. In the course of her treatment, she realized that she needed to avoid threatening her mother's control over her. She was to remain "a good and quiet" pleasing child, secure in the luxury and privilege of her mother's largesse, a young woman who took few risks and expressed little independent ambition. In a vivid transference dream, she saw her analyst as cruelly dominated by the analyst's imagined male analyst. Through the exploration of this dream, the patient recognized the impounded, vengeful aggression that her mother must have lived with as she felt similarly controlled by the wealth-creating grandfather. Her "lost" feeling lifted, and she felt free to pursue a career unrelated to her wealth.

Spouses of the wealthy

Navigating the power dynamics and gender role expectations in marriage is hard enough under ordinary circumstances. Money offers freedom and opportunity but no protection from the kinds of struggles marriage creates. Wealth can amplify and complicate these common challenges. Our society often has asymmetrical gender roles for the spouses of the wealthy. In my experience, wealthy men may use money to bolster a traditional sense of masculine power. Their wives generally seek and find effective ways to define and assert their own power and avoid domination. When the wife has the wealth, traditional assignments of gender authority and power may be challenged. In successful marriages, both partners need to find ways to protect the husband's traditional male sense of strength and power. Insecure men may grow problematically passive-aggressive or distant and resentful when they feel weak, controlled, and impotent. Extramarital affairs are a common expression of this dilemma.

Dilemmas of self-made wealth

To create one's own wealth is to achieve a sense of power and accomplishment in the world. If one's character structure is sufficiently mature, it offers freedom, security, and satisfaction. However, the pursuit of wealth can be seductive and addictive. For some, the potential actualization of regressive oral, anal, phallic, and narcissistic wishes leads to intense oral anxieties about having enough money or anal hoarding, greedy withholding, and anxieties about maintaining sufficient control of the money. For the more narcissistically vulnerable, it becomes the equivalent of phallic narcissist power, drawing in oral and anal unconscious fantasies. When money serves to feed narcissistic wishes or repair narcissistic vulnerability, accumulating more wealth, no matter its reality, becomes a challenge to analyze: "Enough is never enough!" "Greed is good!" "You eat what you kill!" are mantras that may make analysts disoriented and tempted to moralize about the true meaning of life. How does having $20 million make one feel so inferior to someone with $50 million, or $100 million feel "small in the shower" compared to the person with $500 million? Like certain drugs, the pursuit of wealth, of beating the competition, of humiliating your rivals, of "being the king," lose all connection to the reality of the utility of money in life and lifestyle. Often, it is not about doing more, even acquiring more stuff, or having more freedom. It is simply about being bigger and more powerful.

Self-made wealth can ignite infantile grandiosity, omnipotence, and fantasies of repair of all past injustices, inadequacies, or failures (e.g., "I can have everything I want! Nothing is beyond my desire; I am not inferior, I am superior!"). However, this can lead to a compulsivity and impulsivity because nothing is ever enough, and nothing has any value. It may involve the need to control or the misuse or abuse of those who depend on them. The wealthy can feel entitled to vent their frustration and narcissistic rage on the defenseless around them.

Clinically, one encounters forms of crisis when the self-made discover that what they believed would repair damaged narcissism or alienation does not deliver on that promise. They describe feeling intoxicated by, and dependent on, this narcissistic fantasy of having and needing more. When this bubble bursts, they experience demoralization, a sense of emptiness about themselves, and guilt at their neglected relationships. They struggle to accept the need for help. Recognizing and tolerating a dependence on others becomes an important element in the transference.

Fears and guilt

Another pervasive struggle for the self-made is fear of the destructive, revengeful envy of others. This leads to corrosive suspicion, at times correct, that all they are to others is money. The "ghosts" of all those they slew or those they defeated in battle on the way to their wealth can haunt the self-made. Some feel guilt and seek masochistic solutions in the forms of repetitive failed relationships and self-destructive habits or addictions.

For some successful self-made men, it is not the phallic narcissistic meaning of wealth that drives them or a paranoid fear of envy. Rather, a deep and insatiable oral hunger can be the engine of ambition, accompanied by an implacable guilt for having "made it" and left others behind.

A self-made wealthy man in his late 60s came for treatment of depression and a preoccupation with death. His health had been relatively good until a minor incident triggered his morbid fear. He had grown up extremely poor and striven passionately to succeed. He had felt most alive during the years he built his business and his wealth. He was generous to his extended family and quietly philanthropic. Indeed, he never derived much pleasure from his wealth and was the opposite of conspicuous in display. As the treatment deepened and his symptoms of depression lifted, he recognized that he had come to a crisis point in his life. His career and wealth had plateaued; he was planning his succession, and accumulating more money had no appeal. He finally saw that a terror of poverty had been breathing at his back all his adult life, and now a crushing guilt for his success had overcome him. He quipped wryly at one point that he had needed to deny his success and his mortality to "keep the books balanced"—as long as he was striving he was safe. What was he to do with his life at this point? Death seemed to be all that was left for him. This reserved and formal man found himself weeping as he revisited the sad, impoverished lives of his parents in his country of origin. He grieved and mourned deeply for them and recognized that his wealth could not repair their lives. Without embarrassment, he asked for their forgiveness and pledged to find new satisfactions in his life with his family, with his philanthropy, and a surprising comfort in the religion he had abandoned a decade before.

Self-made wealthy women may suffer an additional challenge compared to their male counterparts because of asymmetrical social gender role expectations. The power that comes with wealth, and the work it may have taken to acquire it, may create a sense of being masculine, not feminine. This poses both an intrapsychic and interpersonal dilemma.

Certainly, not all wealthy and successful individuals suffer from this narcissistic addiction. These people come to treatment for other reasons and reveal a healthy perspective on the meaning and value of money. They have not fallen into the trap of addictive narcissistic repair: "the magic number," as several have described it, that allows one to retire, change one's life; the ticket to freedom, security, and opportunity for creativity, altruism, and so on. The analyst who has helped a patient to fulfill this wish may struggle with envy mixed with humbling admiration.

Certain forms of resistance

Resistances in the treatment of the wealthy follow from the ways in which money can offer freedom from awareness and responsibility and license to act. Having a lot of money can serve the patient's need to remain unaware of and avoid attention to meanings of thoughts, feelings, and behaviors.

Action offers formidable resistance through the easy use of money to gratify wishes and whims. Being able to acquire luxuries or leave at a moment's notice becomes a particularly challenging resistance to awareness of transference reactions, and an analytic challenge, especially when it prompts envy in the analyst: How nice it would be to take an impromptu weekend in Paris, the Alps, or a film festival and not worry about the cost; to have the attitude of "I do it because I can do it" when the only consequence is missing the treatment when the analyst wants to make the treatment an emotional priority at the moment when it is just what the patient can so easily and so gratifyingly avoid.

For the wealthy, the analyst's fee and the cost of the treatment may be insignificant to the patient. While the wealthy have good reasons to fear financial exploitation, being billed for missed sessions can be dismissed as of no consequence, or worse, as condescension. Sometimes, the bills are not even seen or reviewed by the patient but simply turned over or sent to an office "that handles these matters." A patient who had been in treatments over several decades was told that the fee was increasing next year and said: "Why do you analysts always insist on mentioning this? I don't know what your fee is; I have not paid attention to it; I trust you. Can we not have to talk about it?"

Another fee-expressed resistance is the failure to pay fees promptly. Some wealthy patients do not attend to their bills promptly whether they write the checks or not. They are either not generally concerned about these obligations or can resist awareness that the analyst is actually counting on the prompt payment of the fee. That the analyst works for a living becomes an interesting shared dilemma of idealization and devaluation. Analysts can struggle about bringing it up because they feel that they should not have to talk about money, because it makes them feel petty and small and reactively sanctimonious and superior.

For the analyst, the patient's wealth is "in the room," and the analyst must reckon with its force. There are common countertransference challenges that arise and demand attention.

WEALTH IN THE MIND OF THE ANALYST

Analysis demands that the analyst live in the shadows of the patient's life, as a private transformative presence maintaining boundaries and finding satisfaction in the work. However, as I have suggested, wealth feeds certain aspects of an individual's narcissism, and narcissism, in analysis and in life, is contagious. Under unrelenting transference pressures, analysts of the wealthy can be subject to countertransference envy and the need to defend against it. The seductive power of wealth and its inflaming of grandiosity may prompt the analyst's defensive idealization and narcissistic identification—the narcissistic satisfaction of being close to wealth and power—and its opposite: competitive devaluation and moral superiority.

With the wealthy, the ethical analyst cannot seek direct financial reward but can wish for recognition and gratitude from the rich and powerful. The wish to be special by being secretly in the patient's life, to be "the analyst to the great," can be expressed in various fantasies of public acknowledgment (e.g., a mention in a book or speech, a named professorship, a scholarship for analytic students, or some other concrete expression of the analyst's role in the patient's life).

Envy can become particularly problematic for the analyst for any number of acute or chronic, personal, and transferential reasons. Especially when being devalued in the transference, the analyst may seek shelter in illusions of analytic moral superiority. As a response to the narcissistic assaults of devaluing resistance and the painful envy of wealth's power and freedom, the analyst may take up the banner of antimaterialism and become pathologizing and moralistic. For example, harsh judgmental interpretations of grandiosity and superficiality, or of a paucity of mature values or genuine concern or empathy, may be signals of countertransference envy.

Analysts are far from immune to their place in society. For some, it is not particularly meaningful, and for others, having a profession represents a significant attainment of social standing, material comfort, and class. This can contribute to an insidious struggle with envy. Analysts can experience a form of "analytic schadenfreude," a private pleasure in the suffering and crisis of values of their wealthy patients. Confronted with limitless material opportunity and freedom from schedule and obligation, analysts may seek refuge in self-satisfaction and illusory superiority of a more meaningful and contributing life.

For the analyst, it is not easy to accept that one is "staff"—valued staff, but staff for the wealthy nonetheless. We value our knowledge, skill, and transference authority, and seeing ourselves as one of a retinue of service providers may not sit well. A fact of life for the wealthy can be the ease with which they can discard and replace parts of their service and material reality. We know that we are replaceable, or at least we should, but the facility or impulsivity of the wealthy to discard what is not useful, not pleasant, and the like can challenge an analyst's composure.

I have found it useful at times to remind myself of certain questions analysts should ask themselves but may be afraid (too guarded or ashamed) to ask. For all treatments, these questions are a form of self-consultation and "analytic hygiene," a form of checking with oneself: What are my fantasies? What might I be enacting? Am I envying? Living vicariously? Getting off on being the analyst to this patient, especially if he or she is superrich? Am I attempting to make myself more important, more needed to the rich? Am I seeking to be the personal consultant, the essential advisor to the patient, to the family, about the money?

WEALTH IN CHANGING TIMES

As elaborated in many of the chapters in this volume, we have been in a time of considerable economic pain and anxiety in this country since October 2008. A severe economic recession has taken hold. Many people have lost their jobs, their savings, and a belief in a secure future for themselves and their families. It is important to consider how this is manifest in the minds of analysts and their patients.

When analysts worry about what is going on in the room, they are simply doing their job. When analysts worry about health, money, family, career, and whatever else may be going on in our outside lives, it can be an unavoidable distraction from our work. Good analytic practice requires us to ask ourselves about how our personal concerns may reflect our participation in the clinical process or how realistic pressures, including financial ones, have an impact on our work.

When we as analysts are worried about money, for whatever reasons, it will intensify envy and the countertransference responses described. This will impair empathic sensitivity to the genuine concerns of the wealthy during financially stressful times. It can be difficult to empathize with someone who has lost the vast majority of his or her wealth but retains more money than the analyst could ever accumulate and have at his or her disposal. The idea of economizing or trimming expenses on luxuries, homes, staff, and trips can seem preposterous to a working analyst, to say nothing of the idea of cutting back on the treatment because of the cost.

Analysts need to be cautious. We need to be aware of the temptation to be dismissive or of an impulse to be critical or contemptuous of such concerns. What the wealthy patient may be experiencing when his or her money is threatened may be a well-shielded crisis in self-definition and identity. This can be an important opportunity for self-examination and reintegration of self-esteem. Sensitively explored, this can reveal aspects of narcissistic vulnerability and entitlement not previously accessible. Despair, rage, paralysis, and impulsiveness can emerge in the treatment as wealth appears to evaporate. Again, it is the meaning of the reality of wealth, not simply the amount of the money. When the wealthy remain untouched at times of financial crisis, fear of the envy of others can be a serious concern. Analyst and patient may collude to avoid awareness of the analyst's envy for fear of its destructive impact on the therapeutic relationship.

Fitzgerald was correct about the rich being different. But, according to legend, his friend Ernest Hemingway supposedly retorted: "Yes. They have more money!" I cannot agree with Hemingway. It is not just the "more." It is, as Fitzgerald described, what more money means and does to people. Money does not buy happiness. Having wealth can be a mixed blessing. For some, it is an empowering gift that offers freedom and creative opportunities; for others, it can be a crippling burden, a "golden prison." As analysts, we must take Fitzgerald to heart and remain vigilant about our own feelings about money, class, and a sense of difference. Analysis is about the exploration and understanding of difference. How the wealthy are different from us as analysts is part of the always-humbling and endlessly fascinating work of analysis.

REFERENCES

Fenichel, O. (1938). The drive to amass wealth. *Psychoanalytic Quarterly*, 7, 69–95.

Fitzgerald, F. S. (2006). Rich boy. In *All the sad young men*. Cambridge: Cambridge University Press, 5–42.

Freud, S. (1905). Three essays on the theory of sexuality. In J. Strachey (Ed. & Trans.), *The standard edition of the complete psychological works of Sigmund Freud*, Vol. 7. London: Hogarth Press, 125–245.

Olsen, P. A. (1986). Complexities in the psychology and psychotherapy of the phenomenally wealthy. In D. Krueger (Ed.), *The last taboo*. New York: Brunner/Mazel, 55–70.

Chapter 4

Analyzing a "new superego"
Greed and envy in the age of affluence

Janice S. Lieberman

In my psychoanalytic practice, which, I believe, is to some extent a mirror of the outside world, over the past decade I have witnessed a "new superego," a companion to "the new ego," a term that was used some 30-odd years ago in discussions of "the widening scope." Those of my patients who possess this new superego seem to be far less guilt ridden (at least consciously) and governed by a different set of values, ideals, and standards of behavior from those who possess the "old classic superego." Concurrently, I have listened to, and worked with, considerably more vocal and ego-syntonic expressions of greed and envy than ever before. Colleagues and supervisees have observed the same phenomenon both in clinical practice and "out there in the world."

I contend that "the new affluence" (still in place after recent economic calamities, who knows for how long), the fact that the world my patients live in consists of large numbers of very wealthy peers who lead extravagant lives, is instrumental in the activation of greed and envy. There is a wide gap between the "haves" and the "have-nots." I will limit myself to the issues of greed, envy, and the new superego as they pertain to matters of money and material possessions. I do not intend to address what they symbolize on a deeper, more unconscious level: love, the penis, the breast, the womb, and so on. Papers published recently in edited volumes by Roth and Lemma (2008) and Wurmser and Jarass (2008) fully address these issues.

I have done an extensive review of the existing psychoanalytic literature on greed, envy, and the superego. Unlike the work of the ego psychologists on the new ego, which adumbrated specific ego functions and how they could become arrested or problematic due to intrapsychic conflict, I have found the major articles on greed, envy, and especially the superego to be highly abstract and nonspecific. It did not seem to matter *what* the patient so greedily coveted or *who* the patient envied or for *what*. Similarly with the concept of the punitive superego, it did not seem to matter *what* the superego selected to punish the patient for or *what kind* of punishment was meted out.

The superego is supposed to perpetuate the culture. But, *what kind* of culture is it perpetuating? Manifest content for the most part has been disregarded, and it is unclear regarding how inferences about latent content were made. Little clinical material has been given to illustrate points made. In addition, the superego is a concept that seems to have gone out of style. In Sandler's (1960/1987) report on his research on the superego, he observed that therapists sorted data in terms of object relations, ego activities, and transference rather than superego, that there was an apparent "a conceptual dissolution of the superego" (p. 18). Brenner (1998, 2002) deconstructed the superego into wishes and compromise formations and substituted self-punitive tendencies for superego. Wurmser (2004) edited an issue of *Psychoanalytic Inquiry* titled "The Superego: A Vital or Supplanted Concept?" The authors of the articles in this issue varied in the importance they ascribed to the superego. I myself find the concept to be of use and hope to resurrect it. It has been my observation that the superego appears wearing a very different cloak from the days when Freud developed his theories of the mind.

Freud developed his theories about the superego over many years. In *On Narcissism* (1914), he conceived of it as derived from the standards of behavior set by the parents and from parental criticism. In *The Ego and the Id* (1923/1960), he saw it as formed from the repression of the Oedipal complex and as standing for conscience in its entirety. According to Loewald (1980):

> Insofar as the superego is the agency of inner standards, demands, ideals, hopes, and concerns in regard to the ego, the agency of inner rewards and punishments in respect to which the ego experiences contentment or guilt, the superego functions from the viewpoint of a future ego, from the standpoint of the ego's future that is to be reached, is being reached, is being failed or abandoned by the ego. (p. 45)

As Lansky (2004) put it so well, superego punishment is manifested in "self-defeating, self-harming, and self-sabotaging thought or action" (p. 153). We psychoanalysts were taught to assume that our patients had well-formed egos and first to analyze the harsh, punitive superego. We were not taught how to work with superegos that are weak or have lacunae. Those with superego lacunae were thought to be unanalyzable or untreatable.

The traditional definition of superego as consisting of the conscience and the ego ideal is based on a generalized model that is highly ethical, moral, and uniform (Ernest Jones, 1948, wrote about its "spirituality"). It has been my observation that the new superego is based on a different, more narcissistically based morality: For many in our culture today *attaining one's high ideal and even "goodness" is reached through physical exercise, diet, and fitness; it also comes from acquiring wealth.* It does not have to come from altruistic deeds or kindness to others or what has been traditionally regarded as "moral" behavior. The oft-heard expression "no pain, no gain" is used by trainers and physical therapists who have in many cases replaced psychotherapists as well as priests, ministers, and rabbis. Excessive exercise and self-starvation creating temporary or permanent damage to the body seems to me to be a 21st-century replacement for the self-flagellation and fasting of yore.

When back in 1925 F. Scott Fitzgerald wrote in *The Great Gatsby* "about how different the rich and from you and me," he was referring to a hidden world of a privileged few who most people did not see or even read about in their daily lives. In the past 10 years, the socioeconomic pie has been reconfigured. At least until a few months ago, not only were the rich getting richer, but also there were many of them, and many of them were known to you and me. This has been well documented (Frank, 2007; Herbert, 2008; Johnston, 2007; Sorkin, 2007). Even in the recent years of recession, the media (*The New York Times, The Wall Street Journal,* CNBC) have been replete with stories about $45-million apartments, $50-million paintings, and those who use their private jets to travel to their multiple homes. The newly rich hire an increasingly large army of experts to tell them where to donate their money and what to give to their children. In our major cities live large numbers of men and women in their 20s and 30s who have earned millions in financial arenas and in the better law firms; some have already retired. They inhabit the increasing number of high-end expensive co-ops and condos being built and eat in four- and five-star restaurants, and their indifference to any thrift or questioning of bills has driven the price of everything upward in the neighborhoods in which they live. The term *affluenza* has become part of our parlance. In these years in which our economy has been in difficulty, the gap has only widened.

There is a clear demarcation between these haves and the have-nots of their own age. At this moment in time, among the have-nots are the higher-educated university professors, scholars, scientists, doctors, psychiatrists, psychoanalysts, social workers: *ourselves and the bulk of those who we see in clinical practice.* Those among us who have in treatment a number of the haves privately complain to one other that our wealthier patients often present greater fee collection issues than those who do not have so much money. Some of our wealthy patients feel entitled because of their wealth to withhold and make us analysts out to be the greedy ones, anxious to collect our fees.

A recent *New York Times* article (Konigsberg, 2008), about a psychoanalyst who charged his wealthy patients $600 an hour, is an illustration of such a countertransference and greed-driven enactment. Frosch (2008) reminded us that Freud (1913) linked money with sex. Freud's loss of control around money influenced his technical position about fees and charging for missed sessions. Frosch's own experience around money and missed sessions led him to believe that many analysts are filled with shame over being dependent on their patients for their livelihood. I would add to this the shame that is felt in some cases when the analyst finds himself or herself in much more reduced financial circumstances than his or her patients. Since October 2008, the potential for reduced circumstances of psychoanalysts who are dependent for their livelihood on patients who have lost or might lose their jobs has increased the potential for countertransference problems in these patients' treatment.

Not much has been written about greedy and envious patients since Joan Riviere (1932/1991) and Melanie Klein (1957) addressed these subjects, but I have found a few excellent references: A panel at the meetings of the American Psychoanalytic Association in 2000 chaired by Cairo-Chiarandini was given the title of Hemingway's (1937) novel *To Have and Have Not*; Wurmser and Jarass (2008) have edited a book about jealousy and envy. There are some writings on the clinical issues that arise when working with wealthy patients (Dimen, 1994; Josephs, 2004; Kirsner, 2007; Rothstein, 1986; Warner, 1991). Kaplan (1991) wrote a clinically based article on greed that served as a rich resource for me. I share with him the observation that greedy and envious people are usually part of the widening scope of psychoanalysis and may need many years of psychotherapy before they can be analyzed. Their greed and envy are syntonic, and the sources of the difficulties they have in life are externalized for a long period of time. Their parents or spouses, even "fate" and "bad luck," are held to blame for whatever misfortunes brought them into treatment. The old-fashioned term *oral-dependent character* seems to apply to many of them. Superego functioning seems remiss.

In this chapter, I address some of the interrelations between the socioeconomic fact of the recent affluence, the activation of greed and envy, and a new set of superego values, the contents of which are quite different from the values most psychoanalysts, including myself, hold. A degree of *concrete specification* is needed. I present clinical examples that are illustrative and make some speculations about a shift in child rearing at the end of the 20th century that I believe has resulted in what we are finding in our clinical practices and observing in our personal lives today.

Kohut (1971) made a distinction between the traditional "guilty man" around which Freudian psychoanalysis has been organized and the more recent tragic "narcissistic man." The former has an internalized superego, formed as an outcome of the resolution of the Oedipal complex. Kohut believed that the central preoccupation of people today is not guilt or moral conflict, but boredom and dissatisfaction. Traditional psychoanalysis has usually begun with a softening of the harsh, strict superego that punishes the person with unbearable feelings of guilt and depressive affect when the person falls short of his or her ideals and values. *It is my observation that traditional superego definitions do not relate to a certain number of people today, some of whom are our patients.*

Greed and envy are on the short list of "the seven deadly sins," along with their companions lust, gluttony, sloth, wrath, and pride. By contrast, in this age of narcissistic man and the recent affluence, we observe a lack of guilt over greed and envy, little apology for hurting others or the analyst, and a history of a lack of consequences for bad behavior. The outgrowth of the age of narcissism is an "age of entitlement." Since this kind of behavior (formerly regarded as "misbehavior") has become so prevalent, and government figures no longer provide us with role models for "good behavior;" it is not really possible to label those feeling "entitled" as "the Exceptions" (Blum, 2001; Freud, 1916; Kris, 1976). They are getting to be the norm.

I believe that such social change and a new social reality have had a strong impact on the psyches of our patients as well as ourselves. *I do not consider this to be "old wine in new bottles."* It is my thesis that what is intrapsychic can be stimulated and amplified by social reality. Waelder (1936) of course emphasized this point with his "principle of multiple function." His inclusion of "external reality," the outside world, as a force on the ego, on the psyche, is something I take quite seriously in my work. But what we call "the relevant social context" is seldom considered in our writings unless it is "early 20th-century Vienna" or "the Holocaust." The state of the world post-1950 is taken for granted rather than examined as a causative factor.

A brief example illustrates how times and my own view of the world have changed. About 10 years ago, a 40-year-old investment banker came into treatment with me. He lived in a Westchester suburb and commuted to the city for work. He discovered that his wife was having an affair with her trainer, and she had asked him for a divorce. He was especially upset about the potential sale of their home and the dividing up of his wealth. He cried because his daughter would no longer have a theater, as they did on their property, and he was afraid that because of this she would no longer be popular with her friends at school. He believed strongly that with less money he could not possibly attract the kind of woman he desired—a physical "10." Despite my keen awareness of his inner narcissistic issues at that time, I had difficulty imagining or relating to his world. It was difficult to feel empathic with this man in order to really help him. Ten years later, the media and what I have personally witnessed in my private life and have heard from my patients have made it so that I can imagine it, although I am still as far from it in my own life financially and value-wise as I was then.

We psychoanalysts can no longer consider ourselves to be upper-echelon earners, if we ever were. The realities of managed care, medication as a solution to dysphoria, and a world in which people have little time for personal introspection are some of the factors that have reduced the number of hours that we can book. As psychoanalysts, we have good reason to worry about the future, particularly because of the recent economic collapse. Many of us use a certain amount of denial in order not to ruin our days (Dimen, 1994; Josephs, 2004). Furthermore, psychoanalysts' ability to accrue wealth is limited by the number of hours we work (I am not referring to those who have been born into or have married into money). Until the recent crisis in the economy in America, psychoanalytic patients in many other fields have had real opportunities to amass wealth. Some have no wish to do so. And some, due to neurotic reasons, do not do so, even when they consciously wish to. Warner (1991) has addressed this topic quite frontally. He asserted that such situations have potential for serious countertransference acting out. He noted that: "Most analysts have middle-class origins. They may share in the frequently found middle-class covert hatred or envy of the rich. … To cover it up the analyst can either show a reaction formation and be excessively ingratiating or act out this hostility by putting down the rich patient" (p. 590). Dimen (1994), in her thoughtful article on money, reminded us that Freud referred to his wealthy patients as "goldfish."

Josephs (2004), in a similarly thoughtful article, has observed that: "It is increasingly assumed that being a psychoanalyst in the United States can no longer consistently provide for the attainment of the current normative American standard of middle-class affluence" (p. 391). He, like myself, has seen a number of young patients who do not know what to do with themselves, are irresponsible, and reliant on their parents to support the treatment. They are envious of his fee. Their parents regularly inquire why the patient needs to go more than once a week. Others have parents who will not give them any money. Josephs remarked that: "These patients are barely on speaking terms with their parents" (p. 400). A few months ago, a woman patient from Argentina told me that she became so angry with her mother who was visiting for a week that she could not talk to her for 4 days. This anger arose because her mother felt that she could not afford to buy my patient an apartment in the West Village of New York.

Most of us who conduct psychoanalysis rely intrapsychically on inner values and are sustained more by the quality of our relationships and experiences than we are by material things. (There are exceptions, of course.) We pretty much accept and make the best of our lot in life. To what extent should our personal values be expressed to patients with different value systems? In a world in which those who "go for the money" are more valued than we ourselves, do we do our patients a disservice if we attempt overtly, or more likely, covertly, to shape them according to the way *we* are? To those of us who have supported ourselves since we were in our 20s, adults who feel entitled to parental financial assistance and refuse to work seem disturbed and are disturbing to us. Today, women who insist that their husbands support them and refuse to work seem also to be disturbed, or at least greedy and spoiled. But, one can ask whether they are just coming to treatment with another set of cultural values. I believe that these are important issues for us to ponder.

The 1980s were a great time on Wall Street. In Oliver Stone's film by that name, the main character, Gordon Gekko, declared that: "Greed is good. Greed works, greed is right, greed clarifies, cuts through and captures the essence of the revolutionary spirit." A new era was launched. Those born between 1960 and 1980, who are roughly 30 to 50 today, grew up with a new value system. It was a time of prosperity in which there was also much self-examination. (In our field, too, Freud was dissected and deconstructed and parts of his theory reassembled by Kohut, Kernberg, Greenberg and Mitchell, and others.) Whatever was previously considered to be sacred was challenged: the Viet Nam war, the institution of marriage, and, in particular, gender roles. When I began my practice in the mid-1970s, antimaterialism, the "greening of America," autonomy, and self-sufficiency were valued. It was a time of feminist uprising: Mothers went back to school and back to work, and some divorced. For a long time, there was little or no backup mothering. Unlike today, when we have in place an army of professional caregivers and excellent daycare centers, the parenting many children received was uneven at best. Latchkey children were met at the end of the day by mothers who were too tired to give them needed attention. Mothers and fathers felt guilty that their children had two parents working; some were guilty that their children had to witness divorce and live in two different places. Misusing psychological and psychoanalytic advice and expertise, they often tolerated the excessive demands of their children, many of whom we are seeing as adults in analysis and therapy today.

Let me fast-forward to the first decade of the 21st century. The kind of separation-individuation most of us worked at in our youth and worked at 20 or 30 years ago with our patients is no longer desired.* Today, many families are more often or not enmeshed. Children, adolescents, and grown children dominate their parents, who are fearful that their children will hate them or, especially, abandon them. Whereas in the 1970s "terrorist" adolescents or "20-somethings" were involved in political causes, in this decade terrorist adolescents and 20-somethings demand money and material things from their parents. We have in our practices young adults who were both emotionally deprived and overindulged at the same time. I have coined the term *masked deprivation* to describe what I have witnessed: Material things are provided but not the kind of psychological attunement needed for children to develop optimally. Many young adults today do not

---

* Freud also, unwillingly, left Brucke's lab when Brucke told him to "get practical." He was engaged and had to earn a living (Makari, 2008).

have the necessary ego strength and frustration tolerance to seek work that will support them. They observe their friends' parents supporting them, buying them apartments, finding them jobs and partners. They do not leave home even when they have physically left home and are tied to their parents all day long by cell phones, BlackBerries, or iPhones. I have seen in my clinical practice, as well as in my private life, the seduction and courting of young married couples, who are taken by the parents of one member of the couple on expensive vacations, promised country houses near these parents and many other luxuries in an effort to keep the family together. In some cases, this happens also to ensure that the *other* family does not get to see the couple or their future children as much.

All the more problematic for psychoanalytic treatment, the parents often pay for and thus compromise or try to control the treatment. In his article on the children of wealthy parents, Warner (1991) noted that "their sense of reality can become distorted because if they get in trouble they know they will always be 'bailed out' and never have to face the consequences of their actions as others do" (p. 579). They externalize, get their doctors to tell them what they want to hear. "Another significant transference problem is the attempted seduction of the analyst through the affluent patient's money, charm or power" (p. 590). Also relevant here is the work of Rothstein (1986). As we know, Freud himself was not immune to this as he sought funds to support his psychoanalytic endeavors. As Kirsner (2007) has noted, Greenson, who wrote a bible of proper technique, stretched the boundaries not only with Marilyn Monroe but also with a number of superrich patients.

At this juncture, I want to make the point that the majority of those I work with, whose parents were able to cut emotional and financial umbilical cords when they graduated from college, do not seem to be plagued by these issues. They found jobs, and if they have conflicts in work or love, these are not encumbered by envy or greed. I can describe them as having *fiber*, moral fiber, something that seems to be lacking in the ever-increasing number of patients I am speaking about. They have reasonable mature superegos and suffer from failure to live up to overly idealistic and unrealistic ego-ideals. Those with the new superego, on the other hand, often were sexually active at a much earlier age, sleeping with their partners in their parents' houses. If they were lazy, or rude to their parents or teachers, there were few or no consequences. Their parents (and their culture) set the bar for good behavior at a very different level from that of previous generations.

Despite the considerable advances women have made in the world at large, some of my young women patients seem to be in particular difficulty. Overgratification and prolonged dependency on parents has resulted in their limited acquisition of basic skills for functioning independently: cooking, furnishing a home, purchasing clothing, paying bills. We have a generation of young women who hire lactation specialists to help them to nurse; specialists to plan weddings, wrap gifts, set tables, choose colors for rooms; personal shoppers to choose a wardrobe and create their "style"; and personal assistants to do it all. Spas have multiplied as this generation demands constant soothing and massage of every part of their bodies as a way of coping with poor anxiety tolerance, the end result of the combination of early overgratification and neglect. Coupled with the expectation that they have successful careers and gorgeous homes is the social expectation that they look perfect and have perfect bodies, requiring hours at the gym and rigorous dieting, further reducing their energy. When I hear about this day after day, I long nostalgically for the days of the greening of America in the late 1960s and early 1970s, when Dr. Spock advised future parents that they could put the new baby in a dresser drawer if they could not yet afford a crib—a far cry from the designer furniture every newborn has to have today. Part of the new superego admonitions is that newborns be provided with the best of everything or their parents will or should feel guilty.

Some of the young men I have seen in my practice have suffered from having had parents who were often absent when they needed them. But now as young adults they are expected to achieve. They are watched over like hawks, and at the first sign of faltering, their parents take over, writing applications to colleges for them, making phone calls and pulling strings to get them into jobs. These efforts are not private, but public, and the young men exchange the shame of potential failure for the shame of letting their parents take over. One male patient, 45 years old, spent hours on the phone with his mother, who counseled every minute of his business deal, hoping that his business success would take him off the dole. It was my contention that the exact opposite effect would occur.

GREED

At this juncture, one might ask just what is greed, and what makes an analyst think that his or her patient is greedy? The assessment of greed from manifest content is problematic because it is so culture and value system specific. "Affluence" is also culture specific. I recall a supervisor of mine in the early 1970s calling a patient of mine "greedy" because she and her friends celebrated her birthday at an expensive restaurant. I assessed this as finally "letting herself have things." Paradoxically, when I needed another control case this same supervisor referred to me as suitable for analysis an educated young man who arrived wearing a T-shirt that said "Outrageous." He hoped to pay me $5 per session and to come 4 days per week. He was a graduate student who was about to marry a wealthy woman. Her father was paying for their honeymoon (the Grand Tour of Europe and stays in five-star hotels) and had also purchased an apartment for them. He had no plans to work for years.

What happens in the treatment when the analyst's personal values, the analyst's notions of what is right or wrong, differ from those of the patient? It creates a complication in the analysis that must be thought about on an ongoing basis. It is difficult to work with sensitivity without seeming judgmental.

One woman patient, Helen, came to treatment because of her overspending many thousands of dollars every month on clothing she did not need but was desperate for. When she walked in the street and she saw a woman better dressed than she, wearing some stylish article of clothing she had not thought to purchase, she suffered a panic attack due to the intensity of her envy. She could not rest until she had purchased a similar item. The sudden realization that she had the wrong point on her boots or handle on last year's handbag would send her into a panic, which was then followed by a shopping spree to try to set things right.

Helen was particularly susceptible to the selling techniques of a luxury department store personal shopper. No amount of analysis (e.g., asking her about her thoughts, fantasies, and moods just prior to a shopping spree) could enable her to check her desire. She was conscious of worrying that her spending was putting too much pressure on her husband and that he might die. She was unable to access her unconscious death wish toward him. Her husband (whom I suspected of having an affair) was unable to assist in her curbing her expenditures either. I surmised that he tolerated it due to his own guilt, but perhaps he was as greedy as she was, since in some couples one member of the pair acts as the agent for the other's less-conscious desires.

Helen reminded me of Joan Riviere's (1932/1991) patient for whom "all pleasures for her must be acquired and enjoyed at some other person's expense" (p. 198), purchasing expensive clothes so she would deprive her husband and children. Riviere discovered that under the jealousy of her patient, who needed a triangle in which to operate, lay a "dominant phantasy." She had to seize or obtain from some other person something the person desired, thus robbing and despoiling that person.

The countertransference pitfalls when working with such a patient are obvious. Steiner (2008) noted "the enormous pressure on the analyst to take sides in an argument in which the moral aspects of the situation come to the fore. ... We tend to step into a superego role which conforms to the patient's internal superego as it has been projected into us" (p. 45).

For another patient, Eleanor, immersed in the world of affluenza, eating large numbers of sweets did make her feel very guilty, but the other behaviors did not. Her closets were so filled with the clothes that she had purchased at bargain prices that she had to rent storage space to contain some of them. The contents of her superego were very different from my own. Greed as a sin originally had to do with gluttony. In today's world, overeating is a sin, whereas purchasing four houses is a subject for admiration. The duchess of Windsor's motto, "You cannot be too rich or too thin!" has become a superego injunction.

ENVY

As Josephs (2004) wrote: "It is vastly underreported in the clinical literature how much session time college-educated professional patients, especially in New York City, spend ventilating their financial insecurities" (p. 390). I have had similar observations. In my practice, I hear patients express envy of their wealthy parents (with Oedipal overtones), successful siblings, friends, colleagues, and neighbors. A number of my patients are chronically envious of me. Their envy serves as a chronic resistance and at times leads to a negative therapeutic reaction. They envy my fee, my professional standing, where my office is located, and so on. When there is a genuine difference between my material reality as seen and that of the patient's, it makes it difficult to help the patient to observe the transferential aspect of his or her reactions. When I first began my practice, I worked with a young married professional woman who seemed to admire me as a potential role model. She was very limited in what she did other than her work and had never been out of New York. One August, the session before my vacation, she casually inquired where I was going. In spite of everything I had been taught, I told her that I was going to Russia, hoping to inspire her to stretch her own geographical boundary. In September, she returned and told me she was terminating. If I had been to Russia that meant I had been everywhere else and that she was too envious to work with me. There was no talking her out of this, and I never saw her again. What I hoped for as a positive identification was totally naïve. At that moment, I became aware of the destructive and often-hidden envy that can stumble any treatment, and why an anonymous stance is usually the best one to take. When thinking about this years later, I believe that I had unconsciously participated in the need of her inner world for an object she could be envious of and destroy.

The *Random House American Dictionary* (1968) defines *envy* as "a feeling of discontent or mortification, usually with ill will at seeing another's superiority, advantages, or success" (p. 402). Laplanche and Pontalis (1973) did not list greed in their compendium, and they referenced envy as limited to penis envy. (Freud wrote often of jealousy and less about envy, which he also limited to penis envy, placing it in the phallic phase.) But, they worked and observed in times different from ours. For Freud, envy was a cognitive event, whereas for Klein (1957) it was first an affect and then linked with a perception. Klein noted the confusion between envy and jealousy. Envy is the earlier and more primitive affect. She defined envy as "the angry feeling that another person possesses and enjoys something desirable—the envious impulse being to take it away or to spoil it. Moreover, envy implies the subject's relation to one person only and goes back to the earliest exclusive relationship with the mother" (p. 181). Klein agreed with Abraham's idea that envy is oral-sadistic and anal-sadistic. She conceived of primary envy of the breast that is constitutional and that does not have to do with frustration (Roth & Lemma, 2008). As part of the death instinct, there is envy of the "intolerable goodness" of the breast; envy arises at the moment when "good" is "not-me."

Klein (1957) viewed greed as mainly bound up with introjection and envy with projection. Kaplan's (1991) reading of Klein is that

> in greed, as contrasted with envy, there is much less recognition of the object and the focus is on possession and supplies. On an unconscious oral level, greed aims to suck out and devour the breast, essentially robbing it of its possessions. While envy has this aim, it additionally seeks to put bad parts of the self into the mother/breast. In this sense greed relates more to introjection and devouring mechanisms while envy is closely associated with spoiling aspects. (p. 512)

Whichever comes first developmentally, I have observed a close connection between greed and envy. Clinically, I have observed greed to be born of envy. The envious feel empty. As they approach getting what they want, they become so greedy that they destroy it. Boris (1990) has noted that "the conversion of greed into appetite is an event of the first importance. Appetite ... is susceptible to satisfaction. Greed is not. In greed ... any gratification only further stimulates the greed" (p. 130). According to Klein (1957), "another defense against envy is closely linked with greed. By *internalizing* the breast so *greedily* that in the infant's mind it becomes entirely his possession and controlled by him, he feels that all he attributes to it will be his own. This is used to counteract envy" (p. 218). Spillius (1993) concurred: "Greedy acquisition can be a defense against being aware of envy of those who are what one wishes one had or were oneself" (p. 1199).

MARGERY

With the following vignette taken from the four-times-weekly psychoanalysis of Margery, I demonstrate the interconnections between greed, envy, and the superego. Margery presented with many issues, both on a neurotic level and on a character-disordered level, but she was self-reflective and conscientious, an excellent patient. I just present here the severest of her character pathology to illustrate clinical manifestations of envy, greed, and the superego.

Margery lied on her résumé, cheated on her expense sheet, and abused salespeople and employees. She shoplifted as a teenager, and her mother seemed as if she did not notice that Margery had a continual change of new clothes. She envied her sisters and most of her friends. Each and every one had all the things she wanted and felt deprived of. She stole small things from the apartments of one of her sisters and a greatly envied friend. For many years, the only way she was able to be with me in the room was to regard me as a "nothing," having nothing she wanted. Although she spent many of her hours speaking of her envy of various figures in her life with whom she would become obsessed, when I inquired from time to time, she told me that she had no thoughts about me when she left her sessions. She averted her gaze entering and leaving my office, never looking at me. I analyzed her sadism, her aggression gone amuck in her life outside my office. The transference was for the most part displaced.

Margery had no man in her life for many years. When one year a kind man from her past came on the scene and confessed that he had secretly been in love with her in college, her sadism and greed reemerged. She made outrageous demands of him, that he buy her jewelry, that he take her to expensive resorts, and that she would only fly first class. He became hostile, then exploded with rage at her. They broke up, and she was back to square one.

Margery grew up in a wealthy suburb of Chicago. As she described it, her mother was unresponsive to her real needs, and her father was preoccupied with his business. Her parents were "keeping up with the Joneses," decorating and redecorating their home and taking fancy trips. Thus, her parents both served as greedy identification figures. In a dream of the first year in analysis, she pictured her mother as a whale: "There was this big fat whale with fins on it. I was holding onto one and someone else to the other. Someone was jabbing a large point into it—maybe me." Her associations: "The whale is my mother, me attacking her and her attacking me. She eats everyone up around her. I hate her enough to kill her. I feel like my whole body is filled with anger and hatred—a limitless well. I feel so much hatred it could kill me rather than her."

When treatment began, Margery did not want to work. She held a series of low-level jobs while waiting for a man to come along and support her. Once when out of a job she remarked how tired it made her to respond to want ads at night. When questioning her why she did not do that in the morning when she was feeling fresh, she snarled "I don't do mornings. I go to the gym in the morning." Margery's unhappiness was palpable, and her mother tried to pacify her by buying her a television, clothes, a fur coat. Nothing worked. She spent her weekends in department stores, and when she had worked up a large debt managed to persuade her father to pay it.

The Oedipal implications of this scenario were not lost on me—Margery wanted what her mother had. Her failures and her guilty self-flagellation (for not having married a wealthy man as did her sisters, for not having a perfect body) seemed to be less from punishment of a structured superego than an unconscious beating fantasy used by sadomasochistic patients (Novick & Novick, in Wurmser, 2004).

In her treatment, she would not permit me to talk much. "Let me finish. ... You are interrupting. ... It's my session. ... I am paying you to listen." But, she was "hungry" for her sessions, came exactly on time four times per week for years. At times working with her felt like being in a cage with a lion. If I moved close, she could bite me. The envious person cannot receive. Taking could be a gift to the giver (Cairo-Chiarandini, 2001). Her sense of inner emptiness was profound. At times, Margery cried in pain that she was so lonesome: She had no friends and was not close to her family. Both sisters had married wealthy men, and her mother preferred them to her.

Despite the emotional difficulties of working with her, requiring constant monitoring of the countertransference, I was engaged in the treatment because I saw positive gains in certain areas. Within 2 years of one another, each of her parents died, and they were no longer available to give her material things. Their enabling her pathology ceased with their deaths. Margery started a small business that grew and grew, and she began to have interactions with a wide range of interesting people. Her self-reflection increased, and she developed a sharp sense of humor. She began to travel and go to museums and concerts. She did, however, continue to abuse her underlings (a displacement from the transference, among other things). She greedily overworked them so that eventually they would sabotage the work or leave her. She was periodically nasty to me, and her response when confronted was: "I pay you, so I can do what I want with you." This abated over several years of reflecting to her what she was doing with me. I began to receive apologetic phone calls after such episodes, which I regarded as a psychological advance.

The treatment might not have moved as far as it did had it not been for some construction taking place on the street outside my office window. One day, about 10 minutes prior to Margery's session, a jackhammer appeared to break up the sidewalk. The noise was deafening. Margery traveled quite a distance to get to my office, which is in my apartment. I made a quick decision to walk her to my study, a neutral book-lined room, where we could work in quiet. She had never been in any part of my apartment but the office and bathroom. She was reluctant to go, but could not think from the noise (and I also was having difficulty thinking because of the noise). She entered the study, began to panic and had to return to my office. After she recovered, she said: "I have enough to deal with just with *me* and not with *you*. I thought the rooms in the back would be small, like my bedroom, but now I know you have a large room and maybe more large rooms, and that is very upsetting to me." The woman who had averted her gaze and seemed oblivious of me had, in the few minutes in my study, noticed a child's game in the bookcase. "Now, I have to think of you as having children, probably grandchildren. I cannot handle it. It means you have had sex, relationships." Margery came to the next session but would not speak about her reactions. She ranted about her anger at an intern who worked for her, about how he messed up the work. Then, she began to forget to come to her sessions, leaving me waiting for her. She wanted to destroy me and the treatment due to her envy. As Segal (1964) has noted, "Strong feelings of envy lead to despair. An ideal object cannot be found" (p. 41).

Now that her envy of me had entered the transference in such a direct way, we were both able to look at it. There were prominent Oedipal as well as oral sadistic components to it. Entering the study felt like a primal scene repetition. Her mother had everything, and she had nothing. Similarly, her sisters had husbands, and she had none. On reflection, I believe that unconsciously I was tired of being excluded and not spoken about in the narcissistic transference, and that entered into my enactment. I felt that sending her away would have felt like rejection to her. Steiner (2008) wrote about the analyst's attempt to regain a position in the transference when ignored.

It took a jackhammer to pierce the defensive skin of indifference to me. In thinking about it, I ask whether I had been colluding with her defense, unconsciously fearing the aggression and envy that lay underneath. What seemed to be a "twinship" transference (Kohut, 1971), a kind of merger, was defending against the pain of seeing me as ahead of her. Margery's treatment calls to mind Carpy's idea:

[T]hat patients who feel aggrieved are unable to mourn the loss of the good experiences they feel they ought to have had. Instead these patients stick to their bad experiences as proof of their deprivation and their right to redress. Acceptance of the loss of the good experiences they have missed out on would mean having to face acute feelings of envy, both of the good object they should have had, and of the self they should have been. Thus better to hate than to mourn. Viewed from this angle being aggrieved is both a narcissistic defense and a defense against awareness of envy. (Spillius, in Cairo-Chiarandini, 2001, p. 1397)

Riviere's (1932/1991) formulation is that jealousy serves as a protection from deeper guilt feelings for a much more archaic form of fantasy: To steal something from another person on an oral-erotic and oral-sadistic basis seems relevant here. One of Margery's earliest memories is of biting her bonnet string as her mother chastised her. As an adult, she was prone to biting sarcasm and ridicule and had the uncomfortable self-punishing habit of biting the inside of her cheek and her tongue. According to Wurmser and Jarass (2008): " 'The narcissistic injury,' the gaping wound experienced by ours and Riviere's patients, is traced by her to the condemnation by the superego. It is viewed as expiation for the unconscious robbing and aggressive impulses ... by the very early 'heterosexual oral-genital envy' " (p. 12). Kaplan (1991) also observed these dynamics.

CONCLUDING REMARKS

Conducting psychoanalytic treatment with the greedy and envious patients of today is a considerable challenge when the content of the psychoanalyst's superego—the notions of right and wrong, the ideals and values—are so very different from theirs. The countertransference must be monitored on an ongoing basis so that the psychoanalyst does not give in to the temptation to say: "You are greedy," "You are envious," "What makes you think that your father should pay your rent?" or "You should not treat your sister so badly because she has just become engaged." These patients are quite provocative, and the analyst must resist the temptation to retaliate. They are also narcissistically quite fragile and keep a tentative attachment to the treatment and to the analyst. On the other hand, the analyst must also not hang back with stony silence, detaching from the patient with sanctimonious disapproval. These patients are in treatment because they are suffering, feel empty, and are trying to fill themselves with what does not fulfill.

I have had some success when I ask the patient to anticipate the reality consequences of his behavior. "What do you think will happen if you do this?" I have asked: "How do you think (your sister) feels when you say that? Does that matter to you?" I have remarked: "It might bother another person to come late for dinner at her sister's house. It does not seem to bother you. How come?" That is, I work with greed and envy by asking the patient to think about his or her actions and thoughts, fostering a capacity for self-reflection. My stance is neutral and empathic. I have also, when material possessions are so coveted, learned to stay with the concreteness and not attempt to ask what the coveted leather chair stands for or the desired co-op apartment means on a symbolic level. By staying with the concreteness, I have found that within time, sometimes many years, these patients feel attuned to and the narcissistic repair affected in the psychoanalytic treatment enables them eventually to think on a more symbolic, metaphoric level (see Lieberman, 2000). Working with greed, envy, and superego that appear in dreams and in the displaced transference further enables these patients to face themselves and to reflect on themselves.

My description of these patients might lead the reader to think of it as a judgmental rant. It does contain some of my frustration working with them as well as with the predominant materialism of our times. I struggle as I listen to them with their maladjustment. I question what would make for optimal "adjustment" to our culture. What is a "healthy conscience"? A healthy, reasonable "ego-ideal"? I examine my own superego, its conscious aspects. I was trained with the adage: "Where id was, there ego shall be; where superego was, there ego shall be." The id today seems to have obtained more supremacy in the psyche as it is allied with the new superego. Again, the new superego insists that one exercise, diet, focus on the body and its appearance, and amass material possessions and wealth. Profound states of loneliness and emptiness seem to be the outcome along with increased reliance on mood-altering drugs, legal and illegal, as well as alcohol.

I wonder what Freud would think about our times? Freud (1921/1959), who cited Le Bon and "the herd instinct," might not have been surprised at the recent Wal-Mart stampede on Black Friday, greed and superego function gone amok, or the behavior of the leaders of Enron and AIG. At the end of his life, Freud (1940) wrote about the superego acting

> the role of an external world toward the ego, although it has become part of the internal world. During the whole of a man's later life it represents the influence of his childhood, of the care and education given to him by his parents, of his dependence on them—of the childhood which is so greatly prolonged in human beings by a common family life. And in all of this what is operating is not only the personal qualities of the parents but also everything that produced a determining effect upon them themselves, the tastes and standards of the social class in which they live and the characteristics and traditions of the race from which they spring. (pp. 122–123)

Would Freud think that the tastes and standards of these times are allied with the death instinct about which he was so pessimistic? Or, would he see the psychoanalyst as the combatant of false and shallow values, and possibly a conqueror?

REFERENCES

Abraham, K. (1924). The influence of oral eroticism in character formation. In *Selected Papers of Karl. Abraham*, trans, D. Bryan and A. Strachey. London: Hogarth.

Blum, H. (2001). The exceptions reviewed: The formation and deformation of the privileged character. *Psychoanalytic Study of the Child*, 56, 123–136.

Boesky, D. (2007). Principle of multiple function: Revisiting a classic 75 years later. *Psychoanalytic Quarterly*, 76, 93–117.

Brenner, C. (1998). Beyond the ego and the id revisited. *Journal of Clinical Psychoanalysis*, 7, 165–180.

Brenner, C. (2002). Conflict, compromise formation and structural theory. *Psychoanalytic Quarterly, 71*, 397–417.

Cairo-Chiarandini, I. (2001). To have and have not: Clinical uses of envy. *Journal of the American Psychoanalytic Association, 49*, 1391–1404.

Dimen, M. (1994). Money, love and hate: Contradictions and paradox in psychoanalysis. *Psychoanalytic Dialogues, 4*, 69–100.

Fitzgerald, F. S. (1925). *The Great Gatsby*. New York: Scribner Classics.

Frank, R. H. (2007). *Falling behind: How rising inequality harms the middle class*. New York: Basic Books.

Freud, S. (1913). On beginning the treatment. In J. Strachey (Ed. & Trans.), *The standard edition of the complete psychological works of Sigmund Freud* (Vol. 12, pp. 121–144). London: Hogarth Press.

Freud, S. (1914). On narcissism. In J. Strachey (Ed. & Trans.), *The standard edition of the complete psychological works of Sigmund Freud* (Vol. 14, pp. 73–102). London: Hogarth Press.

Freud, S. (1916). Some character types met within psychoanalytic work. In J. Strachey (Ed. & Trans.), *The standard edition of the complete psychological works of Sigmund Freud* (Vol. 14, pp. 309–333). London: Hogarth Press.

Freud, S. (1919). The "uncanny." In J. Strachey (Ed. & Trans.), *The standard edition of the complete psychological works of Sigmund Freud* (Vol. 17, pp. 217–252). London: Hogarth Press.

Freud, S. (1959). *Group psychology and the analysis of the ego* (J. Strachey, Trans.). New York: Norton. (Original work published 1921)

Freud, S. (1960). *The ego and the id* (J. Strachey, Trans.). New York: Norton. (Original work published 1923)

Frosch, A. (2008, May 8). Discussion at a panel on money. New York Institute of Psychoanalysis.

Johnston, D. C. (2007, December 15). Report says that the rich are getting richer faster, much faster. *New York Times*, p. C3.

Jones, E. (1947). The genesis of the superego. In *Papers on psychoanalysis* (5th ed.). London: Balliere, Tindall & Cox, 1948, 145–152.

Josephs, L. (2004). Seduced by affluence: How material envy strains the analytic relationship. *Contemporary Psychoanalysis, 40*, 389–408.

Kaplan, H. (1991). Greed: A psychoanalytic perspective. *Psychoanalytic Review, 78*, 505–523.

Kirsner, D. (2007). "Do as I say, not as I do": Ralph Greenson, Anna Freud, and superrich patients. *Psychoanalytic Psychology, 24*(3), 475–486.

Klein, M. (1957). *Envy and gratitude: A study of unconscious sources*. London: Tavistock.

Kohut, H. (1971). *The analysis of the self: A systematic appraisal of the psychoanalytic treatment of narcissistic personalities*. New York: International Universities Press.

Konigsberg, E. (2008, July 7). Age of riches: Challenges of $600-a-session patients. *New York Times*.

Kris, A. (1976). On wanting too much: The "exceptions" revisited. *International Journal of Psychoanalysis, 57*, 89–95.

Lansky, M. (2004). Conscience and the project of a psychoanalytic science of human nature: Clarification of the usefulness of the superego concept. *Psychoanalytic Inquiry*, 24(2), 151–174.

Laplanche, J., & Pontalis, J.-B. (1973). *The language of psychoanalysis*. New York: Norton.

Lieberman, J. S. (2000). *Body talk: Looking and being looked at in psychotherapy*. Northvale, NJ: Aronson.

Loewald H. W. (1962). "Supergo and Time" in Loewald, H. W. (Ed.) (1980) *Papers on psychoanalysis*. New Haven and London: Yale University Press, 43–52.

Loewald, H. W. (1980). Superego and time. In *Papers on psychoanalysis* (pp. 43–52).

Makari, G. (2008). *Revolution in mind: The creation of psychoanalysis*. New York: Harper Collins.

Novick, J. and Novick, K. K. (2004). The supergo and the two-system model. *Psychoanalytic Inquiry* 24, 232–256.

Random House American Dictionary (1968). New York: Random House.

Riviere, J. (1991). Jealousy as a mechanism of defense. In A. Hughes (Ed.), *The inner world and Joan Riviere: Collected papers 1920–1958* (pp. 1104–1115). London: Karnac Books. (Original work published 1932)

Roth, P., & Lemma, A. (2008). *Envy and gratitude revisited*. London: International Psychoanalytic Association.

Rothstein, A. (1986). The seduction of money: A brief note on an expression of transference love. *Psychoanalytic Quarterly*, 55, 296–300.

Sandler, J. (1987). The concept of superego. In J. Sandler (Ed.), *From safety to superego: Selected papers of Joseph Sandler*. New York: Guilford, 17–44. (Original work published 1960)

Segal, H. (1964). *Introduction to the work of Melanie Klein*. New York: Basic Books.

Sorkin, A. R. (2007, December 6). A movie and protesters single out Henry Kravis: Making an issue of private equity wealth. *New York Times*, p. C4.

Spillius, E. (1993). Varieties of envious experience. *International Journal of Psychoanalysis*, 74, 1199–1212.

Steiner, J. S. (2008). Transference to the analyst as an excluded observer. *International Journal of Psychoanalysis*, 89, 39–54.

Waelder, R. (1936). The principle of multiple function: Observations on over-determination. *Psychoanalytic Quarterly*, 5, 45–62.

Warner, S. L. (1991). Psychoanalytic understanding and treatment of the very rich. *Journal of the American Academy of Psychoanalysis*, 19, 578–594.

Winnicott, D. W. (1992). Review of *Envy and gratitude*. In C. Winnicott, R. Shepherd, & M. Davis (Eds.), *Psychoanalytic explorations*. Cambridge, MA: Harvard University Press. (Original work published 1959)

Wurmser, L. (2004) (Ed.) *The supergo: A vital or supplanted concept?* New York: Analytic Press.

Wurmser, L. and Jarass, H. (2008) "Introduction" in Wurmser, L. & Jurass, H. (2008). Jealously and Envy: New Views about Two Powerful Feeling. New York and London: The Analytic Press, pp. xi–xx.

Wurmser, L., & Jarass, H. (Eds.) (2008). *Jealousy and envy: New views about two powerful feelings*. New York: Analytic Press.

Chapter 5

To be guilty or entitled? That is the question

Reflections on Dr. Lieberman's Contribution

Harold Blum

Dr. Lieberman's paper is evocative and raises many important and interesting issues for discussion. This present era can be characterized as a recrudescence of unbridled narcissism in a climate of avarice and envy. Greed has engendered dangerous climate change, plundered the earth, and bankrupted the banks. We have witnessed an extraordinary idealization of affluence and its aftermath of economic disaster. Billionaires became superstars, "masters of the universe," endowed with clairvoyance and omnipotence. Their material success and luxurious lifestyles were celebrated in the media, with public accolades and idolatry.

The cultural shift has been associated with ego- and superego-syntonic avarice, fraud, and related narcissistic entitlements. As F. Scott Fitzgerald observed, "the rich are different," with exceptional power, privilege, and prestige. Those who amassed fabulous wealth were regarded as exceptions, not held to ordinary or traditional ethics. As the gap between the haves and have-nots grew ever greater, so did the awe, envy, and adulation of the superrich by the merely rich as well as people of ordinary means. Dr. Lieberman observed the diminished or absent guilt and shame among the anointed titans of finance and rulers of corporate empires.

The traditional superego appeared, in manifest content, to have been swept aside in their culture of unbridled greed and proud extravagance. Some of the exceptions had been deeply deprived and injured in childhood, fortifying their compensatory demand for limitless gratifications. Avarice is pervasive and is not limited to the affluent. Railroad workers could retire on pseudo-sick leave and collect workers' compensation while avidly playing golf.

Culture has a powerful effect on the personality. Social class, race, religion, and gender may all be objects of primitive splitting into good and bad objects, idealized and valued objects. The power, privilege, and prestige of great wealth are difficult to deal with outside and inside the analytic situation.

In the analytic situation, the analyst may be valued as a beneficial influence or dismissed like an excess servant. In the countertransference, the analyst may be intimidated, antagonized, or envious of the aggrandized elite. The analyst may feel narcissistically gratified by a superstar patient, eager to have a role in the exalted vicariously enjoyed life of the rich or famous patient. The analyst may be offered gifts, tips, and juicy tidbits of information, seduced as the guru of the tycoon—or the opposite, an over-paid employee, indebted to the patient who projects greed and mercenary motives on the analyst. The patient may fantasize, "Since I pay my ana-lyst high fees, he or she is in my debt and under my control." The analyst may begrudge the patient's fame and fortune, and the greedy patient may begrudge the analyst's fee.

Outside the analytic situation, greed and envy play a powerful role, individually and culturally. It may be noted that although envy begins in infancy, the object of envy may change throughout life. Greed and envy may or may not be of equal importance or intensity in the individual and may have different influence on the countertransference of his or her analyst.

In the deeper layers of the unconscious archaic superego, infantile greed is indeed related to narcissism and oral devouring, but greed acquires mean-ing from all developmental phases. Money is real money but is psychologi-cally related to milk, dough or bread, feces, a treasured breast, a penis, a part object, treasured object, glorified self, potency and power, charity and penury, reward and punishment, and so on. It has always been so, with important cultural and historical vicissitudes.

From antiquity, greed and envy required the deterrent biblical command-ment "thou shalt not covet." Greed was one of the seven deadly sins. The biblical Queen Jezebel arranged the execution of the man whose land was coveted by her husband, King Ahab. She was killed by dogs that ate her flesh and licked her blood. In ancient legend, King Midas of Phrygia exem-plified greed. Granted his wish by the gods, everything he touched turned to gold. He touched his food and almost died of starvation. The punish-ment fit the oral crime. Jezebel was eaten, and Midas could not eat.

Our present culture exacerbated the aggressive avarice of the childish human condition. Many financiers made a "killing" and almost killed the financial system. History repeated itself.

The "robber barons" at the beginning of the 20th century coincided with Freud's case publications. In the Dora case, "a young girl 'greedy for love' finds no joy in sharing with siblings." The Rat Man was obsessed with rats and the starved rat boring into an anal gold mine. He dreamt of dung on the eyes—he had an eye for money. His father was a gambler with past debts, and his parents wanted to arrange his marriage to a wealthy girl, similar to such arranged marriages throughout history.

The Wolf Man dreamed of double gifts on his birthday, Christmas day. Very rich, he thought Freud overcharged him, especially compared to his notion of what Freud charged his other patients. He secretly kept knowledge of inherited jewelry from Freud. Later, he elicited Freud's countertransference enactment when Freud collected funds for him after he lost his fortune in the Russian revolution.

Janice Lieberman is "on the mark/money" calling attention to the analyst's ego-syntonic and culturally syntonic countertransference. I could not help but be reminded of my personal experience with the famous analyst R. G., to whom she referred. His analytic relationship with Marilyn Monroe was impaired by his countertransference. He negotiated regarding her movie contracts, took her into his home and thus into his family. In the case of another wealthy elite patient, R. G. screened suitors for marriage to her. Under the aegis of a noble cause, he arranged for her to donate funds to the Anna Freud Center.

I am pleased that Dr. Lieberman has retained the term *superego* despite some suggestions that the concept lacks theoretical explanatory value. The functions of the superego comprise a separate set of internal representations, a separate agency operative in psychic conflict as well as in the group mores of society and culture: "Strengthening of the superego is a most precious cultural asset" (Freud, 1933, p. 11).

What happened to the strong, traditional superego? I do not think that the core of traditional morality disappeared but was somewhat modified by new identifications. The later injunctions and admonitions are grafted onto those of childhood, which remain in the depths of the psyche. There are superego arrests, regressions, deficits, lacunae, contradictions, splits, and greater or less capacity for enforcement of internal and external rules and regulations. The cop is too often not there when needed. Freud (1933) also noted the frequent lack of a reliable superego: "A large majority of men have brought with them only a modest amount of individual conscience, or scarcely enough to be worth mentioning" (p. 61).

The individual superego may be relatively autonomous, but vulnerable to group identifications. As in the military, it is possible to suspend prior strictures against violence and murder into delimited permission to kill (a license to kill, like James Bond). A military superego is temporarily superimposed, not without variable internal conflict. Guilt often returns after return to civilian life. If guilt is not present and cannot be evoked after a significant transgression, it implies that the patient may be a sociopath. The hallmarks of a sociopath are the absence of guilt and of empathy for the injuries inflicted on others. Some of the predators to whom Dr. Lieberman referred may have had sociopathic traits or might actually be sociopaths.

When Masters and Johnson needed subjects for their investigation of sexual response, they thought they would have to enlist prostitutes. Surprise! The medical staff readily volunteered under the aegis and rationalization of important "noble" medical research. Some of the staff, released from prohibition under Master's leadership, engaged in amazing sex acts that were hitherto unimaginable behavior. Some of the staff reported that sex in the laboratory was better than at home.

Dr. Lieberman's fascinating case material evokes issues of conscious and unconscious guilt. The absence of conscious guilt does not preclude unconscious guilt or a wish for punishment. In the case of the woman with "affluenza," she showed no guilt, shame, or remorse about filling her purse by illicit pocketbook sales. However, I doubt that she was guilty about sweets and excess calories. She was likely vainly concerned about her weight and figure; she may have been taunting her analyst about these issues in the transference. Unconscious guilt has to be considered, transposed from theft to overeating sweets. She seemed to plead guilty to a minor infraction rather than accepting responsibility for fraud. Unconscious guilt, often amalgamated with the developmentally earlier affect of shame, can powerfully propel a spectrum of evasion, trivial confession, criminal confession, and false confession. Criminals from a sense of guilt are uncommon yet are responsible for some cases of illegal, punitive, and self-punitive behavior. Those ready to confess to crimes they did not commit have too often found law enforcement too ready to accept the confession. Prosecutors can be greedy for convictions, and police issue traffic tickets even for trivial traffic infractions, which help pay the town taxes.

Dr. Lieberman has delineated and illuminated the pervasive significance of greed and envy, and their influence on the superego, inside and outside the psychoanalytic situation. It has been a personal pleasure to discuss her most thoughtful, timely chapter on a timeless subject.

REFERENCES

Fitzgerald, F. S. (2006). Rich boy. In *All the sad young men*. Cambridge: Cambridge University Press.

Freud, S. (1933). Five lectures on psychoanalysis. In J. Strachey (Ed. & Trans.), *The standard edition of the complete psychological works of Sigmund Freud* (Vol. 11, pp. 3–57). London: Hogarth Press.

Chapter 6

Tight money and couples
How it can help even as it hurts

Brenda Berger

Over 23 years of clinical practice, I, like many psychoanalysts, have worked actively with my patients around issues of money. Most often, money came up in the ways that my coeditor Dr. Newman describes vividly in this book, through the evocative lens of fees. In negotiating and setting them, collecting or not collecting payment for sessions, I have encountered powerful and often very aggressive fantasies, fears, and enactments. These have expressed varied primitive emotions, which my patients could not yet feel or understand. So, we worked together over the years around this loaded topic, arriving slowly at places where my patients could better manage their feelings around money and behave in less-punished—and punishing—ways in their lives.

But, fees were by no means a forefront issue for all my patients. When it came to money, many of them understood what they paid for treatment; they paid on time, accepted slight increases over the years, and were pleased by fee reductions when the need was there. Money just was not the particular vehicle through which they expressed their anxieties. Money was there, a part of life, but somehow in the background.

And then, the stock market crashed in October 2008; suddenly, 21 years into my practice, money burst center stage into my office. It seemed to me that it was on every patient's mind, present in every session (or almost every session), and painfully it was also very much on my mind. Having come of professional age in good financial times, the 1980s and 1990s afforded me a certain relaxed attitude about the rewarding income I could finally earn from the work I love and trained hard to do. But abruptly I was concerned about a diminished retirement account. And my patients were worried about their jobs, their savings, and whether they could afford to continue their treatments with me. Therapy for many had become a luxury item. In short, as I simultaneously offered fee reductions to those in need, I worried about my own income.

Money as anxious reality, money in the transference and countertransference became a challenge as the economy turned downward every day. I was knee deep in the minefield of potentially conflicted interest. I knew firsthand about the messy business described very honestly by Dr. Irwin Hirsch in Chapter 2 of this book, a chapter he aptly titles, "It Was a Great Month: None of My Patients Left."

Though afraid, I was also intrigued and challenged by the myriad ways in which my patients and I managed, expressed, or mismanaged our fears about money. The crisis was immediate for everybody. It felt a little like war, or September 11 again. I was suddenly that much more clinically and theoretically alive.

I also began to think more deeply about people's drive to amass wealth. Turning to Fenichel (1938), I researched the interplay between this instinct to possess and obtain power and the way our social system works to applaud money as a symbol of both power and value. What was of most interest to me were the ways in which patients talked about the impact of the power of money on their relationships.

I was particularly struck by two married couples, one in which a lot of money was gained by the husband during the economic downturn, and another in which a lot of money was lost by the husband. Their cases (presented here as disguised composites for confidentiality) revealed something counterintuitive, paradoxical, and to me dynamically fascinating. In the one case (the E.'s), making millions of dollars actually exacerbated problems in their relationship. In the second case (the Z.'s), losing a lot of money and having less to spend resulted in better communication and more empathic mature connection. As an analyst, I should not have been surprised. A market crash, like any traumatic reality, can, and often does, catalyze revelations, growth, and change in unexpected ways. This chapter examines the question of whether the sudden frightening loss of financial security can sometimes provoke emotional growth, while the sudden appearance of wealth, like all so-called good things, might have a deleterious impact in certain dynamic contexts.

I demonstrate, through the clinical material I describe, the relationship between more or less choice around money, and healthier versus destructive functioning. Specifically, I highlight the value of containing omnipotent fantasies and impulsive behaviors around money in relationships, in therapy and the workplace, such that reality testing is optimized, and harmful grandiosity can be better regulated intrapsychically and intersubjectively.

 Money is a commodity that allows us to obtain real and healthy power and efficacy, but it can also be misused in the business of destructive hubris and control. This I was seeing in my patients, and this we have all seen painfully, particularly since 2008 in many frightening stories of financial greed unregulated in our economy. Most dramatic perhaps was the extraordinary Bernard Madoff sociopathic extreme. Could there be a better lesson than the one Madoff gave us? His was a lesson about how vulnerable we all could be to one man's ability to seduce us through his, and our own, absurdly exaggerated fantasies about the power of making more and more money.

WHEN GLITTER WAS NOT GOLD

Ms. E., an attractive woman of 38, was early in her second marriage when she came to see me. Initially, she did not suggest that her relationship was in trouble, although this emerged over time. She also did not convey that money was any kind of problem. She spoke instead in a giddy way about being extremely wealthy. Her new husband had made, and was continuing to make, huge amounts of money as the economy of the world collapsed. Ms. E. felt that the only problem she had around money was that having so much of it made decisions hard for the couple since they could afford to do anything and everything they wanted. The sky was truly the limit. This indeed was a problem. But with time, it became clear that the couple's indecision around their wealth was only the tip of a much bigger and more disavowed relationship iceberg.

Ms. E. was depressed when she came for therapy. The daughter of two emotionally removed and critical parents, she grew up in a small town in the south. In what she described as a melancholy and angry home, Ms. E. listened nightly to her parents arguing about how trapped they felt both in their marriage and in the enormous burden of having to care for their autistic firstborn son. Ms. E. was the baby in the family. She was very close to her sister, who was 18 months older than she was. This beloved sister had died of cancer a few months before Ms. E. came to see me, and Ms. E.'s loss was really deep. An additional loss for Ms. E. lay in the fact that her first husband had left her for another woman after they had been married for 8 years. Ms. E. divorced him shortly afterward. Two years after the divorce, Ms. E. married her wealthy second husband.

Mr. E. seemed to be somebody who was almost oblivious to his wife's substantial pain. A jet-setting, very busy working man, he traveled all over the world, preoccupied with his ever-expanding financial empire. He showed little interest in Ms. E.'s terrible worry about one of her three sons from her previous marriage. This 10-year-old boy had recently been diagnosed with attention deficit disorder (ADD) and was having difficulties in school. Ms. E. was concerned about her son's schoolwork and personally injured by his acting out in such visible and embarrassing ways. Her idealized firstborn child was failing her as a needed inner ballast against her losses and inner vulnerability.

Although her sessions often ended tearfully, Ms. E tried for much of the time to soft-pedal her sadness. She began sessions in a perky way, a style that denied her actual worry and uncertainty. And, she talked a great deal about her newly acquired wealth. Even through this excitement, I heard with concern about her husband's isolated intoxication with the power of his money. I heard about his buying expensive real estate, about his extravagant donations to schools and hospitals as ways of networking more business contacts and having wings of buildings named after him. I heard about $10,000-per-night hotel bills in Dubai, and a GoldVish cell phone worth a half million dollars, an exclusive item known only to the very rich. All this spending, as well as purchasing expensive cars, he did without discussion or consultation with his wife. It was striking to me how seemingly unconcerned she was about the disconnected new marriage she had made. Ms. E. began drinking several glasses of wine every night.

But we worked, where Ms. E. felt safe to work. Our initial twice-weekly therapy focused on her worries about her son and her ongoing grief around the loss of her sister. Bit by bit, Ms. E. was able to tell me that she got from her sister what she needed (and was unable to secure) from her emotionally depriving parents. Her sister mirrored, soothed, and protectively confirmed her. In those ways, Ms. E. compensated and received some of what Kohut (1971, 1977, 1984) believed to be central food for the self, for the development of ambitions and ideals. Little to none of this restorative relating seemed to be happening in her marriage, and lots and lots of money appeared to be distracting Ms. E. from that fact.

Prior to her second marriage, Ms. E. had worked productively and creatively as a lawyer. She made a comfortable living, and she was proud of her professional identity. Once remarried and financially flush, she gave up her work and seemed rather fragmented. Left by both her sister and her first husband, disappointed and injured by her son, oddly disinterested in her younger sons, without her professional identity to lean on, Ms. E.'s sense of self was shaky. She had millions of dollars but nobody to help her feel needed, important, whole, and adored. And, she lacked the necessary internalizations of those functions to keep her steady.

I continued to feel concerned about her marriage. This concern grew as Mr. E. (his marriage to my patient was his fourth) began to sound more narcissistic to me in character structure. Ms. E., meanwhile, in her sessions with me, attempted defensively to cover her substantial inner anxiety and emptiness by talking increasingly about being wealthy. She seemed on the one hand quite intoxicated with it. Yet, she also attributed many of the couple's difficulties to the abundance of money in their lives. Her husband stalled on all decisions related to family life. Ms. E. seemed frightened and unsettled. I wondered if Mr. E. was taking pleasure, rooted in anal-phase eroticism, in his endless withholding of money and commitment from her (Fuqua, 1986). He had plenty to spend, but held on and on, and would not let go in the service of building a real and settled family life. He could not even agree to buy a furnished apartment they were renting so they could make it their own. I worried that Ms. E. might have retraumatized herself by marrying somebody who, like her parents, sister, and first husband, would leave her again.

In each session, Ms. E. repeated (with what seemed like inauthentic embarrassment) that the couple's struggle was only because their wealth gave them so much choice that they could not decide on family matters. Having all the money in the world, somehow Ms. E. felt to me like a refugee in limbo. Despite being a very intelligent woman, she was blocked in her ability to think about deficiencies in her own and her husband's abilities to plan together, to share and negotiate, to empathize, commit, and engage. It seemed that their money was compensating for too much and was actually impeding them in the whole business of being together in their new marriage.

My countertransference from time to time was a feeling of disgust. It was uncomfortable and quite unusual for me to feel such distaste toward a person I actually really liked, someone who was clearly suffering and who needed help. But so many of my patients, my friends, my family, and I, myself, were all feeling really afraid around the stock market collapse. Ms. E.'s money talk was successfully making me envious. I had to work hard to remember how fragile she was, to keep thinking about how she might be using her money to feel omnipotent, bigger and better than her therapist, to deny that she was a patient, a person in need (Almond, 1997).

Ms. E. paid my regular, not exorbitant, fee for her therapy. She treated this in a matter-of-fact way. She wrote her checks regularly and without incident. But, while she never spoke directly about my fee, she did use her wealth aggressively to reverse her own competitive and empty feelings.

As time went on, more of the real tragedy of her life emerged. Mr. E. showed little interest in working with her on their relationship. He began traveling more without her and spending extravagantly on ever-larger luxury items without talking to her about them.

Tensions between them began mounting, and Ms. E. started to miss sessions with me as she flew around the world to be with her husband. Her Sophie's choice felt palpable to me but seemed unconscious to her. Should she make a home with her children without him, or should she run after her elusive husband, trying to nail down a marriage with a man who seemed to need to be away?

Bit by bit, I felt a parallel process developing. I was feeling about the treatment the way Ms. E. felt about her marriage. While we began with an understanding that she would be in twice-weekly analytic psychotherapy, this lasted only a few months. Then, she was off, away, or somehow too busy to come to regular sessions. I could see what Stone (1979) meant when he wrote, "among the very wealthy, some feel they do not have to adjust to life; they make life adjust to them" (p. 41). Consistent with her defensive style of rationalization, Ms. E. explained this as her needing to keep certain doctors' appointments with her child or having to go on vacations. I was running my practice around her commitments rather than the other way around. In the object relationship being played out, I was her, she was her husband, and I was feeling the difficulty of keeping our relationship alive.

In this transference/countertransference enactment, I worked hard to offer Ms. E. session times so that the treatment could continue at least twice monthly. Her acute depression lifted, but she was in my office much less than what I thought she needed. While it seemed to me that Ms. E. was resisting confrontation with her own vulnerability and her fears around intimacy, anger, and neediness, I was worried about how much confrontation she could tolerate without fleeing completely. I let things go on this way for too long. Perhaps that had to do not only with my sense of her fragility but also with my own financial worries at that time.

As it turned out, when I finally did confront Ms. E. (about 2 months into her acting out around session times), my prediction was sadly confirmed. She fled the treatment in a way that she could not discuss or work through with me. She never returned.

The end was sudden, angry, sad. In response to my suggesting that her infrequent appointments might have something to do with her own struggles around intimacy and worries about her marriage, Ms. E. snapped at me. She claimed that she had never agreed to regularly scheduled treatment, and that my stressing it was about my taking advantage of her money. This was painful, and the opposite was actually true. My confronting her (I think too belatedly), despite my fear that she would leave, was in fact my attempt to care for her.

That I had allowed a less-structured treatment for a few months was complicated. In retrospect, I think it was a combination of trying to titrate my interventions optimally and help Ms. E. with what I believed she could manage. In addition, being human during a time of national economic crisis, I was afraid around potentially lost income. This took me a bit of time to surmount, but finally I recovered my analytic stance and could name the resistant elephant in the room.

At the point that I took on Ms. E.'s withholding of herself and her time from me, I was truly worried about her and her marriage. Her husband was claiming that his spending and commitment stalling were because he wanted the freedom to live his life doing whatever he wanted to do because he had the money to do it. I was very worried that Ms. E. was denying the seriousness of her marital situation.

But, Ms. E. was not yet ready for this hard inner work. Instead, she left her treatment with me, propping herself up through a defensive blaming projection that incorporated a certain reality to pack maximum punch.

She claimed that the only reason I was stressing her resistance to regular sessions was because I needed her money. In that way, she avoided a painful confrontation with the poor little rich girl inside herself. In this way, again, she enacted with me a parallel process in which she played her husband, who often felt that people used him for his money, and I played her, trying to demonstrate, ineffectively, that I actually cared. She resisted facing that she married a wealthy man, but someone who was emotionally quite deprived, who knew little about relating, collaborating, sharing, committing, and being intimate. Their marriage was at risk. If it collapsed, Ms. E. would be just fine on the money front. But, her substantial anxiety revealed that she seemed to know, at least preconsciously, that she had much to lose internally if it were gone.

I believe that more therapeutic work would put Ms. E. in touch with the loss of a very big dream, the dream of a rich white knight who, through money, could save her from herself. At the time that she left our work together, Mr. E. was living in Switzerland. Ms. E. was in New York with her three young sons still in school. It seemed up to her somehow to find a way to both be a mother to them and see her husband where possible.

In time, if she can tolerate a deeper treatment relationship, Ms. E. could be helped to see how her desire to possess a great deal of money through her husband serves a defensive need to "enlarge the compass of her ego" (Fenichel, 1938, p. 6). Such a treatment could address the painful early losses she suffered living with two distant and critical parents. And in remembering and bearing her early pain, Ms. E. could come to understand better her own fears around making emotional contact, something she and her husband avoid in their busy defensive preoccupation with money. In the context of an ongoing, steady, stable therapeutic relationship, Ms. E. could perhaps face that she chose two emotionally unavailable men, depriving herself of what she needs so much more importantly than money.

This case reminded me again that as clinicians, it is often hard to face our therapeutic limits, to curb our own omnipotent fantasies, which are typically less about money and more often about cures. With Ms. E., I came up against the painful realization that we can all only do as much inner work as we can bear at any given time. This is particularly hard to face if we fear (as I did with Ms. E.) that our patients might be hurting themselves by ending treatment prematurely. And as workers (in addition to healers), it is difficult as analysts to confront our limits when financial times are tight because it is then that we must face the uncomfortable and humbling reality that we indeed do depend on our patients for our livelihood.

In the face of the frustrating therapeutic outcome with Ms. E., the Z.'s described next helped me feel more hopeful around the whole business of less being more, both for individuals and perhaps for our society at large. Through the ways in which the Z.'s coped with real fear around losing a job and the substantial money that went with it, by the way they bore all that came with their losses, changing, growing, and healing their relationship even as they suffered, I felt that the Z.'s showed much from which we all can learn.

WHEN LESS BECAME MORE

Ms. Z., a bright and very likable woman, was 35 years old. I saw her twice weekly for 8 years. She initially came for individual therapy shortly after she married her brilliant and dynamic husband, who made a lot of money and was outstandingly successful professionally. Ms. Z. seemed to speak admiringly of her husband when she spoke about his substantial intellect and his ability to provide a very comfortable life for her. Otherwise, she tended toward many complaints about him as childlike, selfish, and indulgent.

Husband and wife both suffered from chronic depression and behaved in childlike ways with each other. Mr. Z. was more agitated, Ms. Z. more weepy, self-abnegating. Their dazzling income was important to Ms. Z., and it kept her somewhat buoyed since she came from a family in which she lacked emotional and financial security. They loved spending, and they tended to opt for the expensive in what they did or needed.

Mr. Z.'s central power in the relationship resided in his ability to earn big money. He demanded that his wife be his on-call mother, whose job it was to cook for him, make his appointments, pack his suitcases for business trips, indulge his snapping at her angrily when she did not jump to his agitated demands. Ms. Z. complied for many years but was tearful and enraged.

A very intelligent and educated woman, she was nonetheless not internally secure enough for the first few years of her treatment to see that she could refuse this role. She could not imagine any way in which she could work toward something more collaborative with her husband. We worked long and hard on how she repeated with her husband her interactions with her demanding, critical father. She had tried as a child to get close with her father by struggling to meet his various frustrated needs.

In the early years of their marriage, Ms. Z. worked in a demanding job in the advertising world. She repeated with her boss some elements of her struggle with her husband and father. She often acted like an overwhelmed child, inducing criticism and rebukes. She then felt as if a failure, frightened, exhausted, and misunderstood by him. She finally left this job, feeling she could not take it anymore. Given her husband's large income, she did not seek work elsewhere.

Ms. Z. came from a family in which her father was brilliant academically but depressed and unavailable, in many ways like her husband. Her mother was cold, narcissistic, depressed, and bullying. Although not the oldest child in her family, Ms. Z. was the identified parent. She was by far the most competent and successful of the four children, which seems to be the way she became the "executive child," a role she repeated in her relationship with Mr. Z. She was often called on for advice when anybody in the family collapsed in either emotional or financial ways. This kind of collapsing was frequent, again a parallel in her marriage. Ms. Z. would take up her role, comply with the family demands, and then be angry, tearful, and victimized in her sessions with me.

Ms. Z. idealized her childhood and her home. She kept her own depression under relatively stable control with medication, therapy, and the joy she got from her three little children. Parenting was truly healing for her. But, being a mother also took enormous emotional and physical energy and brought her disappointment and frustration with her husband into bold relief. His self-preoccupation and agitation with her, and endless exhaustion for all things related to the family, made for constant conflict between them. Each accused the other of being insensitive to what they needed. Collaboration and compromise were difficult for them to achieve. They typified what Cooper (1973/1993) referred to when he said that there is no masochistic defensiveness without narcissistic injury. Both of them demonstrated both ends of the spectrum, with husband looking most often more narcissistic and wife more masochistic. But, they could switch positions and did when it came to their fighting.

In their battles, each was committed to proving that the other was truly the "wrong" one. Each felt victimized by the other, and each demonstrated a blindness to the injury of the other.

Desperate and overwhelmed (but still financially flush), Ms. Z. bought whatever help she needed with the children by hiring nannies. Her husband continued the patterns he learned in his own family, behaving often like a spoiled child who got what he wanted when he wanted it. The notion of postponed gratification was foreign to him. The fact that he made large amounts of money that supported the family in a lavish way seemed to give him extra license to demand and control family life. He treated his wife as if she were an employee, barking orders and checking what she had accomplished at the end of the day.

Ms. Z. felt increasingly exposed and humiliated by the way he treated her privately and publicly. I referred the couple for couples treatment, and her husband remained steadily in a committed individual treatment as well.

His treatment was challenging and effective and gradually he became more of a man and a father. He became less inclined toward bursts of anger toward his wife. But, the husband's narcissistic character pathology intertwined with Ms. Z.'s entrenched sadomasochistic character structure and depressive mood made their work hard.

Enter the stock market collapse in October 2008. A few months later, Mr. Z. was fired because he behaved in a cheeky and rude way with his boss. For the next year, this brilliant man, who had always been gainfully and lucratively employed, was out of work.

Ms. Z. lost her "protector," her problematic knight, but nonetheless her "knight in shining armor." Their lifestyle was extremely expensive with three children in private school. Ms. Z. was very scared and angry. Interestingly, as furious as she was with her husband, something seemed to change in her. She ranted at him, and about him, much less. She seemed to roll up her sleeves to do more internal work than I had ever seen before. As the months of unemployment dragged on, we talked together about the possibility of Ms. Z. going back to work. We finally were digging more deeply beneath her too comfortable dependent position, a position that had been facilitated by her husband making endless streams of money. In an interesting way, as her husband looked more vulnerable and unemployable, Ms. Z. found some empathy for him, something that had been lacking when money was flush and she submitted to his control.

In her therapy sessions, the feeling was strangely different. Instead of the familiar outpouring of her victimization, the bitter listing of her husband's indulgent ways, Ms. Z. began to use her treatment to examine her own evasion of responsibility when it came to earning a living. She was more open to her characterological issue of negating her capabilities, her safe space of feeling like an inept child worthy of criticism.

Through the loss of money, Ms. Z. slowly and painfully unpacked her need for her husband to be a big man through his wealth. She gradually saw that this came from her desire to hide from the world as the frightened child she still, in certain ways, felt herself to be. The couple began quickly to problem solve around money together. It was interesting to see them at last being their very smart selves and collaborative together. They helped each other budget, cut costs, and consider moving. They talked together about the humiliation they felt with their neighbors. And for the first time in years, they were less alone. As fellow sufferers, no longer villain and victim, they fired their nanny together with pain. And, they began to share more of the child care responsibility, a real first in their marriage.

Ms. Z.'s work in her treatment during this very scary time was really impressive. The economic crisis brought her terror up quickly, and she was able to feel it at the core. Impressively, she was able to work with both the present reality limits of their money and to better understand her primitive terrors, which came from having been asked as a child for premature maturity in her family.

It is interesting and encouraging to me to see how this couple, who faced a serious financial setback, severe limits on their money, and injury to their way of thinking about themselves in the world, grew nonetheless. They were gradually more able to be vulnerable and afraid together. As they developed that capacity, they also became more empathic toward each other. They certainly still fell into old patterns, with Mr. Z. wanting to criticize Ms. Z. for this or that way in which she was ineffective. This tended to happen when he felt more financially and professionally powerless. Ms. Z. would then fall into wanting either to rant about her abused mother position or to cry about her overburdened executive child position.

But as a couple, they actually became more genuinely related. This partnership had never happened before they confronted real pain together. As I listened to Ms. Z. in sessions during her husband's long unemployment when their money was so tight, I felt for the first time that they actually loved one another. They seemed to see each other anew, as two actual, real people rather than as omnipotent idealized notions that they could bring forcefully under control (Freud, 1913).

DISCUSSION

These two clinical cases about how money has functioned in the lives of the E.'s and Z.'s obviously do not permit generalization. There are so many differences and intervening variables. Ms. E. was very new in a marriage (her second); Ms. Z. had been married for 12 years and had done some active couples work with her husband. Ms. E. was new to therapy; Ms. Z. had the benefit of 8 years of treatment. The Z.'s were both in their first marriages; Ms. E. was in her second marriage, and she was her husband's fourth wife.

What they do have in common is their age, socioeconomic status, education level, and certain similarities in their narcissistic/masochistic character structures and depressive tendencies and in their husband's financial success and drive for increased wealth. In addition, all four struggled internally with hungry drives and with accepting limits.

As children. Ms. E.'s husband was overcontrolled and emotionally deprived, and Ms. Z.'s husband was spoiled and overindulged. The men's developmental histories, which lacked phase-appropriate empathy with limit setting, are posited by classic analytic theory and self-psychology (Fenichel, 1945; Kohut, 1977) as predisposing them toward pathological narcissism, quite common in wealthy people (Olsson, 1986). Once adults, Mr. E. enacted "freedom fests" with money in manic ways; Ms. Z.'s husband seemed to want to remain an indulged child forever. In this position, he lacked a sense of other at home and in the workplace, behaving often in outlandish and grandiose controlling ways.

Both women were undernourished emotionally and depressed. Both men, in midlife, lacked the ability to enjoy what they had. They needed more and more money to boost their sense of themselves. Their wives needed the husbands' money in ways that also seemed to feed them.

Might money have functioned for them as the good and ever-flowing, never-weaning breast, as Orgel suggested in his discussion of this chapter? As it "healed" them through all it could buy and the pump it provided, they were shielded for a time from feeling the emotional limits of their parents and the men they married. In his discussion of money in the unconscious, Fenichel (1938) suggested that the drive to accumulate wealth is a derivative of infantile narcissism transformed into more realistic needs like achieving power and self-esteem. He also went on to say that possessing money shores people up against several kinds of losses, including the loss involved in weaning, the business of getting and having less.

The problem of generalization notwithstanding, I think this clinical material does help to frame questions about how money perhaps functioned for these patients and for others in our society at large. In trying economic times especially, perhaps we can be buoyed by the idea that lemonade can be made out of lemons, as the Z.'s tried to do as they faced limits to their budget and expanded demands on their collaborative functioning.

Is it possible that external controls facilitated some internal changes in a couple that lacked the capacity to control their impulses, wishes, and needs? Did a sudden serious limit on money, a frightening slap of being fired and unemployed result, in some internal transmuting because sacrifice was enforced and gratification had to be postponed? Did these limits act like a kind of weaning, which facilitated growth and development in the Z.'s?

I had seen something like this in another case I treated also at the time of the stock market crash. It was Mr. R., a man with serious obsessive-compulsive disorder, who had been fired from many jobs because he could not finish his work assignments. But when the market crashed, he suddenly was able to do his work. He said it was because he actually felt the substantial blow to his trust fund, his formerly safe and ever-flowing breast. Only at that point did Mr. R. do his work well. He explained this to me in session, saying that suddenly he "had no choice" but to do his work. Feeling his tight money, something urgent seemed to happen inside him, some counter, or bigger anxiety, that overrode his characteristic obsessive delaying, and he got his work done.

Might Ms. E.'s husband need to come up against an external constraint, a powerful reality test, before he realizes how destructive one can be by living so much under the sway of the pleasure principle? Fenichel (1938) wrote about social institutions modifying the instinct to amass wealth. The modified instinct he said then reacts anew on "social reality through the actions of individuals" (p. 2). Perhaps this is what happened to Mr. Z. when he was fired into a horrible economy and was jobless. He became more humble and object related with his wife. Mr. E. received no such modification from his business world or his wife or any substantial treatment. His grandiosity continued unbridled.

The literature on the developmental sequence from "good omnipotence" (from which self-esteem arises) to a high degree of narcissistic omnipotence (which tends toward destruction of self and others) suggests that destructive impulses are tamed by good-enough mothering (Freud, 1913; Winnicott, 1965). This kind of nurturance might be likened to the therapy that the Z.'s got and the E.'s evaded. Perhaps the Z.'s did better in part because their treatments engaged their underlying aggressive, hungry, injured selves and limited and contained the destructive fantasies that sought enactment through their wealth.

Without this kind of emotional and societal reality testing, with endless money to play with, one wonders what exactly might promote ego development in Mr. E., whose narcissistic pathology puts him more and more at risk for losing yet another family, his fourth.

It is evident in the case of Ms. E. that the myth that money makes people happy is indeed a myth. External limits might help some like the Z.'s in developing inner coping skills, but the converse, having more and more, does not seem to do the same. Ms. E. and her husband's problems are not being solved by external boosts from private airplanes, expensive watches, hotels, cars, works of art, or millions in the bank. Mr. E. did not seem to grasp that doing whatever he wanted to do without attention to its impact on others was not really autonomy. He has yet to discover that he might well still be internally unseparated from, and angry with, his controlling, depriving mother. Despite his huge wealth and power in the world, he seems unable to say an internal, effective "no" to his mother, and he still enacts that "no" against his wife and family and calls it "freedom."

At the metalevel, particularly when money is tight, can we also learn something from the E. and Z. couples and from Mr. R. as well? Can we wonder about the special value of limits, curtailed choice, delay of gratification, struggle, sacrifice, and grieving the loss of fantasized control over life and people?

As analysts, we work repeatedly with men and women in their 30s, 40s, and older with marriages and children under their belts, whose egos are not yet well integrated, who still feel internally very deprived, split, and angry, like the composite cases mentioned. They often try to use money to solve inner needs. They enact accordingly, sometimes with devastating consequences to themselves, their spouses, and their families. Through intergenerational transmission, they promote ongoing cycles of neurosis in their children.

But, might this moment in economic history, this tight-money moment, afford us a special teaching and learning opportunity that we might liken to the important weaning periods in parenting? Can we capitalize on the reality of this time by doing more of what should always be done in any good analysis—focus our patients and ourselves on the value (though painful) of bearing the loss of omnipotence, the loss of limitless choice, and the gains of delayed instinctual gratification?

Considered through the lens of healthy versus pathological narcissistic development, there are parallel lessons and questions at the societal level as well.

Money in America was once a more healthily traded commodity; people had a sense of efficacy and personal engagement around making it and spending it. In the 1950s and 1960s, America seemed to be flourishing in what one might call a healthy developmental way. We were a highly successful country with ambitions and ideals. People were involved with one another on both sides of the transaction. There were those who sold and those who bought goods or made them. There was more awareness of self and other, of actual people. When it came to money, there was more relationship.

Bit by bit, we have moved to a place where 21.3% of the wealth in this country is held by 1% of the people (Domhoff, 2010) and where that 1% of wealthy people do not give back by investing in the American economy, but rather in the Cayman Islands, China, or elsewhere where they get higher returns (Reich, 2010). Every day, workers are increasingly removed from the mass of money produced. Rewards for the power that money brings are enjoyed by very few who exert disproportionate control.

Before the American "Culture of Narcissism" (Lasch, 1978) burst its own omnipotent economic bubble in October 2008, investment banks were packaging ill-conceived mortgages as securities. There was no responsibility to the lender. Money was making money for its own sake. As Thomas Friedman (2010) put it in a *New York Times* opinion column, we were in a "national epidemic of get-rich-quickism and something-for-nothingism (p.11)". The sky seemed to be the limit, or perhaps we imagined there was no limit. After all, balloons and bubbles float—such was our sense of economic grandiosity gone wild.

People who could not actually afford to buy their homes got mortgages, lost them, then lost their homes. Millions of people lost their jobs. Hardworking people watched their savings evaporate, kids who had worked hard to get into and graduate from college, graduated into a world that had no jobs to offer them. Grandiose limitless fantasies about power through money had destroyed so much for many, not only in America, but throughout the world.

We all shook; institutions and people who seemed invulnerable fell. Regulations and limits were debated and battled. Bit by bit, they were implemented. The recovery will be slow, and it is hoped there will be a societal "working through" and real learning from all that was broken.

Of the many possible lessons to be absorbed, I think that Ernest Becker (1975) wrote about the hardest and most important one of all. Referring to the fantasy power of money, he wrote that it radiates "even after one's death, giving one a semblance of immortality" (pp. 81–82). The pursuit of increased wealth gives many the illusion of licking death, a powerful idea indeed, but surely only an idea.

In short, can we learn in these humbling times the lesson that the Z.'s learned, that tight money can help us feel more mortal, and in that important way, just ordinary, limited—what we in fact, actually are? Can we welcome the pain of that as a necessary fall from grace, a curbing and weaning that might lead us away from self-aggrandizing and bring us back to the value of responsibly caring for and engaging with others? In short, can tight money help us, even as it hurts?

REFERENCES

Almond, R. (1997). Omnipotence and power. In C. Ellman & J. Reppen (Eds.), *Omnipotent fantasies and the vulnerable self* (pp. 1–37). Northvale, NJ: Aronson.
Becker, E. (1975). *Escape from evil*. New York: Free Press.
Cooper, A. (1993). The narcissistic-masochistic character. In R. A. Glick & D. I. Meyers (Eds.), *Masochism: Current psychoanalytic perspectives* (pp. 117–138). Hillsdale, NJ: Analytic Press. (Original work published 1973)
Domhoff, W. (2010). Who rules America? Retrieved August 2010 from http://sociology.ucsc.edu/whorulesamerica/power/wealth.html
Fenichel, O. (1938). The drive to amass wealth. *Psychoanalytic Quarterly*, 7, 69–95.
Fenichel, O. (1945). *The psychoanalytic theory of neurosis*. New York: Norton.
Freud, S. (1913). *Totem and taboo*. In J. Strachey (Ed. & Trans.), *The standard edition of the complete psychological works of Sigmund Freud* (Vol. 13, pp. 1–161). London: Hogarth Press.
Friedman, T. (2010, September 12). We're no. 1(1)! *New York Times*, 11.
Fuqua, P. (1986). Classical psychoanalytic views of money. In D. Krueger (Ed.), *The last taboo* (pp. 17–23). New York: Brunner/Mazel.
Kohut, H. (1971). *The analysis of the self*. New York: International Universities Press.
Kohut, H. (1977). *The reconstruction of the self*. New York: International Universities Press.
Kohut, H. (1984). *How does analysis cure?* Chicago: University of Chicago Press.
Lasch, C. (1978). *The culture of narcissism*. New York: Norton.
Olsson, P. (1986). Complexities in the psychology and psychotherapy of the phenomenally wealthy. In D. Krueger (Ed.), *The last taboo* (pp. 55–69). New York: Brunner/Mazel.
Reich, R. (2010, September 3). How to end the great recession. *New York Times*, 21.
Stone, M. (1979). Upbringing in the super-rich. In J. Howells (Ed.), *Modern perspectives in the psychiatry of infancy*. New York: Brunner/Mazel.
Winnicott, D. W. (1965). *The maturational process and the facilitating environment*. London: Hogarth Press, 57.

Chapter 7

Follow the money
Training and fees, fantasy and reality

Stephanie Newman

I had practiced for more than 10 years as a doctoral-level psychologist before graduating from an analytic institute. And though I could finally call myself a psychoanalyst, I was surprised to learn that I had another title: beginner. In the psychoanalytic community, you can work for a number of years and still be considered a cub, a newbie. What an unusual perspective and strange lens through which to view one's accomplishments and professional stature.

But I digress.

This is a chapter about doing treatment and earning a living as a beginning analyst. It highlights money, in all its complexity, in both fantasy and reality, and addresses the particular challenge of maintaining a part-time analytic practice in hard economic times.

The part-time practice option is an increasingly common one for those who are raising families, do not prescribe medication, or are unable to land supplemental work in a hospital setting. And, the current recession presents a double whammy for trainees who work this way: A candidate who works fewer hours sees each patient multiple times per week, often for much reduced fees. Such a candidate is at risk of becoming too dependent on the few individuals in treatment and may need these patients to keep coming in order to pay bills and fulfill training requirements. Having great need for one's patients creates potential problems for treatment and has a potentially harmful impact on the relationships between patients and analyst, to be sure. This is elaborated in the clinical portion of this chapter.

Before considering the clinical material, however, I wish to offer my view on why part-time analytic practice and training is so fraught. If you follow the money, it becomes clear: Working 25 hours a week, 16 to 20 of them at greatly reduced fees, means money becomes tight. Candidates might have real difficulties meeting training and life expenses, even when higher fees also come in dribs and drabs. Throw in child care costs and the numbers are even grimmer—one can almost imagine Suze Orman screaming, "Get a hold of yourself ... your financial situation is out of control!"

Candidates treating low-fee patients in harsh economic times face pressures to build up their practices but may be unable to do so. The old convention of calling or sidling up to senior members of the institute and mentioning that you have "openings" may not work as well because many senior people admit that they also have more open hours than they want. Now more than ever, building a practice takes time, effort, patience, and forbearance. Those who hold Sisyphus up as the symbol of hard work and struggle might want to rethink it, as Sisyphus probably never tried to build an analytic practice.

All this is meant to convey that money matters. When money is tight, it is daunting for individuals and for the field of psychoanalysis overall. For newer analysts starting practices, the future looks intimidating and scary and feels frustrating—all of which is problematic for the treatment situation. After all, no good analyst wants his or her financial fears and practice costs to influence personal work, treatment recommendations, or course of treatment. And, money may become a determinant in the survival rate of analytic institutes, as more and more new analysts find it difficult to complete their training.

As will be elaborated, I treated several patients at very reduced fees while completing the training about which I felt so passionate. I can say, now, as a full-fledged analyst, that despite all of the financial obstacles, I made it through analytic candidacy. And I am glad I did. Things have improved dramatically in the financial sense since I was a trainee. Some of my patients have made gains and have left treatment. Others have realized professional and personal successes, and we have agreed together to raise their fees as our work has continued. Overall, my practice has grown. But, as described so beautifully by senior clinicians like Drs. Jacobs, Hirsch, Lieberman, and Orgel in this book, the issue of fees and finances remains relevant throughout the course of practice.

To shed further light on the complexity of fees in the training situation and to preserve confidentiality, I draw two composite portraits in order to describe two separate enactments around money. These enactments illustrate how different patients used money to repeat with me in the present what they could not consciously remember from the past. They withheld fees and payment as a way to pull me into sadomasochistic entanglements that involved pain, longing, and hopelessness. For them, controlling, depriving, and punishing was their way of loving. And being controlled, hurt, and punished was the way these individuals felt loved (Freud, 1919).

The analysands I describe came to treatment mired in their childhoods and holding themselves back in ways they and I had yet to understand. Feeling stuck in unsatisfying lives over which they felt they had no control, they recreated in the transference their prisons, their lack of control, and their misery. Once the enactments around fees were understood, they had a clearer window into their aggression, pain, and wishes for control.

The relationship among money, control, and aggression is well documented in the literature (Abraham, 1921/1942; Freud, 1908, 1909; McWilliams, 1994; Shengold, 1988, 1989). The meanings of money and the importance of its use as a tool to further analytic exploration are also well established (e.g., Abraham, 1921/1942; McWilliams, 1994).

To discuss the financial realities inherent in training in the current economic climate, I wish to acknowledge briefly the ideas of Freud (1914), Shengold (1988, 1989), and others and to add my contribution to the mix. It is my contention that controversies about fee structures and balances are often used by those with masochistic characters to communicate in action that which they cannot consciously express in words: feelings of aggression and wishes to control, torture, and hurt or punish. Viewed in this way, analysis of patients' attitudes, fantasies, and behavior in relation to unpaid fees and balances becomes a tool through which to understand and work through patients' earliest experiences of suffering, aggression, hopelessness, and despair.

At this point, it is also important to underscore Dr. Berger's conceptualization that candidates often become locked in sadomasochistic enactments (Berger, 2009), such as the ones I describe surrounding money and fees. As the following clinical material illustrates, money is a useful clinical tool. In several of my training cases, it was used to access early experiences and explore transferential themes of wanting to trap, control, and deprive as a way to love and feel loved.

THE WOMAN WHO DID NOT PAY

Ms. D. worked sporadically in a creative field and sought analysis to figure out why she felt anxious and depressed, isolated and alone (she was in her 30s and regretted that she was still single) and why she had needed for most of her adolescent and young adult life to drink and use drugs. I agreed to see Ms. D. four times a week for a moderate fee, paid by her father, and our work progressed, until he abruptly stopped paying, and she stopped looking for work, ostensibly in anticipation of an insurance settlement. Ms. D. and I worked together while a large balance accrued, and analyzed the meaning of her maintaining this balance. I allowed her some latitude, as I liked her and liked working with her, and as she seemed motivated to understand herself and improve her life. I knew that she was a starving performer, often charged rent on a credit card, and ate sparingly—some days no more than a piece of fruit.

Although Ms. D. had stopped paying me, I felt it was important to continue the analysis because she seemed motivated to understand herself and improve her life. I felt that understanding the meanings of her difficulty finding steady work, establishing close relationships, and of her maintaining a large balance, which I began to understand included her acting in a dependent and aggressive manner by depriving me, were crucial to a successful treatment outcome.

After about 5 months in which Ms. D. spoke poignantly of her loneliness and despair and her abusive family of origin, but stayed clear of discussing the balance, despite my gentle prodding, my resentment mounted. Five months felt like a very long time in which not to be paid.

Even though I knew the nonpayment to be a central and important enactment occurring between us, I waited to address this issue. Why I let this go on I know, in retrospect, had much to do with my then status as a candidate and with my belief that it was part of my job to help Ms. D. live through and analyze even the most unpleasant enactments. I know now that I also let a balance accrue because as a candidate I was afraid to make waves, even as I began to feel resentful, trapped, and exploited.

Eventually, though, I felt that things had gone on for too long, and I decided to address the balance and Ms. D.'s underlying dependency and aggression. Several times when I gingerly raised the issue, though, Ms. D. immediately "forgot" what we had been talking about, even as I tried to tread lightly, not to overwhelm her, yet still be direct enough to confront a salient issue between us. In one instance, she fell asleep when I was exploring her failure to pay. On several occasions, she went home to sleep, midafternoon, after sessions. I understood her forgetting and sleeping to be, at least in part, a reflection of her dissociated aggression and rage.

Feeling it was important to help Ms. D. integrate her aggression, I attempted in one representative hour to connect her forgetting, sleeping, and anxiety with her maintaining a large balance (i.e., her aggressive wishes toward me), and I said we could understand the balance as a "communication" to me. She spoke on a very concrete level, refusing to acknowledge there could be any deeper meaning in the balance; rather, it was just that she could not pay me or others until the insurance money hit her bank account. She vehemently denied any aggression toward me and insisted she felt only gratitude. I noticed I felt furious. The hour ended.

As a candidate, I routinely presented case notes to a supervisor. When I vented about Ms. D.'s lack of payment and our inability to discuss the issue, my supervisor suggested that by maintaining a large balance, essentially acting on feelings instead of knowing and feeling them, Ms. D. had succeeded in keeping her aggression toward me out of her awareness, all the while provoking me to treat her just like the abusive father of her youth, who had habitually called her stupid and hit her. We agreed that she was making me suffer, just as she had suffered. She was depriving me, just as she had been deprived.

When Ms. D and I next met, I tried to discuss with her what I believed she had been reliving in the treatment. When, once again, I mentioned the balance, Ms. D. felt attacked and embarrassed and accused me of being aggressive. She asked whether I was going to "throw her out." I pointed out that the feelings that she had might be so threatening that she had to see them as coming from me. I also noted that I had no plans to stop working together—that came from her.

The next hour, she brought in a payment, told me she had called to find out about her insurance settlement, and noted that after our prior session she had felt cared for and had "been pushing it to the limits with me." She continued: "For years I was terrified of being dependent on someone. Every time I am with a man I feel trapped. My last couple of boyfriends always just wanted to trap and control me. ... One even pressured me to have a baby, even though I wasn't ready. Now I am dependent on you and I am terrified. *But, you can never leave ... you have to stay connected to me because I owe you so much money.*" She then commented that she was terrified of getting close to me because close relationships are fraught with danger; people in intimate relationships mistreat and exploit each other.

Once our enactment around the fee and Ms. D.'s underlying aggressive and dependent feelings were better understood, Ms. D. could move forward in various ways. After this point in the analysis, she began to seek full-time jobs and to date men who were loving and available.

THE MAN WHO WANTED FREE TREATMENT

A similar, but more prolonged, enactment involving fees occurred with Mr. R., a single college student who toyed with the idea of becoming an optometrist, but who mostly spent his days feeling resentful about coming from a family that was of "poor means." His father had died when he was young, and his mother had worked a series of "low-paying and demeaning" jobs in sales and food service industries to pay for their "horrible, squalid" apartment and to put food on the table.

Mr. R. resented the other students in the local community college he attended and lamented the fact that he had few friends. When asked about the others in his school, he described them as "a bunch of spoiled rich kids who have had everything handed to them." Mr. R. reported commiserating with his mother about "how unfair it was that others had it so easy and they had to work so hard." When they were not commiserating, Mr. R. felt they had nothing in common and nothing to speak about. Mr. R. said angrily that his mother had nothing to offer; she was cold and "ice water ran through her veins."

At the time treatment began, Mr. R. said he could pay $10 an hour. Since he had minimal income, lived in squalor, and had student loans, I—anxiously—agreed to accept what felt like a very low fee. I agreed because I liked doing analysis, and because I needed one final control case to progress in my training. I also felt that I should take reduced fees; my former analyst had done so for me so our treatment could continue when I returned to school, and reducing fees appeared to be a common practice at the institute. So, I agreed to a substantial fee reduction for Mr. R.—even though I was concerned about committing for a period of years to such a low hourly amount.

Not surprisingly, money was of paramount focus in Mr. R.'s treatment. It was constantly in his thoughts and mine. And indeed, by the midphase of the treatment, his very low fee felt like a noose, tightening around my neck and rendering me a prisoner. In retrospect, I know this was because as a candidate I was subject to certain training realities: I needed a case to progress; it was difficult to find people who were willing and able to come multiple times a week, regardless of the fee; and once I started consulting with Mr. R., I was loathe to stop the treatment, even though it was depriving and not remunerative. I wanted to see the treatment through, but I also resented the difficult work and loss of potential income I was incurring.

During Mr. R.'s analysis, both he and I struggled with powerful feelings of hopelessness, despair, and immobilization. Mr. R. used the sessions to vent. Unconsciously, he re-created with me the situation with his mother in which the only shared experience was one of misery and commiseration; there was no joy. As such, he primarily filled the hours with complaints about the regular weekend and holiday shifts required by his sales job.

When angry, Mr. R. became nonreflective and spoke in a bitter fashion about how hard he had to work. He repeatedly told me he was struggling in school and was worried he would not graduate (all the while secretly maintaining a 4.0 average and applying for scholarships at 4-year colleges).

During one particular session, I noticed I felt increasingly hopeless and frustrated about what felt like a complete lack of progress in the analysis. Mr. R. spent the hour in his usual fashion, recounting feelings of despair and hopelessness. I listened and attempted to get him to reflect on what he was saying, on his anecdotes, patterns, and the similarity to past situations. He just vented. I worried about whether my work with this patient would satisfy the requirements for graduation at the institute.

Late in the session, I listened to Mr. R.'s worries that he had failed a recent series of exams at school: "Maybe I really am incapable as I always thought. ... I feel like throwing in the towel. ... It feels like school is never going to end. I don't think I am ever going to graduate. I feel like I am in prison."

Reflecting on my countertransference as I listened, I realized that Mr. R. had been feeling similarly, like a prisoner for the past 2 years of our treatment, and that those years had felt way too long. I had despaired about my professional future, about his lack of psychological mindedness, and about the low fee I was accepting for this difficult treatment. I had worried that no analytic work was occurring, so the case would not "count," meaning I would never advance in my training.

Hearing that he had felt immobilized and like a prisoner, I realized that I was in a complicated transference/countertransference enactment with him, and that he was finally expressing what I had been experiencing since the beginning of the treatment: Since there was no way Mr. R. would ever get better, there was also no way I would ever graduate from analytic training. I feared I would fail at the institute in a very public way, would be permanently stymied, and would never practice psychoanalysis.

Feeling freer, I suggested to Mr. R. that he seemed to need to present himself as a failure in the treatment room. This observation led to fantasies about his mother's envy of him. He feared likewise that I would not be able to tolerate his successes.

Years into our work, after hearing daily about only how difficult things were, I learned that Mr. R.'s mother had found a new boyfriend, and that she and he had routinely deposited money into Mr. R.'s bank account. With that money, Mr. R. had bought luxurious new clothing and home furnishings. He regularly ate in fancy restaurants and even took a nice vacation—all in secret.

So, after several years of concealing what felt like an economic boon to Mr. R., and in which Mr. R. maintained that he could afford no more than $2 or $5 increases to the fee, it became apparent that he was no longer having money problems—but I struggled to meet expenses. At one point while I was a candidate, many of my hours were spent treating in analysis and therapy those who said they could pay only greatly reduced or nominal fees. I was learning and progressing in my candidacy, but it still felt depriving. I grew poorer while Mr. R. grew richer.

I found out about the improvements in Mr. R.'s financial situation when he graduated from community college. One day, he announced that he had found a job that paid a better salary and offered health insurance. Instead of describing his progress with excitement, though, Mr. R. lamented that things continued to be difficult for him, as he had many expenses and everyone in his life "had their hands out" for his money.

I asked Mr. R. whether he feared I also would ask for more, like all the others. He shot back, "I knew you'd bring this up! I knew it—*you've been waiting*. I know you'll want to take my money if I have too much! Just like my mother. You're just waiting for me to have more so you can raise the fee." A very long pause followed. "This is very expensive for me, you know. Maybe I just can't afford analysis. Maybe I should just go someplace cheaper." I felt outraged. "Cheaper?! Cheaper than $10? Boy would I like to see that," I thought to myself. But, though I felt devalued and angry, I chose to remain silent rather than act on my own as-yet-unprocessed feelings.

Not surprisingly, Mr. R. did not go to another analyst. Despite his feelings of hopelessness and misery, and despite his need to keep the good and the joy out of our treatment, he was deeply connected to me. Over the next months, we analyzed his fantasies about and his fears of envy—his own, his mother's, and mine. He described his own covetous feelings and imagined that others and I wanted to steal anything he had of value. He acknowledged that he also wanted to take things from others. At this point in the treatment, he attended his graduation ceremony.

The next hour after the graduation, Mr. R. spontaneously offered a higher, more reasonable hourly fee of $30 ($120 for four times a week). He volunteered that he had known all along that he could afford more, and he told me about his mother's financial assistance and his pending scholarship applications. He continued to say that although things had become easier for him than he had let on, he did not want to pay me because analysis, even one in which I labeled feelings and made connections, felt "too silent." "It's just like with my mother. ... It feels like you're just sitting back there not doing anything. So, why should I? Why should I give you anything when you don't give me anything?"

After analyzing his feelings about paying, about wanting to hurt and deprive me, and about his fear that his valuables would be coveted by me and others, Mr. R. was able to make substantial improvements in his life. He decided to pursue graduate training in his chosen field, and he found a partner with whom he has a satisfying and loving relationship. He also began to collaborate in the treatment about his progress, not only his set-backs and difficulties. He and I share pleasure in his psychology, his struggles, and his accomplishments. The treatment is richer and fuller for it.

* * * * *

I realize in retrospect that working with several perpetually despondent, hopeless, masochistically provocative analytic patients who kept much of the good out of the treatment, thus depriving me emotionally as well as financially, contributed to my hopelessness about my work and my feelings of imprisonment. That is, the circumstances of my having difficult patients who paid very low fees, my needing to continue working with them due to my own moral compass and sense of what constituted good and ethical treatment, as well as my needing to fulfill the requirements of my institute and the American, contributed to my feeling that I was stuck and suffering in a candidate's prison.

To be sure, not every candidate would experience taking some low fees and being subject to certain requirements as a noose or a prison. I am aware that some of my reactions had to do with my personal countertransference. But, these were reactions I had to the candidate experience.

So, for these reasons, the composite portraits of Mr. R. and Ms. D. are illustrative. Both demonstrate how money can have myriad meanings and how it can be used effectively as a vehicle for patients to express in action powerful aggressive and sadistic feelings and memories, as well as to re-create old sadomasochistic entanglements that they cannot remember or express in words.

Specifically, both used money to "trap" (Ms. D.'s word) or "imprison" (Mr. R.'s word) me, thus expressing a complicated object relationship between them and me. For Ms. D., if she maintained a balance we would be forever intertwined, and I would not leave her. She would show me how love was given and experienced in her family: Love was not kind; there was no mutuality or respect, only one who dominated and punished and one who was subservient. Feeling dependent on me and vulnerable to me, Ms. D. wielded money and the balance as a sword. By withholding payment, she expressed her aggression, power, control, wishes to dominate, submit, hurt, punish, and love, thus re-creating with me her experience of a dominating and cruel parent.

Mr. R. also used money to express powerful feelings of aggression and sadism, as well as wishes to hurt or punish. He felt he was unworthy, repellant, less than, and ugly, inside and out. He got me to see him practically for free—although he admitted in retrospect he could have afforded more—as a way to re-create the depriving and dead relationship with his mother. He felt deprived and desperate, and he lived in abject poverty. He deprived and impoverished me, as an expression of his sadism, aggression, and wishes to punish.

In his fantasy, neither of us would ever improve or progress past abject circumstances; we were tied together as victims. If one of us saw an improvement in our circumstances, we could no longer love each other, and we could not stay together. Success and moving up were tantamount to the loss of a crucial relationship. This would be a loss and loneliness too devastating to bear.

Although Ms. D. and Mr. R. ultimately made some strides, their treatments were difficult to endure, and both progressed slowly. I felt it was my job to tolerate the discomfort, the hopelessness, the ambiguity, and then try to put words to the despair (both mine and theirs). It was my job to tolerate the financial deprivation and try to use it to further analytic exploration.

It follows, then, that the candidate analyst who feels resentful and impoverished by a very low fee, might (with less experience and possibly less ability to do self-analysis) be less equipped to understand his or her own reactions to financial and other kinds of deprivation. The candidate may be embarrassed to report resentment to supervisors who readily share that they took low fees during training. How can a candidate complain about money when supervisors and training analysts routinely lower fees and do not complain—to candidates anyway?

It is also interesting to consider the effect, on the candidate or newly graduated analyst and the treatment as a whole, when patients can and do pay a full fee during a prolonged recession. Briefly, it is worth noting that the full-fee situation also poses difficulties. For example, in a difficult economic climate, what do we say when the patient who can and does pay a high fee looks at a large monthly bill and announces, "This is like a mortgage payment! Analysis is helpful, but is it worth this much money? Is it worth more money than a place to live?"

At such times when confronted by the wealthier analysands whom I have treated, I wondered how to quantify and put a price on happiness and self-understanding—and how to factor in the impact of the current recession. While these are interesting questions, the issues that arise in newer and more senior clinicians working with wealthier patients are beyond the scope of this chapter. (These sorts of challenges are beautifully addressed by Dr. Glick in Chapter 3, "The Rich Are Different.")

Implicit in the present discussion, though, is that it is the lot of the candidate, and sometimes even the experienced clinician, to take fees that are lower than regular ones for analytic treatment. We cannot terminate a patient simply because the fee is too low. And, we cannot just tell a patient who maintains a large balance that we will not see him or her, at least for the short term, when the nature of what we do implies a contract to understand what the patient's actions and nonpayment communicate.

Although trainees have always reduced their fees, I believe that we are in a new world, with different economic realities. With no insurance reimbursement for intensive treatment, and tighter money all around, and in the current zeitgeist that favors pills and quick fixes, analysts might have to rethink fee structures overall if our field is to survive. Institutes might consider financial incentives to help candidates complete their training and build their practices. Now more than ever psychoanalysts need to keep talking about money—not only as fantasy but also as a cold, hard reality.

REFERENCES

Abraham, K. (1942). Contributions to the theory of the anal character. In *Selected papers*. pp. 371–392. London: Hogarth. (Original work published 1921)

Berger, B. (2009, January). *Sadomasochistic Struggles within the Consulting Room: A Candidate's Dilemma*. Paper presented at American Psychoanalytic Association meeting, New York.

Freud, S. (1908). Character and anal eroticism. In J. Strachey (Ed. & Trans.), *The standard edition of the complete psychological works of Sigmund Freud* (Vol. 9, pp. 169–175). London: Hogarth Press.

Freud, S. (1909). Notes upon a case of obsessional neurosis. In J. Strachey (Ed. & Trans.), *The standard edition of the complete psychological works of Sigmund Freud* (Vol. 10, pp. 155–249). London: Hogarth Press.

Freud, S. (1914). Remembering, repeating, and working through (further recommendations on the technique of psychoanalysis II). In J. Strachey (Ed. & Trans.), *The standard edition of the complete psychological works of Sigmund Freud* (Vol. 12, pp. 147–156). London: Hogarth Press.

Freud, S. (1919). A child is being beaten: A contribution to the study of the origin of sexual perversions. In J. Strachey (Ed. & Trans.), *The standard edition of the complete psychological works of Sigmund Freud* (Vol. 17, pp. 179–209). London: Hogarth Press.

McWilliams, N. (1994). *Psychoanalytic diagnosis*. New York: Guilford.

Shengold, L. (1988). *Halo in the sky*. New York: Guilford.

Shengold, L. (1989). *Soul murder*. New Haven, CT: Yale University Press.

Chapter 8

Money and meaning

A senior psychoanalyst comments on Drs. Berger and Newman

Shelley Orgel

Both Drs. Berger and Newman examine the impact of money and fees on the treatment situation. Dr. Berger, in one of the clinical composite cases she describes, relates a successful therapeutic outcome of a female therapy patient (Ms. Z.), whose life choices became greatly restricted due to financial reverses in the current economic downturn. Dr. Berger believes that Ms. Z.'s straightened financial situation played an essential role in determining positive developmental changes. Dr. Newman's cases, also composite portraits, describe how two patients used fees and balances to play out with her aspects of their early relationships.

In the present discussion of these chapters, I narrow my focus to just one of Dr. Berger's clinical vignettes (Ms. Z.) because, like Dr. Newman's patients, she dealt with shattered finances in a harsh economic climate. Although Dr. Berger also presents another example of a woman whose fortunes grew during the current recession, I confine my comments to the three patients who shared the stresses of financial difficulties. I have done this to examine more closely the effects of restricted financial resources on psychological functioning and the many meanings money presents in the clinical situation.

In considering the clinical material of Ms. Z., Dr. Berger's patient, a woman who had great wealth before the current recession, we are reminded of Freud's often-cited idea that it is therapeutically beneficial to set a fee that requires a meaningful sacrifice, the giving up of something (having to choose), but not something essential. As an aside, there have been reports showing that limitless wealth undermines the therapeutic process. I would add that paying huge fees also slights the *meanings* of paying any fee; it narrows the focus of attention to the *concrete amounts* of money changing hands. We have read about analysts asking $600 per session or more from patients for whom it was claimed that such amounts carry no meaning to the very rich and have no negative consequences for the therapy.

As Dr. Newman's treatments reveal, it is also meaningful when a patient pays a very low, or nominal, fee—especially when that patient can pay more.

Confronting and exploring the complex meanings of money and fees is one of the tasks Drs. Berger and Newman have set for us. In other words, while it seems important to charge a fee appropriate to the patient's economic circumstances, much experience and the message of these chapters alert us that we need also to be cognizant of the universal conscious and unconscious meanings of money and to think of the fee as an aspect and determinant of the quality of the relationship. Such awareness would include attention to who assumes responsibility for the payment and to anticipate how the analytic work itself may affect the relationship to the payer and therefore to the future stability of the treatment situation. As analysts, we try to distinguish between what the patient *feels* consciously and reveals unconsciously, in enactments, for example, about paying money or not as a condition for the continuing relationship to the analyst.

These are just two major circumstances in which money issues are inseparable from the total relationship and the therapeutic course and outcome. Aside from working out what the patient can afford, no mean challenge sometimes, many more issues influence what fee we decide to charge. A few questions come readily to mind: what spending money in general means to the patient; the enduring attitudes toward saving, budgeting, withholding substantial resources generally; the complex meanings of generosity as a character trait; and most essentially, the meanings of fantasies of using money to "buy" love, or the reverse—the fantasy conviction that paying money is inimical to a genuine loving relationship, that it negates the possibility of love.

For many of us, our financial situation affects how we believe we are viewed in the world, as adult or child, as man or woman, with esteem or condescension, envy or pity, as one who has or has not. All these self- and object images are embedded in one's character, and inevitably these aspects of one's identity enter into all of one's relationships. Dr. Newman emphasizes how money transactions bring back to life the patient's early self- and object relations in the transference and countertransference. She points out that interpersonal conflicts centered around money can mirror or repeat in new forms sadomasochistic struggles over possession; boundaries; wresting oral, anal, and genital gratifications from resisting objects; rage over frustrations of primitive needs; fantasies of being robbed, coerced to give up body contents and control of sphincters; active and passive fantasies of rape; as well as shame and guilt over acquisitive urges, over greed.

These chapters reveal how struggles over money are used to create a bond that reassures against object loss. But always there is a disquieting sense that something is not right when money is in focus. What one obtains with money never fulfills the universal deep wish for love with no strings: the love a selfless mother has for her adored child, a total acceptance of one's essential, unadorned self. Thoughts about the money asked and paid can never be absent as irritants, stimuli that demand action, and therefore the manifest and unconscious meanings of money must be a part of every dynamic treatment situation.

MS. Z.: WHEN LESS BECAME MORE

Dr. Berger's idea that the economic downturn may require "weaning" seems particularly appropriate in relation to Ms. Z.: During better financial times, she and her husband relished their money as a flowing breast. Dr. Berger provided analytic psychotherapy for Ms. Z., who conveyed that she was helped by it. Nonetheless, it is worth wondering if, through a more intensive psychotherapy or psychoanalysis, this patient might have gained a deeper understanding of her unconscious fantasies concerning the meanings of having wealth and losing it, an understanding that might shed more light on the vicissitudes in her relationship with her husband.

I wonder about what kind of relationship Ms. Z. had with her father, and what the role of money was in the family? She was labeled an "executive child," a position she repeated in her marriage. Forced to be the parentified child, the practical one, I wonder how intensely she longed to *be* a child, to be allowed to be irresponsible, to find unconflicted pleasure in fantasy, playfulness rather than having to attend to practical realities. And perhaps her symptoms reflect this conflict. Her home feels to me to have been a depressing one, with much complaining, arguing, people blaming each other, hardly a "fun place." What kind of drinker was the father? Happy? Belligerent? Abusive?

Ms. Z.'s husband is described as a spoiled child who lived out the childhood of which Ms. Z. felt cheated. Their money allowed him to be the indulgent parent freed from personal responsibility to "be a man." He could "drink" from it as from an ever-flowing breast. When the flow stopped, and when "weaning" was imposed on him, he mobilized himself, with the help of his own therapy, to take steps toward personal responsibility. One would expect that these changes would have disrupted Ms. Z.'s characterological masochism, a threat to her need to see herself as the suffering responsible one—for her father and brothers in the past, for her children in the present. One feels she was conflicted about accepting and attempting to use her husband's earlier affluence to fill a kind of bottomless well of emotional deprivation. To use financial resources for this purpose made her feel like an inept child deserving criticism. She is angry that she cannot let herself *be* "the frightened child she feels herself to be" and to accept her wishes to be taken care of as her husband is able to feel.

I think the change in the financial situation—which allows them to be more vulnerable and afraid together—has had therapeutic effects and has helped them to integrate previously split-off parts of themselves. Each seems to accept being both child and adult, that one identity does not require negating the other, that these needs—to enjoy the pleasures of adulthood *and* childhood, motherhood and fatherhood—could exist in both of them. Correlated with this, there seems to be a breakdown of barriers between masculine and feminine identities, responsibilities, prerogatives. Each is better able to accept aspects of both roles in the other. Perhaps for Ms. Z., the economic "crash" repeats her mother's pregnancy and then the birth of her baby sibling—her loss of the breast. But this time, with the very significant help of therapy, it has not been traumatic. It seems rather to have the effect of supplying a needed developmental stimulus that allows her to experience adult relationships—with her husband and therapist—as enriching rather than depriving. This time, the added responsibilities did not necessitate angry, masochistically tinged withdrawal and resented precocious pseudomaturity. As a result, the deeper pleasures of adulthood are more available to her.

A few further questions arose in reading about Ms. Z. One thing we share with our patients is concern about money. Fee issues are important to all of us; therefore, Dr. Newman's emphasis on the meanings of fees applies also to Dr. Berger's practice. I understand that Dr. Berger was willing to lower her fee for Ms. Z. when her circumstances changed. I am curious about how this was handled and about how it affected the treatment? The meaning of the fee can be incorporated easily into sadomasochistic aspects of a relationship. So, the meanings to Ms. Z. of paying for treatment or of being offered the gratification of a lowered fee would be complex and important to explore.

Second, having to deal with economic problems in this period brings the situation of some candidates closer to that of those more senior colleagues who have financial problems and stressful practice situations. Probably most analysts face a dilemma when deciding to recommend more intensive treatment—analysis—versus less-intensive treatment at potentially higher fees per session. Drs. Berger and Newman, sensitive to the current economic pressures on their clients, demonstrate a flexibility and willingness to make treatment affordable to patients who do not have, or who came to have less after the economic downturn.

Third, how has the changed economic situation for Ms. Z. made it more possible for Dr. Berger to identify with her patient's struggles, her neediness—to have more empathy with these conflicts and feelings than she could have had earlier?

To generalize, then, the meanings of money, economic circumstances, the fee, and the like to the *patient* are also bound with such meanings to, and the material circumstances of, the therapist/analyst. Dr. Newman's chapter tackles this issue sharply and openly and so forms a nice complement to Dr. Berger's paper.

MS. D.: THE WOMAN WHO DID NOT PAY

I first consider Ms. D. and limit my questions to just a few: Dr. Newman's report contains much that is interesting and raises many questions that deserve discussion. We all feel we are being treated to an embarrassment of riches.

Ms. D.'s father stopped paying for the treatment, and Dr. Newman writes, "Ms. D. and I continued to work together while a balance accrued. ... over the next few months, meeting four times a week, we attempted to analyze the meanings of her maintaining a large balance. I allowed her some latitude as I liked her, and liked working with her. She seemed motivated to understand herself and improve her life."

Reading this, I wondered: How much did Dr. Newman communicate *unconsciously*, and how much did Ms. D. understand *unconsciously*, that *she would* take care of this patient, as her father would not, *if* this patient acted the part of a considerate person who *seemed* "truly motivated (*consciously*) to figure out how to improve her life." In other words, would not both of them, but mainly Ms. D., be inhibited in expressing the anger that must have been welling up in them both? I cannot help wondering how much of a transference/countertransference agreement they forged that accepted her version, that she was helpless to influence her father's iron-fisted authority.

Dr. Newman seems not to have questioned very deeply her liking and sympathy for Ms. D. as someone ground under the heel of a tyrannical father, who suffered "reality" frustrations and deprivations, and who claimed it was others' refusals to give to *her* that was the essential reason she could not give to others, most particularly to her analyst.

It is most relevant to our discussion that Dr. Newman did not press her patient about the growing unpaid balance because she "believed it was part of" her job "to live through and analyze even the most unpleasant enactments." Her assumption at the time seems to have been that candidates need to accept a masochistic submission to the institute authorities, just as her patient needed to accept such a position while waiting for an inheritance (the masochist's promised reward). Her "inheritance," becoming a loved daughter of Freud, a recognized member of the analytic community, would follow if she was a submissive candidate. "It was my job."

What we may fruitfully discuss here, then, would be how much of what she believed at the time a candidate must go through reflected *her* psychic reality and how much these conditions are imposed on candidates in general in analytic training. She faced similar questions later when she and her patient eventually confronted their positions in the world and in their relationship. Out of this self-reflection came insight and active work to resolve their enacted sadomasochistic impasse.

Here is what happened: After 5 months without being paid, Dr. Newman brings up the unpaid balance and the fact that Ms. D. did not talk about it. Her "gingerly" way of introducing the subject sounds somewhat defensive, as if she feels guilty of "attacking" this nice young woman with a club of reality. The patient's response of forgetting, sleeping, and anxiety sounds as if she immediately and totally shut out Dr. Newman and her words by a process akin to dissociation. I would speculate that she was warding off rage that felt overwhelming and destructive. Dr. Newman, for her part, was identifying herself with Ms. D. in her role as supplicant, while Ms. D. became the unbudgeable, opaquely unreadable father, keeping *her* out of the loop. Dr. Newman "began to feel resentful, trapped, exploited," as she assumed the accustomed "castrated" position her patient had assumed in relation to her father.

What Dr. Newman seems unable to say to her patient at this moment (because she is a candidate who cannot make waves?) is something like: "By not paying me or talking about the balance, you are unconsciously attacking me and injuring me. I wonder about your response when I bring it up. I expressed my sense that it is hard for you—you do not consider that it may be hard for me, just as your father, you believe, doesn't consider *your* feelings and *your* reality."

I would speculate that if Dr. Newman held her patient more responsible for what was going on it would have disrupted the mutual enactment sooner and would have meant to her patient that she *really* did want her to change, that she really envisioned her becoming an adult—therefore, that she is not like Ms. D.'s father. And in fact, a few days later, Dr. Newman does make such a useful intervention.

Ms. D.'s pseudostupid response revealed her passive aggression clearly. An aspect of the pseudostupidity would be her unquestioning belief that her aggression is only in response to others; that her mind is, as it were, an empty, innocent vessel, passively expecting to be filled with, and reacting to, what others put into it, including their aggression. Dr. Newman's persistent successful work eventually led to the patient asking if she would "throw her out." Her answer, that she had no such intention, led her patient to believe she really meant what she was saying. It marks a turning point in this analysis. Shifting from being the object of others' intentions, Ms. D. now speaks as *subject* about *her* wishes, fears, and need for an unbreakable tie to be achieved by something they both want—money. But money now seems to represent more than just a source of oral gratification.

Ms. D. could be called a moral masochist by Freud's definition. Here are a few of Freud's (1924) comments on this kind of character (in the male):

Through moral masochism morality becomes sexualized once more (e.g., in the form of unconscious fantasies of being beaten by the father). The Oedipus complex (through whose sublimation morality has been internalized) is revived and the way is opened for a regression from morality to the Oedipus complex ... a large part of his conscience may have vanished into her masochism. ... Masochism creates a temptation to perform sinful actions in order to provoke punishment (from the power of Destiny, a projection of the superego into the outside world). The masochist must do what is inexpedient, must act against [her] own interests, etc. (p. 169).

This is what Ms. D. seems to have done when she speaks as "subject," not just as passive victim of her father's bonds and aggressive hold over her.

MR. R: THE MAN WHO WANTED FREE TREATMENT

Dr. Newman also is bravely honest and self-revealing in this report of the man who wanted free treatment. She tells us she was ambivalent about beginning the treatment at $10 per session. I think she would agree that at the outset she had not understood all the meanings and consequences to both of them of her "generosity." She tells us she needed one more case to be eligible to graduate, and that she felt sorry about the patient's circumstances.

As with Ms. D., she notes that she loved doing analysis. We also learn that her own analyst reduced *his* fee when her circumstances changed, and that doing this was a common practice at her institute. We might conclude that she needed at that juncture in her analytic education to identify with idealized analytic figures in order to strengthen her not-yet-firm sense that she indeed was becoming such an analyst herself. (I analyze; I *am* an analyst.) In fact, I believe such imitative identifications, as Jacobson labeled and described them years ago, are a universal early step in students' development of an analytic identity. What complicates the situation was Dr. Newman's not fully confronting the likelihood that she might well have conveyed her initial ambivalence about accepting *this* patient. This communication may have markedly influenced the direction the analysis took in the early months. This clinical instance raises a generally applicable question about the advisability of accepting a patient in analysis about whom one feels such conscious ambivalence.

I wonder whether Mr. R.'s angry rants about life's injustices might have been intensified by his sense that he was not accepted wholeheartedly *and* by his unconscious identification with his analyst's own conscious and unconscious feelings about the terms she *had* to agree to as a candidate. Dr. Newman, hoping that her patient (child) would thrive and thus affirm her ability to nurture and express gratitude to her for having been chosen, was instead met with resentment: Her patient elaborated rancorously about those who are given more because they are first, not second, choice.

Dr. Newman writes that she felt herself to be "a prisoner of the analysis. ... His fee was like a noose around my neck. ... I was imprisoned by my own moral compass and sense of what constituted good and ethical treatment." Dr. Newman's difficulty in accepting her human feelings, *her* needs, including, I assume, needs from her childhood, clashed ever more severely with what she believed the moral authorities of the institute required as the "correct analytic attitudes." This patient felt to her like a half-dead child whom Dr. Newman could not nurture into active life and responsiveness. The half-strangled newborn was strangling the desperate mother. The noose was around both their necks, a suffocating tie, but not a bond. Neither could survive and grow, be freed from this entanglement. Dr. Newman expresses all of this in her condensed statement: "I was imprisoned by my own moral compass."

Here, I would like to suggest a somewhat different narrative the analyst might propose as a possible way to get beyond this impasse. What if the analyst had said something like: "You feel I don't really want you to be my patient; that I have to work with you. I have given this idea of yours some thought and will continue to do so. It is true that you pay me a reduced fee; *that* is real and meaningful to both of us. You may believe I don't really accept you mainly because you don't give me enough money. And you try to tease me about what money you secretly have, and withhold from me. You believe I want more and more. But actually, I think the focus on money offers you what feels like an acceptable, believable reason you don't feel wanted. Otherwise, you would have to face your lifelong sadness that there is something basic, deep, unchangeable in you that will always leave you feeling you are 'bad,' unlovable, a failure, second, never first choice. What you label your bad luck also helps you to deny these feelings that come from inside. I think you are afraid to know how much you want to be wanted by me—totally, unconditionally—since you cannot believe it can truly ever happen and you will be left humiliated and defenseless."

Would this approach, conveyed in a series of interventions, have shortened the prison term of both Dr. Newman and her patient?

As with Ms. D., when she told Mr. R. she was not thinking of firing him, there is a moment in Dr. Newman's report that seems to be a point of breakthrough. I am referring to Mr. R. telling Dr. Newman that he had graduated with a 4.0 average.

Rather than envying her patient for these successes, and rather than coveting them or wanting to take them for herself, as apparently was the case with Mr. R.'s mother, Dr. Newman took pleasure in Mr. R.'s possession of them. Previously, Mr. R.'s position has been: You want everything, to give me nothing, and this is the role I am enacting with *you*. Mr. R. must also have known that his analyst was a student; yet, she could *still* take pleasure in Mr. R.'s accomplishment, his brilliant graduation. Dr. Newman demonstrated that it was not a zero-sum situation between them in which only one of the pair could thrive. In the next session, Mr. R offered to share more of what resources he had with his analytic partner.

Dr. Newman's persistent efforts to analyze these individuals who seemed like adversaries bent on her surrender and defeat, obtaining their pyrrhic victories, shows admirable strength of character. However, when doing the "job" required by the institute becomes of major importance, the work is made more trying, more of a chore, relatively less rewarding. These first experiences not infrequently inflict an emotional blow to a young person eager to do analysis. I vividly remember these feelings from my own candidacy. Early in one's clinical analytic experience, it is difficult to hold the steady conviction that it is the *desirable* intensification of the transference attachment that has brought into bloody life these patients' threats, demands, negativism, and wounding attacks and not the analyst's inadequacy or the patient's unanalyzability.

It is tempting to overlook patients' needs to test, through masochistic provocation, the enduring strength of the relationship and the analyst's commitment to it, particularly when they pay low fees to a younger person. And, it is hard for the beginning analyst truly to believe that the patient is terrified that his or her aggressions will damage or destroy the new object the patient has come to need so badly, and that he or she will be abandoned, depleted and alone.

The individuals presented by Dr. Newman seem to have in common that they have grown up still depending on others to supply them with essential ingredients for their survival and growth. And these others, in the patients' early lives, have often given and withheld, promised and reneged, over-gratified, and unexpectedly frustrated these people (see Ms. D. especially). Their masochistic characters attach to others by creating sadomasochistic relationships with those who represent their primary objects. They have brought these needs and ways of relating wholesale into their analyses. It is to the analyst's credit that these analysands have felt able to test via strenuous enactment whether they can use her in this way.

There is reason to infer that their early objects (e.g., Ms. D.'s father, Mr. R.'s mother) were teasing and judgmental, and that these were the early objects with whom their children identified and from whom they projected their patterns of aggression onto the analyst. I believe it requires much experience and self-analytic reflection for analysts to become able to grasp and contain these projections (to internalize them partially and temporarily) while simultaneously sampling their latent emotional responses to them in themselves, identifying their origins in the patient, but also finding shared resonances with their patients' psychologies in their own mental lives—and using this mixture of projection and introjection to "understand" what the patient is communicating both in and out of awareness. Being able to achieve such delicate balances makes it possible to approach a position of relative neutrality. We can appreciate how difficult this is to achieve.

Given the nature of these individuals' early relationships, and given their way of relating to Dr. Newman, identification with the aggressor comes to mind as a central defense mechanism in the analytic work she describes. Identification with the aggressor is a developmentally intermediate step *toward* superego formation in that primitive aggression can be internalized and directed against the self, yielding self-criticism, need for punishment. I think it is related to the depressive position of Melanie Klein. Virtually simultaneously, in the regressive direction, the aggression is projected onto the object, who may then be regarded as a persecutor who justifies the attack. This stance is analogous to Klein's paranoid-schizoid position.

When Dr. Newman gingerly brought up the fee, I suspect she was responding to an expectation of such a paranoid response. Ms. D. actually "refused" to take in what she was saying; a kind of negation occurred in which the patient could claim, in effect, I won't swallow this, own it, it is coming from you. Her very existence as an autonomous, boundaried being may have demanded her refusal.

Perhaps here another dimension of the meaning of money can enter into our discussion. To the patient, the fee *is* for the analyst. It is always imposed on the patient, and its very necessity tends to evoke sadomasochistic interaction. In this sense, it resembles the injunction to say everything that comes to mind or to mandate the use of the couch when these are presented as requirements for the treatment process to go forward. In this sense, also, the analyst is an aggressor; the patient must submit. Freud's original rationale (rationalization?)—that the fee is in the interests of the analysis and lessens resistances and so on—is to be questioned.

Actually, by the 1920s, Freud and many of his followers offered free and low-fee analyses and concluded that the treatment worked just as well with those analysands. For patients whose own overwhelming feelings of potential starvation, needs for nurturance, total acceptance, endless narcissistic affirmation—for such people, the idea that the analyst needs something from them, has personal desires—can be unbearably threatening. This awareness dethrones them from their position of unique specialness in the same way as do other basic assaults on their illusions of total narcissistic omnipotence analogous to submitting to weaning or bowel-and-bladder training.

Dr. Newman's experience is that her patients became vengeful, evoked rage in her, and led her to provide low fees and allow large, unpaid balances, and provide treatment without payment for months and years. I would speculate that Dr. Newman's talent and empathy reflect at the same time a kind of thinness of self-object boundaries in that she could not easily protect herself from internalizing and making her own, sharing, for an extended period of time, her patients' early painful experiences of wanting to hurt and punish her. These are ego qualities—a particular vulnerability and sensitivity—that one finds in some artists and some especially gifted analysts. With time, experience, and self-reflection, Dr. Newman was able to keep a flexible but clearly differentiated boundary between her self-representation and her patient's projection of his or her own internal objects. One could say she became aware of, and could better work with, her countertransferential experience of projective identification. And the work moved forward, becoming more gratifying and less stressful.

Insofar as conflicts over money can ever be resolved, it is required that *both* analyst and patient can be gratified; and that both can accept that the fulfilled life and pleasure of one *gives* to the other rather than takes away. If this state of being can be achieved, and it is achieved rarely, there would be no necessary conflict between having and giving; one wants the other to have and to be. Does this not define this thing we call love? Money cannot buy it, but ideally money need not be the cause of sacrificing it and losing it.

REFERENCES

Freud, S. (1924). The economic problem of masochism. In J. Strachey (Ed. & Trans.), *The standard edition of the complete psychological works of Sigmund Freud* (Vol. 19, pp. 159–170). London: Hogarth Press.
Jacobson, E. (1954). The self and the object world. *Psychonanal. St. Child.* 9: 75–127.

Chapter 9

Money, love, and hate

Contradiction and paradox
in psychoanalysis*

Muriel Dimen

The way analysts talk, behave, and feel in relation to money is replete with an uneasiness that is the surface manifestation of a deep, psychocultural contradiction between money and love that cannot be thought, willed, or wished away. For the clinical project to succeed, this contradiction can and must find a temporary, reparative resolution in the paradox between love and hate. This essay takes up the question of money in the spirit of the Marx-Freud tradition, in postmodern perspective, and through several languages, not only psychoanalysis, but social theory, anthropology, and less centrally, feminist theory as well. It addresses money's unconscious and emotional resonance, and its cultural meanings; money's clinical and theoretical vicissitudes in the context of cultural symbolism and economic change, as well as the class position of psychoanalysis and the psychology of class itself; and money's relational meaning in transference and countertransference.

Since most psychoanalytic discourse about money takes place informally, it seems appropriate to begin in anecdotal style. When I first mentioned to colleagues my intention to write about this topic, I was greeted with what you might call a less than enthusiastic response. "Why are you talking about money?" asked one, quite startled. Another found the proposed title a bit inappropriate and wondered if it oughtn't be changed to something like "Between Commerce and Trust." It's almost as though money were in fact not quite a suitable topic for our distinguished community. Something we don't talk about, at least in public? A little unsavory, perhaps? Or vulgar?

This was not the first time I'd met with psychoanalytic unease about money. Consider Dr. French, as I am calling him, a colleague to whom, many years ago, I referred a patient's husband. The man had a cash business (no, he wasn't dealing drugs) and, like his wife, paid his analyst in cash, just as anyone in his subculture did whenever buying anything. Shocked,

---

* This chapter originally appeared in *Psychoanalytic Dialogues*, 4(1), 1994, pp. 69–100. Reprinted with permission.

Dr. French shook his hands as if to rid them of dirt and said to me with an embarrassed smile, "It's, well, money just doesn't belong in the consulting room."

It begins to look as though Freud was right, doesn't it? Recall his (1913) ubiquitously quoted observation: "Money matters are treated by civilized people in the same way as sexual matters—with the same inconsistency, prudishness and hypocrisy" (p. 131).

Freud and his contemporaries might not have shared Dr. French's feelings about cold, hard cash. If they had, they probably would have written about it; to my knowledge, the only classical reference to the matter is Abraham's (1921/1953) certainly accurate diagnosis of severe anality in people who insist on paying not only analysts' bills but even the smallest sums by check (p. 378). Nevertheless, our forebears, themselves uneasy about money, recognized the deep desire that its dilemmas simply vanish. They thought hard about money's relation to development, character, and pathology. Abraham's (1921/1953) and Jones's (1918) attention to its place in anal characterology develops Freud's (1908) original insights about its psychosexuality, "the sexual and especially the anal erotic significance of money" (Aron & Hirsch, 1992, pp. 39–40), ideas that are certainly familiar enough and to which I return later. Ferenczi (1914/1976) augmented this line of reasoning by assigning money a role in development; he argued that the adult attachment to money represents a socially useful reaction formation to repressed anal eroticism. Fenichel (1938/1954) suggests that anal-erogeneity is made use of, and strengthened, by a social system based on the accumulation of wealth and competitiveness.

The approach to money taken by Ferenczi and Fenichel was political as well as psychoanalytic. Ferenczi (1914/1976), for example, concludes that the "capitalistic instinct ... contains ... [both] an egoistic and an analerotic component"; standing at the disposal of the reality principle, "the delight in gold and the possession of money ... also satisfies the pleasure-principle" (p. 88). Fenichel (1938/1954) points out that what he identifies as the drive to amass wealth is born with capitalism, adding that in pre-capitalist, tribal society it did not exist, while in a future classless society, it would have disappeared (p. 108). They were not the only classically trained psychoanalysts who wanted to unite two of the three great and diverging arteries of 19th-century European thought, Marxism and psychoanalysis (to put them in their chronological order; the third and temporally intermediate one is Darwinian evolutionary theory). While it is unlikely and probably not desirable that these two grand theories will meld into a single perspective encompassing nothing short of human life itself, nevertheless the dialogue between them has been fruitful and remains compelling. Not only Ferenczi and Fenichel but such luminaries as Edith Jacobson, George Gero, and Annie Reich received their intellectual formation during a time heady with progressive politics and psychoanalytic discovery. While some, like Wilhelm Reich and Erich Fromm, kept striving for synthesis, others abandoned their politics, a yielding impelled more by their Holocaust-driven escape to an anticommunist United States (with its medicalized and anti-intellectual psychoanalysis) than by the inherent incompatibility of two cherished and imaginative comprehensions of human possibility (Jacoby, 1983).

Taking up the question of money in the spirit of the Marx-Freud tradition (a project already called for by Rendon, 1991) but adding a postmodern perspective, I consider money's vicissitudes in the psychoanalytic relationship a topic that is theoretically immediate as well. Freud's discussions about money as a practical matter (1913) and money as a psychological matter (e.g., 1908) may appear in separate essays (see Whitson, n.d., p. 3). But their distance in print represents only the map of his thought, not their lived geography. In the light of recent psychoanalytic and social thought, money's clinical and theoretical locations turn out to be more proximate than might at first appear. Developments in psychoanalytic theory—such as the Kleinian understanding of love and hate, the Winnicottian notion of paradox, the interpersonal assessment of countertransference, and contemporary relational arguments about the simultaneity of one-person and two-person psychologies—and developments in social theory—such as social constructionism, critical theory, and postmodernism—permit a synthetic and evolving interpretation of money in the psychoanalytic relationship that is both clinically relevant and theoretically responsible.

On reflection, it becomes clear that a theory of money cannot derive from psychoanalysis alone. Consider Freud's only partially theorized perspective. His ideas on the psychosexuality of money, which pre-date his instructions about its handling in the clinical setting, in essence constitute the sole intellectual frame for his practical considerations. Money is, Freud (1913) says, to be approached in the consulting room with the same matter-of-factness as sex, for while money has a narcissistic dimension, being "in the first instance ... a medium for self-preservation and for obtaining power ... powerful sexual factors are [also] involved in the value set on it" (p. 131). The way analysts address it ought then to serve psychotherapy. By speaking with frankness, Freud says, he furthers the educative project of psychoanalysis; he shows patients that "he himself has cast off false shame on these topics, by voluntarily telling them the price at which he values his time" (p. 131).

As for the rest, for the principles on which Freud (1913) bases his policy of leasing his time and setting his fee, he speaks from "ordinary good sense" (p. 131). He speaks as a practical man of the world who must consider his material existence by charging for all time leased and regularly collecting his debts (pp. 131–132). The arrangement of leasing one's time, he observes, is "taken as a matter of course for teachers of music or languages in good society" (p. 126). He is faithful to his beliefs, not only his own theory of treatment but what is closely related, his ethics. In elaborating his ethical position, he reviews the behavior of other professionals, concurring in, or distinguishing his own practice from, theirs. He has, he tells us, desisted from taking patients without charge or extending courtesy to colleagues' kin for three reasons. For one thing, free treatment stirs up resistances to, say, the erotic transference in young women and to the paternal transference in young men, who rebel against any "obligation to feel grateful" (p. 132). For another, charging a fee preempts countertransferential resentment of patients' selfishness and exploitativeness (pp. 131–132). Finally, he finds it "more respectable and ethically less objectionable" to avoid the pretense to philanthropy customary in the medical profession and to acknowledge straightforwardly his interests and needs (p. 131).

The common sense from which Freud reasons is, however, like any informal system of "folk" or cultural knowledge, embedded in unexamined presuppositions. It combines, in effect, the expectations and prejudices customary for his class with his personal needs and predilections, and thus contains unarticulated ideas about issues that are only now being theorized in psychoanalysis—such as the patient's experience of the analyst's subjectivity (Aron, 1991) or the relation between one-person and two-person psychologies (Ghent, 1989; Aron & Hirsch, 1992)—or have, only since Freud's time, been anatomized by social thought, like the economic and political place of the helping professions, the social class of analysts and patients, and the psychology of class (Sennett & Cobb; 1972, Ehrenreich, 1989). Such vantage points being absent either from classical theory or from psychoanalytic thought altogether, it is not surprising that, until recently, so few analysts have considered the matter of money systematically. Whatever the other resistances to this topic (and I get back to them shortly), the intellectual tools to study it have been missing.

I want here to refurbish the intellectual tool kit by conversing in several languages, not only psychoanalysis but social theory, anthropology, and, less centrally, feminist theory as well. I decode money's unconscious and emotional resonance, as well as its cultural meanings. I track its clinical and theoretical vicissitudes in terms of cultural symbolism and economic change, as well as the class position of psychoanalysts and the psychology of class itself. Through both an examination of Freud's dicta and feelings about money and a clinical example, I render its relational meaning in transference and countertransference.

MONEY IN PSYCHOANALYTIC QUESTION

If Freud and his contemporaries were laconic on this matter, his followers have become exponentially voluble as the psychoanalytic century has worn on. The bibliographical entries in the anthology *The Last Taboo:*

Psychoanalysis and Money (Krueger, 1986) are few and far between until the 1960s, when they begin to cluster; and then in the 1970s and 1980s they positively blizzard. Here we are in the 1990s, trying to climb out of what has been termed a "recession" but has really been a depression, which has nipped at, if not bitten into, the practices and pocketbooks, and psyches of most psychoanalysts in private practice. Just in the last 3 years, there have appeared two more books on the question, one a general anthology (Klebanow & Lowenkopf, 1991) and the other about the fee (Herron & Welt, 1992). All cover quite a range of topics, from fee setting, personal philosophies about fee policies, and the relation between gender and money to managed health care and the effects of free treatment.

The snowballing discussion of money has a history, part of which is cultural. Psychoanalysis's "last taboo" fell during a period when a lot of other icons were being broken too, as, simultaneously, the class position of professionals was subtly but permanently shifting. If the 1960s (the "we decade") saw the blossoming of sexual expression and the 1970s of narcissism (the "me decade"), then the 1980s (the "greed decade") made the admission of the desire for money and the accumulation of wealth at least more common if not more socially acceptable. But, we might ask, acceptable to whom? Surely not stockbrokers and corporate raiders. Wall Street's expression of greed may well have had to do with the wildest financial party since the roaring 20s, a party perhaps even more avaricious than the age of the robber barons. But people who trade in money are supposed to be on good terms with selfishness; helping professionals are not. Instead, they are supposed to value money only for its ability to serve a modest standard of living. What was surprising in the 1980s, then, was the seemingly sudden acquaintance with covetousness on the part of professionals.

Psychoanalysts' heightened interest in money, not to mention their greed, had, however, more than a decade behind it. It was, in fact, a response to, and expression of, a long, slow slide in their socioeconomic fortunes. The 1960s were a watershed in a century-long trend; until then, the gap between rich and poor in the United States had been steadily decreasing. After that, the gap began to yawn. The middle class, from which traditionally have come most analysts and analysands, began to shrink, indeed, to decline; presently, middle-class people can no longer count on owning their homes or sending their children to college without impoverishing themselves (Newman, 1988; Ehrenreich, 1989). By the same token, the insurance reimbursements that subsidized their psychoanalytic treatment have dwindled, bruising both those in need of therapeutic help and those who make their living by providing it.

This decline in middle-class fortunes coincided with a boom in the helping professions, which in turn further reduced professionals' share of the pie. The extension of parity to psychologists and social workers by insurance companies, the increasing participation of social workers in the psychoanalytic profession, the proliferation of "media shrinks," and the flood of self-help books—these belong to the expansion of psychotherapy to all levels of the middle class, even to the working class. Part of the democratizing trend in psychoanalysis (Havens, 1989, p. 142; Zaphiropoulos, 1991, p. 242), this growth also belonged to a cultural change that might be called the "therapization of America." The evolution of a therapy-sensitive culture in which people are knowledgeable about, and receptive to, psychotherapy, in which consumers assume the right to question and choose among all medical authorities, and in which psychotherapy is packaged by managed health care has, ironically, also reduced analysts' incomes. The more competition there is among providers of mental health care, the fewer the patients and the lower the fees for each privately practicing analyst (Aron & Hirsch, 1992; Chodoff, 1991, pp. 254–256; Drellich, 1991, pp. 159–161); the more knowledge consumers have, the more they question analysts' authority and resist the imposition of what have sometimes seemed to be arbitrarily high fees (see also Herron & Welt, 1992, p. 171).

As psychoanalytic pockets slowly emptied, psychoanalytic journals began to fill up with articles on money. Comparisons would be interesting. In other countries, say, Sweden, where the middle class remains or has become economically secure, as it was in Freud's time, are these issues handled differently? Are they addressed systematically? Or are they ignored, as, in fact, they were in Europe and the United States until, for all intents and purposes, 30 years ago? Or take the obverse: Will psychoanalysts in Eastern Europe begin formally to consider the clinical and theoretical problems money presents as their practices leave the public domain of (medical) hospital care and enter the private market?

THE DISTURBANCE OF MONEY

In responding, if only unconsciously, to this recent (and perhaps permanent) downturn in the American economy, however, analysts are noticing merely what has been there all along. In saying this, I am revising Durkheim's (1930/1951) classic sociological position, codified in his paradigmatic study of suicide. Durkheim (1938) drew a parallel between medical and social science: If studying illness reveals the nature of health (as, indeed, Freud himself, 1905, argued), then, he said, studies of social pathology should reveal the basis for social order and hence the true nature of social life. That social life is normally orderly, however, can no longer go unquestioned. A deconstructive, postmodern approach, which, perhaps not strangely, finds a harbinger in Freud, suggests otherwise. Taking a Foucaultian tack (Flax, 1990, p. 36), I argue that studying social disorder reveals instead the normal lines of discontinuity and conflict that are the fault lines along which cultural evolution and changes in inner life occur.

So, with money and psychoanalysis: Just as we learn from "hysterical misery" about "common unhappiness" (Freud, 1895), so if we look into disrupted economics, we come on money's ever-present, complicated meaning in psychoanalysis and thence the normal difficulties of the work. Several recent articles teach us a lot about the underrecognized countertransferential effects of analysts' economic dependence on their patients that these parlous times make visible. While their work allows us to see that you and your patients want you to be as invulnerable as a tenured full professor, you actually feel about as secure as a part-time adjunct. Yet, analysts have been so uncomfortable with their own feelings of need and greed (Aron & Hirsch, 1992, p. 255) that they have tended to treat money as a psychological problem for patients and merely a practical one for analysts (Whitson, n.d., p. 3). Indeed, analysts' dystonic relation to their own dependence may constitute the biggest single counterresistance in regard to money (Aron & Hirsch, 1992, p. 243; Whitson, n.d., p. 3). Herron and Welt (1992) concurred and developed the theme: "The issue … isn't that greed exists [among psychoanalysts]; rather, it is how that greed is responded to; how it is aroused, frustrated, or met" (p. 48; see also Shainess, 1991).

Analysts' pecuniary need of their patients, however, is not only a discrete countertransference problem. As we can see from Freud's by now well-known financial preoccupations, it is an inevitable thorn in their sides that demands as much inspection as their other basic needs vis-à-vis patients, their needs for, for example, love and respect, power and gratitude. Throughout his 17-year correspondence with Fliess (Masson, 1985), Freud writes periodically about his money-related worries, as well as about the times when his income feels to him adequate. It's quite clear not only that his cash flow is uneven but that this unpredictability breeds cynicism. For example, he prefers American patients for their hard currency (Gay, 1988) and writes, on January 24, 1895, "Mrs. M. will be welcome; if she brings money and patience with her, we shall do a nice analysis. If in the process there are some therapeutic gains for her, she too can be pleased" (Masson, 1985, p. 107). Notice also his reference to his wellborn, well-to-do patients as "goldfish," once on September 21, 1899 (p. 374), and another time on September 27, 1899: "The goldfish (L. von E., and S. by birth and as such a distant relative of my wife) has been caught, but will still enjoy half her freedom until the end of October because she is remaining in the country" (p. 375). Such mordant humor ought not gainsay Freud's famous largess toward some of his patients, for example, the Wolf Man (1918). Still, since he complains, on September 15, 1898, of sleeping during his "afternoon analyses" (Masson, 1985, p. 303), can we not imagine that, sometimes, the most desirable capacity of a patient's purse may have detoxified her less alluring capacity to make him nod off? In any event, Freud's pervasive, if intermittent, focus on money and its ups and downs of anxiety, cynicism, optimism and the like suggests that the roller coaster of comfort and fear about income so familiar to contemporary analysts is doubly determined: The product of hard times, this anxiety may also be an aggravated variant of a pattern actually inherent to the work not only of psychoanalysts but, as we see in a moment, of most helping professionals.

In the last generation or two, analysts have had a far smoother economic ride than Freud, and those made anxious by money were more likely to be in the beginning stages of practice. For example, at the beginning of the affluent 1980s, when my practice was relatively new and supplemented by an academic position, I made my anxiety known to my supervisor, a very senior and well-known analyst of interpersonal persuasion. His reply was, "You can do your best work only when it's become a matter of indifference to you whether you gain or lose an hour." While he seemed to be saying that one can work well only when money is out of the picture, I would now put it another way. It's not that money is relevant to analytic work only when times are bad. When times are good, it's relevant by its absence; then, we're like TAPS, which is what the disabled call the rest of us, "temporarily abled persons." From our present perspective of financial doubt, then, we might wonder whether the mid-century lack of competition among analysts was simply a constant or, instead, an active agent of countertransference. For example, if financial uncertainty now unsettles analysts, can financial security make them smug? Was it such smug sincerity, as well as, perhaps, character, that led another prominent analyst, during the ironically but wistfully termed "golden years" of psychoanalysis (the late 1950s/early 1960s to the stock market crash of 1987), to decline patients older than 40 because he thought them less able to change? Can complacency distort analysts' respect for patients' neediness, transforming empathy into pity? Could such a countertransference amplify the vexing popular mistrust of psychoanalysis itself?

These questions intersect another vital clinical issue, the countertransference symbolism of money. Do psychoanalysts not face a dilemma of safety that money actually symbolizes? If feeling unsafe threatens to impede the analyst's confidence and hence competence, is it also possible to feel too safe (Greenberg, 1986)? There's a necessary insecurity: Psychoanalysts cannot guarantee their method will work, for success depends on a relationship being established and maintained, and the sustenance of relatedness is a day-to-day affair (P. Bromberg, personal communication). More. Current emphases on clinical process, on the importance of not knowing too precisely where you are in a session, suggest a need for analysts to tolerate a certain amount of danger (Bion, 1980; Eigen, 1986). Indeed, they develop Freud's insistence on not pressing the patient for linear sense: In explicating the value of the fundamental rule, Freud (1913) cautions, "A systematic narrative should never be expected and nothing should be done to encourage it" (p. 136). Only in this atmosphere of unsafety can we expect to come upon the new and/or the forgotten. Hence money's rollercoaster effect becomes a convenient, rationalized, and inevitable container for the nonrationality and uncertainty of psychoanalytic process. While not arguing that the uncertainty of earning a living in capitalist society guarantees the feeling of risk necessary to analytic process, I insist that the anxiety money generates cannot be banished from the consulting room. On the contrary, it is endemic to the particular sort of work analysts do (e.g., Chodoff, 1986). Analysts, it turns out, are not alone in their unease about money matters. They share it with everyone else in their class, a class called the "professional-managerial class" (Ehrenreich & Ehrenreich, 1979; Ehrenreich, 1989) that came into being between 1870 and 1920 (the birth period, note, of psychoanalysis, as well as the robber barons). Professional-managerial work ranges from law and medicine to middle management, from social work and psychotherapy to education, from academe to journalism. It entails what is crudely called mental labor but is better characterized as labor that combines intellect and drive with considerable, although not total, autonomy and self-direction (Ehrenreich, 1989, pp. 38, 78).

Professional-managerial work is not only a livelihood. It is also a means of power and prestige, and a shaper of personal identity. Because it involves conceptualizing other people's work and lives (Ehrenreich, 1989, p. 13), it confers authority and influence. Indeed, it was arguably the chisel that the then-emerging middle class used "to carve out" its own socioeconomic place, its own "occupational niche that would be closed both to the poor and to those who were merely rich" (p. 78). Finally, by providing the opportunity for creativity and discovery in regard not only to one's work but also to one of its chief instruments, one's self, it enters—indeed, expresses, reflects, and generates—one's identity.

This kind of work renders the professional-managerial class an elite. But, and this is Barbara Ehrenreich's main point in *Fear of Falling* (1989), it is a highly anxious elite. For one thing, members of this class know that their power, privilege and authority can make their clients envy, resent, and hate them (and, analysts would add, idealize them). For another, they, like their clients, also sometimes suspect, even if secretly, that because they do not produce anything visible or tangible, they do not actually do anything real; as such, not only does their work seem worthless, it also cannot match their own or their clients' idealization. Because their only "capital," so to speak, is, as Ehrenreich writes, "knowledge and skill, or at least the credentials imputing skill and knowledge" (p. 15), their high status is insecurely founded. Unlike real, material capital, she continues, skill and knowledge cannot be used to hedge inflation, nor can they be bequeathed. They must be renewed by and in each person through hard work, diligence, and self-discipline. Consequently, members of the professional-managerial class, like anyone in any class but the highest, fear the misfortunes that have overnight sent even middle-income people sliding into homelessness and indignity, a fear that Melanie Klein and Joan Riviere (1964), to whom I shall return, liken to that of children who imagine being orphaned or beggared as punishment for their unconscious aggression (p. 109, n. 1). They fear falling through the economic and moral safety net, hence Ehrenreich's aptly titled *Fear of Falling*. They fear "falling from grace," the title of another book by Kathy Newman (1988) on a similar topic; they fear losing their financial status, their elite position of authority, the work they love and their identity as moral, beneficent persons. Rooted in the very work of professionals, then, this anxiety about felt fraudulence and looming loss is actually built into the role of analyst in a class-structured society.

CLASS, COUNTERTRANSFERENCE, AND ALIENATION

Like all social institutions, class has powerful unconscious resonance. In the most general sense, class refers to the material aspect of society and the way it divides and joins people along a ladder of economic and political power. By definition, class is hierarchical; the relation between classes is determined by their economic and political superiority or inferiority to one another. To put it more crudely, class distinctions are about money and its unequal distribution in society. Conversely, money represents the veritable or potential differences in power among individuals and among groups. It indicates not only differences of class but those constituting other hierarchies, like race, ethnicity, gender, sexual preference, and so on. Money, in other words, is symbolic of the fault lines webbing and cracking a psychological and social reality in which difference is the nucleus of hierarchy (Dimen-Schein, 1977, pp. 88–92). The hierarchy of privilege organized by class, status distinctions, the unequal amounts of money people have— these trigger not only greed but envy, excite questions of self-esteem, invite oedipal competitions.

The fault lines of class and other hierarchies show up systematically in transference and countertransference. To return to our exemplar: If, in his most despondent moments, Freud felt greed and cynicism toward his "goldfish," he was unreflectively contemptuous of the middle class and benevolently condescending toward those poorer than he. Addressing the petit bourgeois reluctance to pay for psychoanalysis, Freud (1913) argued that the restored health and increased "efficiency and earning capacity" afforded by treatment made therapy less expensive than it appeared. Therefore, he concluded; "We are entitled to say that the patients have made a good bargain. Nothing in life is so expensive as illness—and stupidity" (p. 133).

As for the poor, he opined that the best psychoanalysis could supply was "a practical therapy of ... the kind which ... used to be dispensed by the Emperor Joseph II" (1913, p. 133). Known as the "emperor of the beggars"

(1780–1790), Joseph, in good Enlightenment fashion, used on occasion to live among the poor so he could come to know at firsthand what they needed (C. Fink, personal communication). It would not, of course, have occurred to either the emperor or the physician what we take for granted today, that poor people might actually have been able to articulate at least some of their own needs. Still, while Freud (1913) regrets the inaccessibility of psychoanalysis to the impecunious, he acknowledges that "one does occasionally come across deserving people who are helpless from no fault of their own, in whom unpaid treatment does not meet with any of the obstacles [including secondary gain] that I have mentioned and in whom it leads to excellent results" (p. 133). Nevertheless, in his relation to such poor patients as he might have taken on, his paternalism would have had to be analyzed. That it would not have been is a foregone conclusion. As we have known from his unconscious sexism, the emotional structure of socioeconomic hierarchy does not appear on his map or on that of classical psychoanalysis.

From a psychoanalytic perspective, one might see in Freud's intermittent dyspepsia about his patients a symptom of what has been called the "money neurosis" suffered by the bourgeoisie in Vienna and other European cities in the late 19th century (Warner, 1991). From a political perspective, one could label it "classism," or class prejudice. If we put psychoanalysis and politics together, however, what we discern in Freud's heart is the social malaise called "alienation." What I mean by alienation is not so much estrangement or disaffection but the cause of these feelings. Hear, for example, the dysphoria of a supervisee who reported thinking, during a difficult session, "I wouldn't be sitting here if I weren't doing it for the money." His guilt, bewilderment, loss, hate, and self-hate proceed from the way money, which permitted him to do his work, nevertheless stole from him its pleasures and meaning. When money is exchanged in a capitalist economy, both buyer and seller—patient and analyst—come to be like commodities, or things, to one another because they enter into relation with each other through the mediation of a third thing (money) that, simultaneously, separates them. As money wedges them apart, so it estranges them from themselves, a distancing that creates anxiety in both (Amar, 1956/1976, p. 286; Marx, 1964, p. 113; Mészáros, 1975, pp. 178, 186). This theft of the personal satisfaction you take in work and in your relationship to those with whom you work is alienation, the process by which your labor and its fruit become alien to you because of the very socioeconomic structure that lets them be (a defining point that deserves particular emphasis here because it tends to be omitted from psychoanalytic discussions; e.g., Fromm, 1966; see Struik, 1964, pp. 50–52; Mészáros, 1975, p. 36).

Alienation, in short, is the estrangement of people from their activity, their products, other people, and themselves (Ollman, 1976, p. 135). An occupational hazard of modern life, it is core to psychoanalysis. As Masud Khan (1979) writes in the preface to *Alienation in Perversions*: "In the nineteenth century two persons dictated the destiny of the twentieth century, Karl Marx and Sigmund Freud. Each ... diagnosed the sickness of the western Judaeo-Christian cultures: Marx in terms of the alienated person in society; Freud, the person alienated from himself" (p. 9). And, of course, we would add today, "herself." Elsewhere, Khan (1972/1974a) calls psychoanalysis the "inevitable result of a long sociological process of the evolution and alienation of the individual" in the West. Freud's genius, he declares, was "to evaluate the situation and give it a new frame in which [the alienated] could find [their] symbolic, therapeutic speech and expression" (p. 131). Extending Khan's point, I think of psychoanalysis as the perfect therapy for a culture of alienation, for in it you pay a stranger to recover yourself. Paradoxically, psychotherapy that is bought and sold under conditions of alienation generates a "dis-ease" in both the person who pays the stranger and the stranger who is paid, and that needs treatment too. In a way, then, my goal is to explicate how alienation filters into transference and countertransference and how clinical process, by exploiting it, transcends it in a momentary, utopian, and reparative fashion.

COMMERCE AND PSYCHOANALYSIS

This explication requires a further and ethnographic inquiry into money's cultural and psychological significance. As the agent of alienation, money has acquired many kinds of meaning. One psychoanalyst observes that it "is esteemed, yet ... condemned" and traces this familiar ambivalence to twin polarities—one, the dichotomy between the "altruistic, selfless, humanistic sacrificing ethic" of the Judeo-Christian tradition and the acquisitional, individualist values of capitalism; and two, Puritanism's conflict, in which hard work and thrift are valued, but their material rewards may not be enjoyed (Krueger, 1986, p. 4). Another notes the contradiction between the philanthropic inclinations of psychoanalysis and the custom of fee for service (Gutheil, 1986, p. 182); he thus echoes Freud's admonition that the analyst be immune to demands for charity routinely placed on the medical profession lest they obstruct one's ability to make a living.

But what is money? Money is so deeply embedded in our culture, daily life and history that it tends to stay just out of definition's reach. Indeed as many years of teaching anthropology showed me, one's own culture is often intangible until it is compared with another. Like any institution, psychoanalysis has its own subculture. Let me, then, switch the conversational perspective once again and look at money anthropologically. A most important conclusion from the lengthy anthropological debate about money is that money objects are not present in all cultures (Dimen-Schein,

1977, pp. 197–199). Money, in other words, is not cultural bedrock. Instead, it comes into being under particular political, economic, and/or ecological conditions. For example, under some circumstances, the circulation of goods and services does not require money but instead is carried out by barter or by conventionalized equivalences. In other situations, different kinds of money have evolved, varying not only in substance (rock, shell, bead, metal, paper) but in their use and function.

After much cross-cultural comparison, then, anthropologists have come up with a universal definition of money, that, spelled out, helps us see, as if anew, money's meaning in psychoanalytic context: Money is any material object that performs one or more of the following five functions—a medium of exchange, a standard of value, a unit of account, a store of value, and a standard of deferred payments. While there may be different objects serving each different function in any one society, the first function tends to be controlling; whatever is the medium of exchange likely serves the other functions too. Finally, money itself may be a commodity, as it is in capitalism, where you buy it with what we call interest, that is, with more of the same (LeClair & Schneider, 1968, p. 468).

According to this less than exciting definition then, there's nothing mystical about money; it is, among other things, a matter of commerce. As Freud saw, however, this plain fact notoriously renders clinicians uneasy. After all these years, psychotherapists still "want to nurture their image as beneficent purveyors of good rather than as individuals who are at least partially involved in commerce" (Tulipan, 1986, p. 79), suffering its alienating effects as much as their customers. Even the notion of fee for service goes gently by the rough implications of trade, civilly suggesting the fair-and-squareness of being paid for the work you do so that you, like your patients, may use what you earn by your labor to buy what you need to live. But commerce? No. That we find tawdry and petty, the very opposite of the trust and professionalism on which psychoanalysis depends (Herron & Welt, 1992, p. 4).

Still, commerce is a cornerstone of the psychoanalytic edifice. It is not the only cornerstone, but it is a primary one. We sell our services to make our living. Oh, yes, sometimes analysts see patients for free. Some even argue that it may be necessary not to charge certain kinds of patients in order to treat them at all (Jacobs, 1986). But even to say "for free" suggests the norm, that analysts engage in trade (see also Horner, 1991, p. 177).

Without money, then, there's no psychoanalysis at all. But with it comes an unavoidable anxiety, an anxiety to which I attribute my colleagues' initial disgruntlement, as well as Dr. French's shock. Indeed, I would be quite surprised were anyone able to think through this topic without a moment or two of anxiety. Just in case that anxiety has in the present instance proved elusive, perhaps I may offer some assistance. Think, for instance, of that moment when you learn that your analytic patient who comes four times a week has been fired and will have to discontinue treatment. That first dip on the Cyclone at Coney Island has nothing on it. Or turn it around: You have taken on a new patient at your very highest fee for a long-term analysis. To take a milder example, you find out that a colleague's practice has doubled while yours has only maintained, or even dropped an hour or two. Suppose it's even the reverse, and you feel merely the queasiness of dismayed triumph: You have got more hours, income, or both than a friend who badly needs the money.

Are these suggestions extreme? Perhaps there are clinicians to whom the loss (or gain) of, let us say $600 a week or about $25,000 a year has no emotional resonance. If so, then the extremity of these examples may have something to do with the history recounted earlier: Analysts who came of age before and just after the middle class began its recent, but silent, descent in the 1960s are likely to be very differently positioned and to have been initially less worried than those whose practices began in the last 15 or 20 years. The original work experience of the last generation may well have created a basic sense of ease, financial optimism, and professional security no matter what the current economy.

Nevertheless, psychoanalytic anxiety in relation to money has always sufficed to create the tacit prohibition on asking people how many hours they carry or what fees they charge unless you know them very well. Of course, it's never in the best of taste for professionals to inquire about each other's income. The traditional ideology of the professional-managerial class is that they work for love, not money or power—although, as we have seen, the 1980s saw some segments of this class reverse their priorities. Still, I do not suppose it would surprise anyone to find that in order to protect themselves from their anxiety about money and the alienation contextualizing it, psychoanalysts depict their pecuniary practices in ways that are, at best, confusing. Let me illustrate with an anecdote. I remember an informal and anonymous survey about fees taken at a retreat sponsored by the New York University Postdoctoral Program in Psychotherapy and Psychoanalysis. One of the obstacles to evaluating the results of this most unscientific investigation is the difference between what people say they do and what they actually do, and sometimes this difference is further complicated by gender. While I can't here anatomize the question of gender difference in presentation of professional self, it's absolutely true that in answering the questionnaire, all the women said they had a sliding scale, while each man declared one bold fee. Yet, we all know male analysts, both senior and junior, who "reduce" their fees, to use that rather cool and complacent euphemism for bargaining. The alleged tendency of women to charge lower fees (Herron & Welt, 1992, p. 174; see Liss-Levenson, 1990) may be at times a fact, and at others, an artifact of the same asymmetrical self-presentation: Although men may charge the same fees as women, offer sliding scales, and the like, saying so publicly is probably inconsistent with their gender identity, in contrast to women, whose self-sacrifice accords more with cultural and intrapsychic expectations of women. To let the men off the hook I also have a female colleague who, in order to conquer her own anxiety about her recently increased expenses (as well as, perhaps, to make me anxious), rather loftily announced that she was now "taking" patients at higher fees. (And I always think, "How nice of her!")

THE CONTRADICTION BETWEEN MONEY AND LOVE

The point is critical: The way analysts talk, behave, and feel in relation to money is replete with uneasiness, an uneasiness that is the surface mani-festation of a deep, psychocultural contradiction that cannot be thought, willed, or wished away. In the marrow of our culture, this contradiction is embedded in the matrix of our work. It inhabits our souls. And it will not disappear until the very bones of our society change, for like all social con-tradictions, it is a relation between contraries that are historical and there-fore mutable but only by a political change that resolves their opposition. All we can do in our work is to find a temporary and utopian resolution to it, and I return to that later.

For now, let us proceed with the contradiction between money and love, for that is what I am talking about. Money and love, the twin engines that make the world go round, at least the world as we know it, do not go together at all. Worse. They negate, undo one another, and their contra-diction funds alienation. While money may be a matter of commerce, it is, like any material object, social practice, or cultural symbol, simultane-ously a matter of primitive passion. Freud knew this. He called money the "Devil's gold," an image he found in European folklore. The Devil, say the tales, gives his lovers a parting gift of gold, which, upon his going, turns to excrement (Freud, 1908, p. 174). (By the way, witches were said to have made a similar present to their lovers; neither gender has a monopoly on love's cruelties.) Freud's psychosexual interpretation of this extravagant and primal metaphor addressed what it means to consort with what he called "the repressed instinctual life." For example, he noted how the image con-trasts the most precious and the most worthless of substances, money and feces, and considered how this contrast sublimates anal eroticism (whence Ferenczi's discussion). This interpretation is, of course, right, brightly illu-minating, for example, Dr. French's distress about the mess that base and dirty money made in his office, the scene of noble motives and high-minded encounters.

The aspect of Freud's interpretation that awaits elaboration, however, is the relation between the gift and the act; what needs unraveling is the rela-tion between the Devil and his lovers so that we may, in turn, decipher the relation between money and love, as well as the relation between those who exchange both, and therefore the place of money in psychoanalysis. Freud and the European folktales had something very subtle in mind, and if you have ever been loved by the Devil, you will know what I mean. Shakespeare did. Recall sonnet 129, which begins:

> The expense of spirit in a waste of shame
> Is lust in action,

and ends with this couplet,

> All this the world well knows; yet none knows well
> To shun the heaven that leads men to this hell.

Follow me, if you would, through a brief exegesis of this poetry, which takes us where we must go, along the nonlinear road from love to hate. When the Devil has left you, you know not that you have been fooled, but that you have fooled yourself. Your feelings, yearnings, longings have betrayed you. You now see you knew all along that what you thought was pure gold was false, that what you thought would uplift you only degrades you. You have searched to be better than you are, in fact, to be the best you can be. The Devil's betrayal crumbles your dreams, destroys the ideal self into which you have breathed life by imagining it in the other's form. In the end, you become less, not more, than you hoped to be. This degradation, then, is the Devil's gold: The Devil's gold is a gift, not a payment. It is a gift given after passion is spent. But, instead of honoring an encounter that, we must assume, was glorious, as glorious as love, this gift degrades it. Gold given to mark love becomes worse than nothing, degraded desire and lost illusions. Hopelessness.

That capacity to make everything less than it is and so to make us doubt what it was we had in mind when we worked so hard to get it—that capacity, says Freud, is what money has. That's why it's the Devil's gold. Money is a pact with the Devil. That's what Marx (1964) said expounding on Goethe (and having also just quoted Shakespeare):

> That which is for me through the medium of money—that for which I can pay (i.e., which money can buy)—that am I, the possessor of the money. The extent of the power of money is the extent of my power. ... Thus, what I am and am capable of is by no means determined by my individuality. I am ugly, but I can buy for myself the most beautiful of women. Therefore I am not ugly, for the effect of ugliness—its deterrent power—is nullified by money. I, as an individual, am lame, but money furnishes me with twenty-four feet. Therefore I am not lame. ... Money is the supreme good, therefore its possessor is good. (p. 167)

If, as Marx (1964) goes on to tell us, money can "transform all [your] incapacities into their contrary," why would you not sell your soul to get it? If money can get you whatever you need, then it "is the bond binding [you] to human life ... the bond of all bonds" (p. 167). But then what can you get yourself? Money can create all that we are and desire and, by the same token, destroy it. Marx therefore asks, "Can it not dissolve and bind all ties? Is it not therefore the universal agent of separation? It is the true agent of separation as well as the true binding agent ... of society" (p. 167). The agent of alienation, it absorbs all creative power into itself, robs people of their own potential; just as money transforms imperfections into powers, so it "transforms the real essential powers of [human beings] and nature into what are merely abstract conceits" (p. 168–169). In a way, money occupies the place in modern society that kinship has in premodern culture; it is the cultural nerve center, the institution that organizes economic life, structures social relations, underlies political power, and informs symbol, ritual, and systems of meaning. Kinship, however, unlike money, can't be taken away from you; as the aphorism has it, "Home is, when you go there, they gotta take you in." In contrast, "money ... is the alienated ability of [hu]mankind" (p. 167). That's why it's the Devil's gold.

In our culture, money has the same unconscious effect no matter in what trade it is used. By reducing everything to a common denominator, it robs everything and every person of individuality and thereby debases what it touches. That is one reason we like to separate it from love and distinguish the profane, public sphere of work, trade, and politics from the sacred, private space of intimacy, love, and relationship. Perhaps that is also one reason that, in the families with which we are familiar and in which men have conventionally been the breadwinners in the public sphere that has traditionally been their province, men, more than women, have tended to think of the money they bring home as their nurturing gifts; decontextualizing money, they can thereby deny the alienation that otherwise robs them of their integrity (Rapp, 1978; Dimen, 1986). As feminism has taught us, of course, these domains mix in a way that makes the personal political, so that men, too, feel about money and love the way a blue-collar worker, described by Richard Sennett and Jonathan Cobb (1972) in *The Hidden Injuries of Class*, felt about having to put in overtime to send his son to college: Aghast to find himself hating his kid, he said, "Things were touching that shouldn't touch" (p. 200).

Money degrades because it makes everything the same. Some kinds of money are called by anthropologists "special-purpose" money, because they can be used in exchange only for particular objects or services; they are contrasted with the "general-purpose" money to which we are more accustomed, money that can buy anything that can be bought. One of the most famous ethnographic examples of special-purpose money is the jewelry used in the system of ceremonial exchange known as the Kula Ring and practiced in the Trobriand Islands of New Guinea; it was studied by Malinowski (1922/1961), who had quite a lot to say to psychoanalysts. Through ritualized ceremonies of bargaining, chiefs of different villages or islands would exchange with regular trading partners bracelets and necklaces made of shells. With any given partner, a chief would give necklaces and receive bracelets, or vice versa; necklaces would go clockwise from island to island and bracelets counterclockwise. The individual's aim in this exchange was to acquire prestige, of which each shell ornament carried a different amount created by, and registered in, the history of the exchanges it had undergone.

This special-purpose money could not be used in any other direct exchange. For example, the chiefs' trading expeditions also occasioned market trade in utilitarian goods in which the ornaments played no role. Commoners would accompany the chief on his voyages, in return for the chance not only to bask in his glory but also to haggle for food, tools, and the raw materials that they could not produce or forage at home. On the trading voyages, the jewelry and the utilitarian goods circulated in completely separate spheres; voyagers could not buy oars with necklaces, for example. Commoners were not, however, excluded from prestige circulation. On certain ceremonial occasions, to demonstrate political loyalty, they would transfer some of their own goods to the chief, in return for which he, on still later and formally unrelated occasions, would give back ornaments that could then become the basis for a commoner's climb up the prestige and political ladder (Dimen-Schein, 1977, pp. 215–217; Malinowski, 1922/1961).

There is a crucial distinction between special-purpose and general-purpose money: Whatever is transacted with special-purpose money tends to retain its individuality, indeed, is embedded in the relationship governing the transaction; general-purpose money, in contrast, is a "universal equivalent; since everything becomes translatable into it," it makes everything symbolically the same (Dimen-Schein, 1977, p. 197). For example, in Manhattan (as of this writing), $1.25 can buy, and thus means, both a subway token (itself a sort of special-purpose money) and, let us say, a frozen yogurt. While special-purpose money is linked only in particulars, general-purpose money measures everything by the same standard; we may think, for example, that a frozen yogurt has the same price as a token, say, $1.25, but we won't think that $1.25 and the yogurt cost the same, that is, that each can be exchanged for a token. While tokens will always represent one's relationship only to the subway or a subway clerk (or, perhaps, the taxi driver who will occasionally accept a token as a tip in lieu of the change a passenger cannot find), that $1.25 will indiscriminately represent one's relationship to everyone and everything, from the subway and yogurt clerks one gives the money to, to the bank and the (automated) tellers one gets it from; from the Sunday paper for which one pays the newsdealer

$1.25, to that most appealing pair of shoes of whose less than appealing $250 price it is a mere half of 1%.

General-purpose money, or a universal medium of exchange, nullifies the particular meaning of any object or transaction, destroying its individuality:

> As money is not exchanged for any one specific quality, for any one specific thing or for any particular human essential power but for the entire objective world ... from the standpoint of its possessor it therefore serves to exchange every property for every other, even contradictory, property and object; it is the fraternization of impossibilities. It makes contradictions embrace. (Marx, 1964, p. 169)

In capitalism, money is a universal medium of exchange. Although everything is not in fact for sale, in principle it is. Since the same standard, whether the dollar, ruble, or yen, quantifies everything, then money erases all differences between things, levels all qualities, eliminates all particularity. Money reduces everything to its abstract capacity to be exchanged. The car assembled in Detroit, the hamburger flipped at the Moscow McDonald's, the ad created for a candidate or dish detergent in Tokyo— what these things signify is not anyone's desire for, or consumption of, them but what they have in common, their cash value.

THE PARADOX BETWEEN LOVE AND HATE

We come to what happens when that most general of things, money, pays for that most personal of experiences, the psychoanalytic journey. The psychoanalytic relation, like love, is highly particular. So particular is it that, at its most intense, in the heat of an analytic encounter, no generality seems to apply to it at all. For example, one has to work very hard to think about what is happening, to recall or develop the theory or construct suited to clarify the complex relation that is transpiring. In fact, this doubled tension, the struggle to engage and the struggle to conceptualize, is one mark of the curative power of psychoanalysis, making it quite distinct from ordinary intercourse.

This particularity, however, is regularly undercut by the money that permits it. As analysts, we all know how rapidly our narcissism or, as Freud would have called it, our self-preservative instinct leads us to equate the loss of an hour with a bill we'll have to find some other way to pay; how disjunctive, that is, contradictory, this thought is to the personal relation that we are also about to lose, with the feeling of loss that looms; and how dysphoric the hunch that our patients perceive these feelings (Aron & Hirsch, 1992; Whitson, n.d.). As patients, who of us has not wondered just which of our analysts' bills our own treatment services? Or thought that we are replaceable by some other patient with enough money to pay the fare for their own personal journey? What's so personal and particular then? In fact, it's so painfully bizarre to go from the feelings of special love, meant only for one's analyst or one's patient, to the money that allows those emotions to flower but could also be used to buy many other things or could disappear in a flash, that one represses the connection and asks, as did my colleague, "Why are we talking about money?" That monthly bill rasps against the poignant longings for love that bloom in the psychoanalytic contact. It threatens to destroy them, turn them to shit. Like the man said, things touch that shouldn't.

When love turns to hate, it seems wise to move from Freud to Klein. In the psychoanalytic contact, as in the psyche, as, indeed, in our culture, the contradiction between money and love threatens to transform love into its seeming opposite; hate in turn threatens to annihilate relatedness altogether; and analysts, not unlike infants, feel the paralysis of terror. Money incites hate, if only because there is never enough of it to go around. But, according to Melanie Klein and Joan Riviere (1964) in *Love, Hate and Reparation*, this twist of social fate resembles the vicissitudes of dependency that they see as the understructure of society, relatedness, and love. Riviere stresses

> the degree of dependence of the human organism on its surroundings. In a stable political and economic system there is a great deal of apparent liberty and opportunity to fulfill our own needs, and we do not as a rule feel our dependence on the organization in which we live— unless, for instance, there is an earthquake or a strike! Then we may realize with reluctance and often with deep resentment that we are dependent on the forces of nature or on other people to a terrifying extent. (p. 5)

While this emergency recognition of dependence may typify only our own culture and even only certain groups within it, what Riviere goes on to say is probably universal. Not only, she says, does dependence become awful when external events deprive us of what we need. Such terror also inheres in love. The "possibility of privation" tends "to rouse resistance and aggressive emotions," a murderousness that forebodes doom (1964, p. 7). What such loss feels like to the infant is what it unconsciously feels like to the adult: Your world "is out of control; a strike and an earthquake have happened ... and this is because" you love and desire. Your "love may bring pain and devastation" to you and to those you love, but you "cannot control or eradicate" either your desire or your hate (p. 9). Hate is a condition of love, as love is a condition of life. You must love in order to live, but loving also means hating.

This, then, is the paradox of my title, the paradox of love and hate to which Klein, and later Winnicott and Guntrip, introduced us. I do not hold, with Klein and Riviere, that these primal passions of love and hate are constitutional. Nor do I hold with Guntrip (1969, p. 24) that only one of them, love, is what we begin with. I prefer what I call the big bang theory, in which love and hate are co-born. Their mutual birthing is what makes their relation paradoxical, for paradox denotes the indissoluble tension between contraries that themselves never change, are transhistorical, atemporal, universal. The paradox of love and hate comes into being through the primal relationship; these passions take their shape and meaning from their passage through the emotional and structural net of that intimacy in which they likewise participate. Love and hate, emerging together, become mutually meaningful in the context of failure, when babies and mothering persons disappoint each other, when, as the earlier Klein seemed to argue, babies, in hating the primary caretaker, also first sense their love, and when, as Winnicott (1945) taught us, parents, to their often denying dismay, feel for their babies what they long ago learned to disavow, the dreaded hate that portends the death of their newborn and miraculous and reparative love.

That we must absorb, indeed, relish this paradox so as to do our best work, we have learned from Winnicott (1945) and from Searles (1965), as well as from Khan (1970/1974b), who says: "One could argue that what is unique about the clinical situation is that the analyst survives both the loving and the hating of the patient as a person, and the patient as a person at the resolution of the relationship survives it, too, and is the richer for it" (p. 111).

THE LANDLADY OF TIME

That paradox is an acquired taste we've all learned from our clinical work. For example, last year, I moved my office to a new and, I would say, upscaled location; while my furnishings are substantially the same, the setting itself is far more elegant and professional than the old one. Most of my patients, including Ms. Rose, as I will call her, were pleased with their new environment. They read it as a sign of surging hope for their therapeutic progress and, not coincidentally, a sign of hardiness in me, an ability to survive their aggression.

About 6 weeks after this move, Ms. Rose, whose low fee is nevertheless a struggle for her to pay, took the opportunity to push on with her analytic work. She missed an appointment, one she had rescheduled because of an upcoming conference. The next time she came, she sat up on the couch and looked me in the eyes. With icy fury, she challenged me: "Suppose someone has an accident?" she asked. Suppose they were in the hospital? Would I charge them? I should note here that Ms. Rose had been in treatment with me for slightly over 5 years. She then explained that she had missed her session because her alarm clock had failed to work. Rageful that she would have to pay anyway, she declined to call to tell me what had happened; I should say that I tried to telephone her but never reached her. Her diatribe intensified. Must she, she wanted to know, be responsible for everything? Could we not share the responsibility? Somewhere in here, I said that the basis for my charging her was my commitment of time. "Of course," she said, "I understand this is a business; you have to guarantee yourself an income. But what about my interests?" The schedule was for my convenience, not hers. It's often inconvenient for her. Oh, she knew the answers: She had to conform to my schedule because I wanted her to face the reality principle. I would not change it, so she had two choices, to pay or not to pay. Anyway, why should she rely on my judgment that she needed more than one session a week? Then, like an archer at last loosing her bow, she let fly her final question: "What are you, the Landlady of Time?"

Ms. Rose is a poet as well as a graduate student in political studies, and if her rage made my heart beat in anger, her metaphor hit me right in the solar plexus. I felt all the emotions of the rainbow—guilt, recognition, anxiety, excitement, hate. After all, Freud said that analysts lease their time. And one of the dilemmas with which I am trying to deal here is what happens when money turns our work into a commodity just like any other. Indeed, it did not escape my notice that Ms. Rose had granted me a perfect illustration of my present argument, which I had already begun to think about. Her knowledge of my inner life was, in certain respects, as unerring as her poetic aim.

At this, for us, unprecedented point of mutual hate, we continued. I said that while she appeared to be asking about my policies, she in fact often seemed to assume my reply. She agreed. She also concurred with my view that she was treating this clash like a pitched battle and added that her anger meant not that she would not continue to analyze this situation with me but that she was no longer letting her relationships go unquestioned. She then observed that it was odd to feel the same way about our relationship, since, of all the people she had been questioning, I was the one who had been kindest to her. I asked, by way of interpretation, Where else should she bring her anger? Where hate but where she loves? She nodded in agreement. I added, correctly but in a fit of bad timing that spewed straight from my anger, that it was about time she was doing this, to which she coldly replied that she knew I would say that. She then began to list my unfairnesses in regard to money, some of which I acknowledged, others of which I contested. At session's end, I wished her a good trip. Her scornful smile said, "Who needs your good wishes?" Two weeks later, when she returned, she gave me a cartoon, in which a therapist is saying to a naked turtle, "I see you're coming out of your shell."

Every clinical moment is overdetermined, and many elements had fused to make Ms. Rose's rage combust. What I would like this vignette to illustrate is my contention that in the psychoanalytic contact, the contradiction between money and love can be resolved only if we transform it into the paradox between love and hate. The Devil's gold turns love to shit only when you cannot live out the hate with the one you love. What Ms. Rose and I did was to live the contradiction together, risking the hate that seemed to be killing us, tolerating imminent annihilation until she found a way to survive it, until the paradox of love and hate presented itself to her in what Ghent (1992) has characterized as the "somewhat altered consciousness that prevails in a spontaneous moment of creativity" (p. 9).

While the disparity in our financial, social, and ethnic status (I am white, Jewish, and a full-fledged member of the professional-managerial class, to which Ms. Rose, fair-skinned, Afro-American, and from a lower-middle-class family, aspires) had always been apparent and sometimes attended to, the envy, greed, fear, and hate stimulated by these economic and cultural differences had become far more accessible in my new surroundings. Until now, Ms. Rose had denied the contradictory dimension of our strange intimacy and could feel only fragments of her love and hate. My new office, which flagged not only my standing and authority but her own aspirations for the best for herself, now permitted her to move the contradiction between money and love into the center of the relationship, where it produced the hate that it always does. There were precursors. For example, shortly after I opened the new office, we began to discuss her ways of skirting shame. One day, she noticed a most offensive but, in this context, strangely appropriate odor emanating from the lovely garden onto which my casement windows open. Sniffing carefully, she said, "Why, it smells like cats." Then she giggled. I asked her about the giggle. She tentatively answered, "Well I just thought, you smell like a cat."

Once the river of hate began to rage, once she finally woke up, opened her eyes, and, in shock, saw me for who I am, that is, the Landlady of Time, not only the money-hate but all the others, all hate itself, could fill the space between us. Her rage was the sound of her shell cracking, heralding the emergence of the self we had previously called the waif in the cave. Naked, that waif emerged, angry yet/and still loving. Her discovery of the paradox, that it was strange to doubt me, even though I was the one she had felt to have been most caring during her years of personal and professional difficulty and struggle, created this utopian moment in which there began to grow another kind of love, the kind of bond you have with someone only when you have shed blood together. Since then, Ms. Rose has let me in on her thought that perhaps analysis is not always the most important thing in her life. She has owned more of the analytic work and, in return for permitting me to write about this encounter between us in a way that disguises her identity, has asked to see this paper; she has, in fact, read this version. Finally, she is no longer my tenant in the cave of psychoanalysis; she has also made us into an interracial and otherwise nontraditional family: In her last dream, she wondered what I saw in the little black girl I had adopted when there were so many white ones around. Hate having been accepted along with differences and inequities between us, she could begin imagining her own, still untenanted loveliness.

CONCLUSION: FROM CONTRADICTION TO PARADOX, AND BACK

Money, along with its coordinates, space and time, belongs conventionally to what has been labeled the analytic "frame." I would like, in concluding, to argue that the frame, which Langs (1973) calls "ground rules," ought to be treated as part of the picture too (see also Horner, 1991; Herron & Welt, 1992, p. 11). While analysts and patients often find the ground rules irritating, not only their outlining of, but their presence inside, the consulting room in fact potentiates the utopian moment that makes treatment work. They enter the symbolic play the frame permits: "When there is a frame it surely serves to indicate that what's inside the frame has to be interpreted in a different way from what's outside it. ... Thus the frame marks off an area within which what is perceived has to be taken symbolically, while what is outside the frame is taken literally" (Milner, 1957, p. 158). Because money while a constituent of the frame is also in the picture, it can be played with as symbol as well as literally exchanged. Thus, in bourgeois culture, as I have argued, a money relation is thought not to be a love relation. Money appears to negate love, producing the hate that signs their contradiction. But the psychoanalytic situation is a case where money permits love, where, for a moment, the culture can be upended, where you can love even where you would most expect to hate, where you would not get to love unless money were exchanged, where money in fact guarantees the possibility of love, and where, therefore, the contradiction between money and love, and the hate it generates become safe.

We know this from Freud, even though, in this instance, he did not appear to know what he knew. His own case histories reveal that the money relation and, hence, alienation entered his patients' lives through their families. Gallop (1982), a Lacanian feminist literary critic, points out that "the closed, cellular model of the family used in ... psychoanalytic thinking is an idealization. ... The family never was, in any of Freud's texts, completely closed off from questions of economic class. And the most insistent locus of that intrusion into the family circle ... is the maid/governess/nurse" (p. 144).

The governess, an omnipresent and essential member of most bourgeois European families, was always from the lower class. She symbolizes, in the unconscious and text alike, the very "financial distinction" that also comes to characterize the relation of Freud and all analysts to their patients. Gallop (1982) reminds us, in this context, of Dora's dismissal of Freud, the 2 weeks' notice she gave him with the same courtesy she would have used upon firing a servant (or a servant, on quitting, would have given her). Gallop argues that for psychoanalysis to provide the radical encounter of self with self it promises and to contend, I would add, with alienation, "Freud must assume his identification with the governess" (p. 146), because, rather "than having the power of life and death like the mother has over the infant, the analyst is financially dependent on the patient" (p. 143).

To put it more concretely, unless money may leave the frame and enter the picture, psychoanalysis must renege on its promise. The very economic transaction that distinguishes the psychoanalytic relationship from ordinary intimacies renders the transference sensible; money mediates one-person and two-person psychologies, their ambiguous, paradoxical, and contingent interface made possible and manifest by money's unavoidable but necessary and definitive arbitrariness, by what, in a way, Freud (1913) would have called the reality principle (Ms. Rose, it turns out, was right). "The fact that the analyst is paid ... proves that the analyst is ... a stand-in" (p. 143). Payment, in other words, grounds the possibility of genuinely new experience in the analysis, as well as that of remembering, repeating, and working through the past: The old happens with a newcomer who would never, without money, have been known and whose job it is to interpret both the old and the new. Reciprocally, the money relation also unveils the countertransference, in the service of whose understanding analysts must be willing to confront, internally and, when indicated, interpretively, both the discomforts and the pleasures of money's powerful place in psychoanalysis.

In a respectful view of psychoanalysis as seduction, Forrester (1990), another Lacanian literary critic, argues:

Psychoanalysis treats money as if it truly were the universal means of exchange, and patients do behave as if they could buy love. ... The analyst ... plays on the fact that patients do not know what they mean, nor do they know what money will buy. It is insofar as they do not know these things that seduction begins. And with seduction, the questioning of the contract and the calling into question of authority ... begins. ... The original seduction is thus that offered by the contract—namely that it is just a contract. ... Its means of accomplishment is the free speech whereby one of the parties will contract the disease of love that the other will cure by treating the proffered seductive words as if they were simply the universal means of exchange. (p. 47)

At the heart of psychoanalysis, this most private of encounters, lies society, just as at the heart of public life lies the alienation psychoanalysis tries to cure. Psychoanalysis is not revolution, and it doesn't make the contradiction between money and love go away. But for a brief, utopian moment, it permits transcendence. In the psychoanalytic contact, the contradiction between money and love, a relation between contraries that can be transformed, finds a temporary, reparative resolution in the paradox between love and hate, a relation between contraries that never changes. The possibility of transformation distinguishes contradiction from paradox: Contradiction bears resolution; paradox does not. Or, rather, as Ghent (1992) has recently said, the only resolution of paradox is paradox itself, here to inhabit, without rushing to relieve, the tension between love and hate, a tension that also preserves the memory of the contradiction between money and love it resolves.

The lesson of contradiction is perhaps easier to remember than that of paradox, which is, in turn, one of the easiest to forget. That money negates love, this we know preconsciously and needs, I think, only to be surfaced to stay in consciousness. But paradox is different; it is relearned each time it is lived. This is perhaps what Freud (1923) was trying to capture when he said that "love is with unexpected regularity accompanied by hate (ambivalence)" (p. 43). That love and hate go together, this is an analytic commonplace. But that, in the hot moment of loving or hating, we never remember that they do, this, perhaps, is wisdom.

REFERENCES

Abraham, K. (1953). Contributions to the theory of the anal character. In D. Bryan & A. Strachey (Trans.), *Selected papers of Karl Abraham, M.D.* (pp. 370–392). New York: Basic Books. (Original work published 1921)

Amar, A. (1976). A psychoanalytic study of money. In E. Borneman (Ed.) & M. Shaw (Trans.), *The psychoanalysis of money* (pp. 277–291). New York: Urizen Books. (Original work published 1956)

Aron, L. (1991). The patient's experience of the analyst's subjectivity. *Psychoanalytic Dialogues, 1*, 29–51.

Aron, L., & Hirsch, I. (1992). Money matters in psychoanalysis: A relational approach. In N. Skolnick & S. Warshaw (Eds.), *Relational perspectives in psychoanalysis* (pp. 239–256). Hillsdale, NJ: Analytic Press.

Bion, W. R. (1980). *Key to memoir of the future.* Perthshire, UK: Clunie Press.

Chodoff, P. (1986). The effect of third-party payment on the practice of psychotherapy. In D. W. Krueger (Ed.), *The last taboo* (pp. 111–120). New York: Brunner/Mazel.

Chodoff, P. (1991). Effects of the new economic climate on psychotherapeutic practice. In S. Klebanow & E. L. Lowenkopf (Eds.), *Money and mind* (pp. 253–264). New York: Plenum Press.

Money, love, and hate 125

Dimen, M. (1986). *Surviving sexual contradictions*. New York: Macmillan.
Dimen-Schein, M. (1977). *The anthropological imagination*. New York: McGraw-Hill.
Drellich, M. (1991). Money and countertransference. In S. Klebanow and E. L. Lowenkopf (Eds.), *Money and mind* (pp. 155–162). New York: Plenum Press.
Durkheim, E. (1938). *The rules of sociological method*. Glencoe, IL: Free Press.
Durkheim, E. (1951). *Suicide* (G. Simpson, Ed., J. A. Spaulding & G. Simpson, Trans.). New York: Free Press. (Original work published 1930)
Ehrenreich, B. (1989). *Fear of falling*. New York: Pantheon.
Ehrenreich, B., & Ehrenreich, J. (1979). The professional-managerial class. In P. Walker (Ed.), *Between labor and capital* (pp. 5–48). Boston: South End Press.
Eigen, M. (1986). *The psychotic core*. Northvale, NJ: Aronson.
Fenichel, O. (1954). The drive to amass wealth. In H. Fenichel & D. Rapaport (Eds.), *The collected papers of Otto Fenichel* (2nd ed., pp. 89–108). New York: Norton. (Original work published 1938)
Ferenczi, S. (1976). The ontogenesis of the interest in money. In E. Borneman (Ed.) & M. Shaw (Trans.), *The psychoanalysis of money* (pp. 81–90). New York: Urizen Books. (Original work published 1914)
Forrester, J. (1990). *The seductions of psychoanalysis*. Cambridge: Cambridge University Press.
Flax, J. (1990). *Thinking fragments*. Berkeley: University of California Press.
Freud, S. (1895). Psychotherapy of hysteria. In J. Strachey (Ed. & Trans.), *The standard edition of the complete psychological works of Sigmund Freud* (Vol. 2, pp. 253–305). London: Hogarth Press, 1955.
Freud, S. (1905). *Three essays on the theory of sexuality*. In J. Strachey (Ed. & Trans.), *The standard edition of the complete psychological works of Sigmund Freud* (Vol. 7, pp. 125–245). London: Hogarth Press, 1953.
Freud, S. (1908). Character and anal erotism. In J. Strachey (Ed. & Trans.), *The standard edition of the complete psychological works of Sigmund Freud* (Vol. 9, pp. 167–175). London: Hogarth Press, 1953.
Freud, S. (1913). On beginning the treatment. In J. Strachey (Ed. & Trans.), *The standard edition of the complete psychological works of Sigmund Freud* (Vol. 12, pp. 123–144). London: Hogarth Press, 1958.
Freud, S. (1918). *From the history of an infantile neurosis*. (Volume 17: 1–124). Hogarth Press, 1955.
Freud, S. (1923). The ego and the id. In J. Strachey (Ed. & Trans.), *The standard edition of the complete psychological works of Sigmund Freud* (Vol. 19, pp. 3–68). London: Hogarth Press, 1961.
Fromm, E. (1966). *Marx's concept of man*. New York: Ungar.
Gallop, J. (1982). *The daughter's seduction*. Ithaca, NY: Cornell University Press.
Gay, P. (1988). *Freud*. New York: Norton.
Ghent, E. (1989). Credo: The dialectics of one-person and two-person psychologies. *Contemporary Psychoanalysis, 25*, 200–237.
Ghent, E. (1992). Paradox and process. *Psychoanalytic Dialogues, 2*, 135–159.
Greenberg, J. (1986). Theoretical models and the analyst's neutrality. *Contemporary Psychoanalysis, 22*, 87–106.

Guntrip, H. (1969). *Schizoid phenomena, object-relations and the self*. New York: International Universities Press.

Gutheil, T. A. (1986). Fees in beginning private practice. In D. W. Krueger (Ed.), *The last taboo* (pp. 175–188). New York: Brunner/Mazel.

Havens, L. (1989). *A safe place*. Cambridge, MA: Harvard University Press.

Herron, W. G., & Welt, S. R. (1992). *Money matters*. New York: Guilford Press.

Horner, A. J. (1991). Money issues and analytic neutrality. In S. Klebanow & E. L. Lowenkopf (Eds.), *Money and mind* (pp. 175–182). New York: Plenum Press.

Jacobs, D. H. (1986). On negotiating fees with psychotherapy and psychoanalytic patients. In D. W. Krueger (Ed.), *The last taboo* (pp. 121–131). New York: Brunner/Mazel.

Jacoby, R. (1983). *The repression of psychoanalysis*. Chicago: University of Chicago Press.

Jones, E. (1918). Anal-erotic character traits. In *Collected papers* (pp. 438–451). Boston: Beacon Press.

Khan, M. M. R. (1974a). On Freud's provision of the therapeutic frame. In *The privacy of the self* (pp. 129–135). New York: International Universities Press. (Original work published 1972)

Khan, M. M. R. (1974b). Montaigne, Rousseau and Freud. In *The privacy of the self* (pp. 99–111). New York: International Universities Press. (Original work published 1970)

Khan, M. M. R. (1979). *Alienation in perversions*. New York: International Universities Press.

Klebanow, S., & Lowenkopf, E. L. (Eds.). (1991). *Money and mind*. New York: Plenum Press.

Klein, M., & Riviere, J. (1964). *Love, hate and reparation*. New York: Norton.

Krueger, D. W. (1986). Money, success and success phobia. In D. W. Krueger (Ed.), *The last taboo* (pp. 3–16). New York: Brunner/Mazel.

Langs, R. (1973). *The technique of psychoanalytic psychotherapy*. Northvale, NJ: Aronson.

LeClair, E. E., Jr., & Schneider, H. K. (1968). Some further theoretical issues. In E. E. LeClair, Jr. & H. K. Schneider (Eds.), *Economic anthropology* (pp. 453–474). New York: Holt, Rinehart & Winston.

Liss-Levenson, N. (1990). Money matters and the woman analyst: In a different voice. *Psychoanalytic Psychology*, 7(Suppl.), 119–130.

Malinowski, B. (1961). *Argonauts of the Western Pacific*. New York: Dutton. (Original work published 1922)

Marx, K. (1964). *The economic and philosophical manuscripts of 1844* (D. Struik, Ed. & M. Milligan, Trans.). New York: International Publishers.

Masson, J. (Ed.) (1985). *The complete letters of Sigmund Freud to Wilhelm Fliess 1887–1904*, ed. and trans. J. M. Masson. Cambridge, MA: Harvard University Press.

Mészáros, J. (1975). *Marx's theory of alienation* (4th ed.). London: Merlin Press.

Milner, M. (1957). *On not being able to paint*. New York: International Universities Press.

Newman, K. S. (1988). *Falling from grace*. New York: Free Press.

Ollman, B. (1976). *Alienation* (2nd ed.). New York: Cambridge University Press.

Rapp, R. (1978). Family and class in contemporary America: Notes toward an understanding of ideology. *Science and Society, 42*, 278–300.

Rendon, M. (1991). Money and the left in psychoanalysis. In S. Klebanow & E. L. Lowenkopf (Eds.), *Money and mind* (pp. 135–148). New York: Plenum Press.

Searles, H. (1965). *Collected papers on schizophrenia and related subjects.* New York: International Universities Press.

Sennett, R., & Cobb, J. (1972). *The hidden injuries of class.* New York: Vintage.

Shainess, N. (1991). Countertransference problems with money. In S. Klebanow & E. L. Lowenkopf (Eds.), *Money and mind* (pp. 163–175). New York: Plenum Press.

Struik, D. J. (1964). Introduction. In D. J. Struik (Ed.), *The economic and philosophical manuscripts of 1844: Karl Marx* (pp. 9–56). New York: International Publishers.

Tulipan, A. B. (1986). Fee policy as an extension of the therapist's style and orientation. In D. W. Kreuger (Ed.), *The last taboo* (pp. 79–87). New York: Brunner/Mazel.

Warner, S. L. (1991). Sigmund Freud and money, In S. Klebanow & E. L. Lowenkopf (Eds.), *Money and mind* (pp. 121–134). New York: Plenum Press.

Whitson, G. (n.d.). Money matters in psychoanalysis: The analyst's coparticipation in the matter of money. Unpublished manuscript.

Winnicott, D. W. (1975). Hate in the countertransference. In *Through paediatrics to psychoanalysis* (pp. 194–203). New York: Basic Books. (Original work published 1947)

Zaphiropoulos, M. L. (1991). Fee and empathy: Logic and logistics in psychoanalysis. In S. Klebanow & E. L. Lowenkopf (Eds.), *Money and mind* (pp. 235–244). New York: Plenum Press.

Chapter 10

Working with children, adolescents, and young adults

The meaning of money in the therapeutic situation

Pamela Meersand

Over the last 2 years, widespread financial anxiety has led many parents toward increased interest in their children's emerging ideas and habits around money. In my practice as a child and adolescent psychologist and psychoanalyst, I have encountered numerous situations wherein families have been forced to adjust living and educational circumstances, cope with the return of previously autonomous young adult children to financial dependency, and make changes in the fees and frequency of a child's therapy. Often, parents are reluctant to discuss such issues with children: They express uncertainty about their youngster's ability to grasp financial exigencies and worry about burdening children with adult concerns.

This chapter discusses how children think and feel about money by examining the development of monetary concepts and the meaning of money in the therapeutic situation. Shifts in children's mental capacities and perceptions, the role of parents in child treatment, and the feelings evoked in the clinician are discussed as they influence the overt behaviors and more hidden fantasies that surround money. Particular emphasis is placed on psychoanalytic views of child treatment and development and on the involvement of money in children's conflicts and fantasies.

Between the early preschool years and young adulthood, thoughts and feelings about money undergo substantial modification. Increasing intellectual and social capacities, developmental trends, and parental attitudes are major influences on the meaning that children attach to money and financial interactions. Throughout the course of development, periods of mental transformation give rise to new ways of thinking, relating, and fantasizing; within psychoanalytic theory, such shifts are linked to the Oedipal (preschool), latency (elementary school), adolescent, and young adulthood stages of growth. During these maturational phases, each of which involves a set of emerging abilities and developmental challenges, the child's sense of self and experience of the outside world—including the therapeutic situation—are reorganized.

In treatment, a child's inner life is likely to be revealed through play and action; unlike the primarily verbal nature of adult therapeutic interactions, these are the dominant modes of communication. When the patient is a preschool or young school-aged child, psychoanalysts and other dynamically oriented clinicians conduct their work largely within the context of the child's creative play, building on the child's narratives and characters to elaborate themes and internal conflicts. A 4-year-old's pretend game of "store" or an 8-year-old's handling of "Monopoly money" can provide a window into the youngster's emerging conception of finance and its role in adult relationships. Adolescents, under novel pressure from sexual feelings and social expectations, often reveal their fears and fantasies via impulsive or defiant action, rather than in quiet discussion with their therapist: Attitudes toward money and reactions to the parent-clinician money arrangements are likely to be demonstrated through behavior.

In contrast to adults, children in therapy have little decision-making power and often no direct involvement in the handling of fees. Bills and payments are exchanged between clinician and parents, and children are often not privy to the specifics of these transactions. The common exceptions are older adolescents and young adults, who may initiate their own treatments and assume partial financial responsibility and whose parents tend to have far less contact with the therapist.

Nonetheless, even very young children begin to demonstrate some awareness that their parents pay for treatment and attach meaning and fantasy to these arrangements. Oedipal-aged youngsters are avidly curious about the private matters of the adult world and are prone to feeling excluded and diminished by affairs beyond their understanding. During the latency period of development, children possess a clearer grasp of the specific value of money and the rules governing its use; they are keenly aware of the power of money for acquiring prized material possessions and may protest the expenditure of family resources on therapy. In adolescence, the knowledge that parents pay for sessions can be swept into conflict and struggles for autonomy: The teenager's casual or openly defiant attitude toward attendance can reflect efforts to separate from adults and fears of being controlled. For the young adult who cannot yet manage to pay for his or her own therapy, the need for parents' continued financial involvement may evoke feelings of guilt and inadequacy.

The child therapist's reliance on parental support and involvement further complicates the role of money in the treatment situation. Parents' intense feelings about their child and that child's problems and reactions to their youngster's private, exclusive therapy relationship may be expressed via the handling of treatment fees. Late payments, inadequate notice of upcoming family holidays, or protests over having to pay for a teenager's missed sessions can all reflect unresolved feelings about the child and the child's therapist. At times, such sentiments are communicated from parent to youngster, either directly or more subtly; these may elicit guilty and anxious reactions in the child, who worries about the financial burden of therapy. When parents are divorced, multiple fears and resentments can find expression in their handling of shared financial responsibility for the child's treatment.

For the child clinician, the relative helplessness and dependency of young patients can make it challenging to devise and maintain consistent treatment parameters, including financial arrangements. A sense of protectiveness toward the child, a feeling of responsibility for the developing personality, pressure from the parents, and special conditions (e.g., the child with special needs or the at-risk adolescent) can evoke the therapist's own guilt, fears, and discomfort with fees.

CHILD DEVELOPMENT AND PERCEPTIONS OF MONEY IN THE TREATMENT SITUATION

Throughout the course of development, the child's acquisition of new mental capacities and structures transforms his or her experience of events and relationships. Psychoanalytic views of childhood and adolescence place these psychic shifts and reorganizations at the center of the child clinician's conceptualizing and interpretive work; age-typical intellectual, communicative, and relational abilities are always kept in mind, along with the particular pressures and vulnerabilities that characterize each psychosexual stage of development (Abrams, 2003; Abrams, Neubauer, & Solnit, 1998; Gilmore, 2002). Within the psychoanalytic literature, there is little work that focuses specifically on the child's changing perception of money in the treatment situation. However, a rich collection of child case studies offers numerous examples of children's feelings and fantasies about money, particularly as these relate to their understanding of the clinician's fee. A select few of these are briefly described (e.g., A. Freud's vignettes as recorded by Abend, 1987; Fraiberg, 1955, 1966; Karush, 1998; Richards, 1998; Sandler, Kennedy, & Tyson, 1980), along with some examples from my own work.

Within the neighboring disciplines of developmental and social psychology, empirical research in children's money concepts has revealed the impact of multiple factors: Unfolding cognitive capacities, emerging social understanding, and parental practices have all been found to influence beliefs and attitudes (Berti & Bombi, 1981; Thompson & Siegler, 2000). Often, such studies employ a Piagetian model of intellectual development, wherein the growing child acquires increasingly complex and organized mental structures; each period of development is characterized by particular modes of thinking and social understanding, which shift as maturation proceeds (Piaget, 1926, 1951). Such a framework is consistent with psychoanalytic notions of evolving mental capacities. When considered together, these developmental theories provide a rich, integrated view of the child's changing thoughts, feelings, and fantasies about money in the therapeutic situation.

The oedipal years: Ages 3 to 5

Preschool children possess a rudimentary grasp of money and its functions. As Piaget's extensive body of work revealed, the young child's intellectual style is impressionistic and intuitive rather than logical. The distinction between imagined and reality-based events is not consistently grasped (Fonagy, 1995; Mayes & Cohen, 1992), leading many authors to employ the term *magical* in their description of the Oedipal child's thinking.

The beginnings of numerical and measurement concepts, however, are demonstrable: Preschoolers can recognize size and shape, distinguish big from little, and count a small set of objects. Three- and 4-year-old children are aware that money may be exchanged for goods, although they fail to grasp the reciprocal nature of monetary exchanges; in other words, they tend to see buying and selling as separate rather than related activities (Thompson & Siegler, 2000). The precise value of money is not yet understood, and children tend to assume that any coin may be used to purchase any item (Berti & Bombi, 1981). Nonetheless, some studies revealed that even preschoolers make certain judgments about money; for example, they may manifest a dismissive attitude toward pennies, referring to them as "junk" (Brenner, 1998). Even within the empirical literature, in which the major focus of interest is the child's acquisition of specific and measurable skills, money is viewed as a subject that begins to accrue meaning and emotional significance early in life.

Young children's social understanding is very limited, making it hard for them to consider the motivations and intentions involved in money transactions. They do not yet fully grasp that behavior is driven by inner thoughts and feelings; moreover, they struggle to understand that other people's needs and desires may differ substantially from their own (Fonagy, 1995; Mayes & Cohen, 1992). Despite this, research has demonstrated that preschool children begin to make links between familiar conditions and the demand for a particular service, such as hot weather and the increased level of activity at a lemonade stand (Siegler & Thompson, 1998).

Psychoanalytic views of the Oedipal child add further dimension to empirical studies by elaborating the child's fantasy life and identifying age-typical conflicts and vulnerabilities. During the Oedipal phase, children display avid curiosity about all aspects of the private adult world, with particular interest in the mysteries of sexuality and reproduction. Dominant themes include painful feelings of exclusion from adult activities and intense desire for the special belongings and accoutrements that are perceived as defining the adult experience. The possession of money, and the mystifying arrangements that surround it, are viewed as part of the exciting grown-up world in which the preschool child longs to participate.

Language and pretend play abilities are well developed by the age of 3 or 4, and such feelings and fantasies are expressed openly to interested adults (Cohen, Marans, Dahl, Marans, & Lewis, 1987).

In analytically oriented therapies, the clinician and young child play together, making meaning from the narratives and characters that the child creates. Psychoanalysts view pretend play as a natural, growth-promoting developmental capacity that offers a unique view into the child's inner world, promotes identifications with important adults, and provides a sense of mastery and agency during a time when children often feel small and powerless (Birch, 1997; Gilmore, 2005; Solnit, 1987). The following clinical example, taken from my treatment of a 4-year-old girl, illustrates the meaning that an Oedipal child attached to money, despite her limited cognitive understanding; for this child, money acquired great value by virtue of its association with her mother:

Rachel arrived to our session proudly wearing her mother's beaded necklace and clutching a toy pocketbook, which she excitedly opened to reveal prized possessions (her older sister's nonfunctioning cell phone, three tiny toy bears, and some money, which she eagerly and accurately described as "real"). She immediately announced that she wanted to play "pretend store," and that she would be the mother shopping for her children, and I would be the shopkeeper. "The store owner doesn't need a lot of money," she declared, handing me three wrinkled dollar bills and a number of dull-looking coins. "I get the shiny ones because I'm the Mommy. The dollars aren't nice." In my role as store owner, I wished aloud that I could have some shiny pennies for my cash register. She retorted that, "Only the Mommies get the fancy things," and then enthusiastically told me about a "castle ball" that her mother and father had attended the previous night (in reality, a yearly dinner at her father's firm); she described her mother's "shiny" jewelry in detail.

Latency: The school-aged child

As children begin the grade-school years, their increasing capacity for logical thinking, improved self-regulation, appreciation for social rules, and growing interest in the wider world contributes to greater autonomy and vastly enhanced availability for learning (Piaget, 1951; Shapiro, 1976). Psychoanalytic views of latency suggest a period of relative calm and cooperation during which the former preschooler's passionate curiosity about parental sexuality is relatively softened, and the world of fantasy and imagination yields gradually to reality and instruction-bound games. The latency child is deeply interested in fairness and rules and has expanded his or her relational investments into the world of school and friendship (Becker, 1974; Mahon, 1991).

By 7 or 8 years of age, children begin to acquire increasingly differentiated and precise knowledge of money concepts. Basic money facts are internalized: Children reliably identify different coins and have mastered their monetary value. These skills can be demonstrated by their handling of simple word problems (e.g., calculating the amount of change to be received when a purchase is made). Latency-aged children understand that there are rules that govern money exchanges, and they comprehend the reciprocal relationship between buying and selling (Berti & Bombi, 1981; Brenner, 1998; Piaget, 1951; Thompson & Siegler, 2000).

This developmental period is characterized by a greatly enhanced capacity for grasping the thoughts and feelings of other people, allowing the school-aged child to empathize with multiple viewpoints (Fonagy, 1995; Mayes & Cohen, 1992). The notion that the therapist performs a service and in turn is paid by the parents, the idea that consistent financial arrangements are relied on by all parties, and the realization that the therapist desires and needs to receive money are all increasingly understood. One 9-year-old girl in psychoanalysis, angry at her loss of autonomy and freedom during afterschool hours, revealed her ambivalent feelings by threatening me that she would "tell my parents not to pay you"; she then folded her arms and glared heatedly at me, waiting for my response. Some days later, she apologized and confessed that she had worried excessively about the effect of her remarks; specific concerns included that I would tell her parents of her rudeness, and that I would refuse to continue her therapy. Karush (1998) described similarly guilty and conflictual feelings in a latency child, revealed by his "forgetting" to pay her back after borrowing a very small amount of money to purchase a gift for a sibling.

The latency child's increasing knowledge about money, in combination with a growing interest in peers and an age-appropriate love of collecting, contributes to keen awareness of what others possess and to a growing sense of the power of money and the potential desirability of purchased goods. Newly acquired planning and organizing skills allow the school-aged child to devise steps for acquiring coveted belongings. In contrast to the Oedipal child, who is content with pretend play, the latency child's desire is for real possessions.

Such tendencies lead the school-aged child toward greater awareness of specific costs and family resources, which may cause negative feelings about the money spent on therapy. Anna Freud (as quoted in Sandler et al., 1980) suggested that these reactions are common: "If children learn about the money paid for treatment, they always feel that this is a terrific waste, and they do so whether their feelings toward the analyst and analysis are positive or negative" (p. 10). She described the disgruntled response of a boy, with a good treatment alliance, on learning her fee: He calculated aloud how many train tracks he might purchase with an equivalent sum of money. Fraiberg (1955) recounted a similar case, wherein an 11-year-old girl's mother disclosed the fee paid for her treatment; the child complained bitterly to Fraiberg about how much money her parents were wasting. However, latency children may also be vulnerable to other, deeper worries about the therapist's need for payment; Fraiberg (1966) described one girl who articulated a fantasy of the analyst as a blackmailer, who will refuse to continue her treatment unless the family provides more and more money.

Teenagers and young adults: From the onset of puberty to financial and personal autonomy

In the psychoanalytic view of adolescence, major developmental tasks involve the loosening of ties with the parents, the establishment of a separate personal identity, and the integration of new, sexual feelings and fantasies; action-oriented behavior, rebellious attitudes toward adults, and increased peer affiliations may serve to strengthen a sense of autonomy and protect against fears of passivity and infantilization (Blos, 1967; Chused, 1990; Shapiro, 2008). The well-known adolescent tendency toward impulsive and risk-taking behavior can evoke strong feelings in the therapist, creating unique challenges in the treatment of this age group.

The intellectual development of adolescents involves a vastly enhanced capacity for abstract and flexible thinking; they can approach complex problems with efficiency, generate and keep track of myriad possibilities, and contemplate hypothetical situations (Piaget & Inhelder, 1958). Complicated, theoretical economic concepts, such as profit, trade, and banking, can be understood (Thompson & Siegler, 2000). Moreover, the adolescent is both emotionally and intellectually engaged by ideas and can integrate complex money and social notions, such as poverty and inequality.

Becky, a 15-year-old girl whose initial depression had improved significantly during the course of our treatment, began to describe intense feelings of guilt that accompanied the realization that her best friend, who was enduring a painful breakup, did not possess adequate family resources for private therapy; this led to frequent heart-felt remonstrance about injustice and the need for social action. The following treatment scenario illustrates multiple adolescent trends, including the following: Becky's heightened awareness of the financial arrangements between her parents and me, an emerging social conscience, her keen understanding of the thoughts and feelings of diverse individuals, and rebellious inclinations toward adults.

When I went to the waiting room to meet her, Becky was seated next to another girl; they were leaning toward each other, engrossed in heated and intimate discussion. Becky looked at her meaningfully as she rose and followed me into the office; as soon as the door was closed, she began cajoling me to "give this session to my friend while I wait outside"; the story of the other girl's breakup with her boyfriend, need for support, and limited financial resources was described with feeling. She revealed that they had hatched a plan, earlier that day, wherein Becky would "donate" her session so that the friend could "at least have a decent conversation with an adult who isn't crazy." I acknowledged Becky's sincere desire to ease the friend's suffering and commented on the generous feelings that would impel her to give up something she herself was finding helpful. The discussion continued, as she assured me that it would be just this once, and that she herself was doing well. Attempting to be tactful, I nonetheless pointed out that her parents would, in effect, also be involved in providing this session for her friend. "I thought of all that," she quickly responded. "This is all confidential, so they'd never know they were paying for her." After a moment of silence, she asked, somewhat playfully, "Am I putting you in an awkward situation?"

Unlike a younger child, Becky was well able to maintain multiple perspectives and motivations in mind: She knew that I would maintain her confidentiality and understood that she was involving me in a form of financial deception, at her parents' expense. The entire situation was clearly titillating to her and her friend, who had been eagerly planning their joint appearance at Becky's session all day and had discussed in detail the arguments they could marshal to convince me. At the same time, the friend's distress and Becky's compassion, along with her sense of guilt about her own financial resources, were very genuine. In her efforts to prevail, she recruited her considerable verbal and abstract abilities and asserted that the "higher principle" was meeting the needs of her friend, whereas the issue of who paid for what was relatively unimportant. Indeed, she elicited in me a sense of discomfort over my failure to spontaneously embrace the girls' plan; I felt rigid and insufficiently idealistic. Nonetheless, I was not willing to see an unfamiliar child without her parents' knowledge, and I did not wish to ignore the complex, and partially aggressive, feelings that motivated Becky's behavior. I agreed to a compromise, and the friend joined us for a part of the session.

Adolescents are well aware that possession of money conveys power and independence to the owner, and that it may be used to promote popularity within the peer group. Often, they are highly motivated to earn their own money and to have decision-making power over how it is spent. Their grasp of the financial arrangements in therapy makes this a topic that is easily swept into ongoing conflicts with adults and struggles for self-sufficiency. Action is a typical and powerful vehicle for adolescent communication: Missing sessions or arriving late are effective methods for expressing defiance and demonstrating contempt for adult rules and concerns. A 13-year-old boy, whose parents had recently agreed that he could walk himself to therapy, had skipped one session to socialize with friends; although he knew that I would not relate this single episode to his parents, he elected to tell them, casually adding the inflammatory "information" that he and I had decided he could miss as many sessions as he wanted since they had to pay in any event.

Older teens and young adults are often still financially dependent on their families; in the past 2 years, as economic opportunities have declined, the need for children in their 20s to remain at or return to their parents' home has become increasingly common. However, therapists who work with these age groups often have little contact with parents and may elect to have none at all, even when they are fully responsible for the treatment fee. Relying on the young adult to arrange the financial aspects of therapy and to convey the information to parents can be burdensome for the patient and may create misunderstanding and confusion for all involved (Abend, 1987; Escoll, 1987).

Research on the attitudes of college undergraduates suggests that they are susceptible to parental feelings and anxieties about money (Lim & Sng, 2006). However, older adolescents and young adults may feel guilty and ashamed about their family's continued financial contribution to their treatment even when there are sufficient resources and the parents willingly support the therapy. Halpert (1972) described an obsessional 21-year-old girl who worried intensely about the financial pressure that she perceived that therapy placed on her parents; she described the sense that her monetary needs had drained the strength from her father and caused him to fall ill. A young adult patient of mine, who worked long hours and earned a very modest income as she trained in her field, insisted on splitting the fee for analysis with her aging, financially comfortable parents; nonetheless, she fretted continuously about keeping them from their retirement and "running through their savings."

In addition to guilt and worry, young adult patients may have other, complex reactions to their parents' financial involvement in treatment. Richards (1998) described a 23-year-old woman whose complaints about the fee and professed concern about the financial strain on her parents served to mask her own frustration and anger that she could not yet pay for herself. Other young patients may resist the transition to adulthood and seek to perpetuate a childhood situation by refusing to assume financial responsibility of any kind. One 24-year-old man, who was unemployed and whose parents paid for treatment, protested my practice of giving him the monthly bill. On one occasion, he described that he "exploded at my parents" when they asked him to bring me a check, observing that "money makes me nervous. I'd rather not know the specifics. I don't like to look at the bills, or think about the cost. It's my parents' problem, not mine."

WORKING WITH CHILDREN AND THEIR PARENTS

Parental support is an essential component of child psychotherapy. Clinicians grapple with the tension between their young patients' need for confidentiality and autonomy and the pivotal role that parents play in providing needed developmental information, facilitating the treatment process, and creating a growth-promoting environment at home. In the past, psychoana-lytic practitioners tended to limit parent contacts once treatment was under way; parents were seen primarily to establish therapy, make the necessary arrangements, and ensure a positive alliance. More recently, thinking about parent work has expanded, in recognition of the critical role the child's major attachment figures play in ongoing development (Novick & Novick, 2008; Yanof, 2006).

Even when parents are rarely seen, however, their handling of financial arrangements can reflect powerful feelings about the child, a sense of exclu-sion from the special treatment relationship, and resistance to the therapy (Hoffman, 1993; Sandler et al., 1980). In situations of divorce, unresolved feelings about the former spouse, and resentments about a changed relation-ship with the child, may also be expressed through money; the therapist's efforts to have contact with and elicit support from both parents cannot always prevent the emergence of negative reactions.

For example, one divorced mother informed her impulsive 11-year-old daughter that her father would not pay for summer camp because he believed that her ongoing treatment with me was too expensive. Not sur-prisingly, parental hostilities escalated following the girl's immediate, con-frontational phone call to her father. Although he had previously supported the treatment and we had frequent contact, the father's anger soon extended to me; his fears of losing a formerly close relationship with his child, sense of having been manipulated by the mother, and overall feelings of pow-erlessness all contributed to his refusal to continue sharing the costs of therapy. Although I had been working with the girl for over a year, and he had previously supported the treatment, he could not overcome the notion that I "sided" with his ex-wife. The child's treatment was soon abruptly terminated, as he withdrew not only his financial support but also his con-sent for her to be in any form of therapy.

During tumultuous times of development, an alliance with the parents is crucial; clear understanding about payment arrangements—including, for example, the therapist's particular policies around challenging situations, such as an adolescent's missed sessions—is essential to establish before treatment gets under way. However, the child's provocative behavior, or the parents' unrealistic expectations for quick relief, can erode previously positive feelings and threaten the verbal contract. Meeting with the parents may help reestablish their trust and patience but can undermine the older child's sense of privacy.

THE CHILD CLINICIAN AND MATTERS OF MONEY

Treating children arouses unique feelings in the therapist that may influ-ence the therapist's attitudes and behaviors toward money, making it hard to balance personal needs with those perceived in the child. When working with very young children, strongly protective reactions can be evoked by their real and imagined helplessness and vulnerability; the adolescent's impulsive, risk-taking behaviors may elicit intense anxiety in the clinician (Chused, 1988, 1990). Moreover, the psychoanalytic literature espouses a tradition emphasizing the special requirements of children and the responsibility to treat them; there are specific references to sacrificing fees when necessary, particularly in high-risk situations, such as adolescent suicidality (Sandler et al., 1980; Eissler, 1974).

Hoffman (1993) observed that the child therapist must grapple with various dilemmas, such as when a parent with resources nonetheless insists on a low fee, and make decisions based on personal needs and tolerance. However, an acute awareness of the child's ongoing development, and of the particular vulnerabilities and opportunities that accompany developmental shifts, can complicate the therapist's behavior around money matters and make it hard to establish consistent financial practices.

A recent example involved a young adult, who had been in twice-per-week treatment with me since midadolescence and whose age-appropriate desire for self-sufficiency had slowly emerged; a very difficult relationship with her parents was further complicated by their continuing involvement in paying for her therapy. She worked full time and went to school at night, supporting herself on a very modest income; it was clear that, on her own, she could only manage a minimal fee. Our long-standing relationship, her growing desire for independence, and my knowledge of the conflictual parent-daughter ties were major factors in my willingness to renegotiate our fee, so that she could fund treatment on her own. Her willingness to discuss these various perspectives, and her empathy for multiple points of view—including her parents' intense wish to maintain control over her—facilitated the process of changing the fee arrangements. While complex considerations enter into any financial accommodations that clinicians make with older adult patients, this young woman's developmental needs had special significance to me and ultimately outweighed my reluctance to accept much-reduced payments.

* * * * *

In the current climate of economic anxiety, many parents have shown increasing interest in their children's relationship with money. However, open discussion of this topic at home often causes adults significant discomfort; they hesitate to transmit their own worries and fears and feel uncertain about their children's level of understanding.

This chapter has explored children's and adults' thoughts, feelings, and fantasies about money by reviewing developmental research and examining perceptions of the financial arrangements in child therapy. Beginning in the preschool years, emotional significance is attached to money, but its real value is poorly understood. School-aged children acquire increasingly accurate and sophisticated notions about both monetary and social concepts; they appreciate notions of fairness, comprehend simple transactions, and can plan ahead and save for future purchases. Adolescents empathize with the needs and perspectives of multiple individuals and envision larger and more abstract societal and economic issues: They are engaged by such notions as generosity and social justice. Young adults are often highly motivated to assume financial responsibility for themselves and are aware of their parents' economic pressures and concerns; their self-esteem may suffer when they are forced to remain dependent on family resources.

Finally, parents themselves attach emotional meaning to money and may use or withhold financial resources as a way to express feelings about their children. A basic developmental framework, as well as a sense of their own vulnerabilities, can help parents initiate discussion about money, set realistic expectations for young children's attitudes and behavior, and ultimately encourage the older child's development of enduring principles and values.

REFERENCES

Abend, S. (1987). Evaluating young adults for psychoanalysis. *Psychoanalytic Inquiry*, 7, 31–38.

Abrams, S. (2003). Looking forwards and backwards. *Psychoanalytic Study of the Child*, 58, 172–186.

Abrams, S., Neubauer, P. B., & Solnit, A. J. (1998). Coordinating the developmental and psychoanalytic processes: Three case reports. *Psychoanalytic Study of the Child*, 54, 87–90.

Becker, T. (1974). On latency. *Psychoanalytic Study of the Child*, 29, 3–11.

Berti, A. E., & Bombi, A. S. (1981). The development of the concept of money and its value: A longitudinal study. *Child Development*, 52, 1179–1182.

Birch, M. (1997). In the land of counterpane: Travels in the realm of play. *Psychoanalytic Study of the Child*, 52, 57–75.

Blos, P. (1967). The second individuation process in adolescence. *Psychoanalytic Study of the Child*, 22, 162–186.

Brenner, M. (1998). Meaning and money. *Educational Studies in Mathematics*, 36, 123–155.

Chused, J. F. (1988). The transference neurosis in child analysis. *Psychoanalytic Study of the Child*, 43, 51–81.

Chused, J. F. (1990). Neutrality in the analysis of action-prone adolescents. *Journal of the American Psychoanalytic Association*, 38, 679–704.

Cohen, D. J., Marans, S., Dahl, K., Marans, W., & Lewis, M. (1987). Analytic discussions with oedipal children. *Psychoanalytic Study of the Child*, 42, 59–83.

Eissler, K. R. (1974). On some theoretical and technical problems regarding the payment of fee for psychoanalytic treatment. *International Review of Psychoanalysis*, 1, 73–101.

Escoll, P. J. (1987). Psychoanalysis of young adults: An overview. *Psychoanalytic Inquiry*, 7, 5–30.

Fonagy, P. (1995). Playing with reality: The development of psychic reality and its malfunction in borderline personalities. *International Journal of Psychoanalysis*, 79, 39–44.

Fraiberg, S. (1955). Some considerations in the introduction to therapy in puberty. *Psychoanalytic Study of the Child*, 10, 264–268.

Fraiberg, S. (1966). Further considerations on the role of transference in latency. *Psychoanalytic Study of the Child*, 21, 213–236.

Gilmore, K. (2002). Diagnosis, dynamics and development: Considerations in the psychoanalytic assessment of children with AD/HD. *Psychoanalytic Inquiry*, 22, 372–390.

Gilmore, K. (2005). Play in the psychoanalytic setting: Ego capacity, ego state and vehicle for intersubjective exchange. *Psychoanalytic Study of the Child*, 60, 213–238.

Halpert, E. (1972). The effect of insurance on psychoanalytic treatment. *Journal of the American Psychoanalytic Association*, 20, 122–133.

Hoffman, L. (1993). Discussion of Dr. Padouva's case. *Journal of Clinical Psychoanalysis*, 2, 110–113.

Karush, R. (1998). The use of dream analysis in the treatment of a 9-year-old obsessional. *Psychoanalytic Study of the Child*, 53, 199–211.

Lim, V. K. G., & Sng, Q. S. (2006). Does parental job insecurity matter? Money anxieties, money motives and work motivation. *Journal of Applied Psychology*, 9, 1078–1087.

Mahon, E. J. (1991). The "dissolution" of the Oedipus complex: A neglected cognitive factor. *Psychoanalytic Quarterly*, 60, 628–634.

Mayes, L. M., & Cohen, D. J. (1992). The development of a capacity for imagination in early childhood. *Psychoanalytic Study of the Child*, 47, 23–47.

Novick, J., & Novick, K. K. (2008). Expanding the domain: Privacy, secrecy and confidentiality. *Annual of Psychoanalysis*, 36, 145–160.

Piaget, J. (1926). *The language and thought of the child*. London: Routledge & Kegan Paul.

Piaget, J. (1951). *Play, dreams and imitation in childhood*. New York: Norton.

Piaget, J., & Inhelder, B. (1958). *The growth of logical thinking from childhood to adolescence*. New York: Basic Books.

Richards, A. K. (1998). A terrible joke: Humor in the analysis of a young woman. *Journal of Clinical Psychoanalysis*, 7, 95–113.

Sandler, J., Kennedy, H., & Tyson, R. L. (1980). *The technique of child psychoanalysis: Discussions with Anna Freud*. Cambridge, MA: Harvard University Press.

Shapiro, T. (1976). Latency revisited: The age of 7 plus or minus 1. *Psychoanalytic Study of the Child*, 31, 79–105.

Shapiro, T. (2008). Masturbation, sexuality and adaptation: Normalization in adolescence. *Journal of the American Psychoanalytic Association*, 56, 123–146.

Siegler, R. S., & Thompson, D. R. (1998). "Hey, would you like a nice cold cup of lemonade on this hot dry day?": Children's understanding of economic causation. *Developmental Psychology, 34*, 146–160.

Silverstein, S. (1974). Smart. In *Where the sidewalk ends* (p. 35). New York: Harper & Row.

Solnit, A. (1987). A psychoanalytic view of play. *Psychoanalytic Study of the Child, 42*, 205–219.

Thompson, D. R., & Siegler, R. S. (2000). Buy low, sell high: The development of an informal theory of economics. *Child Development, 71*, 660–677.

Yanof, J. A. (2006). Discussion of Anna. *Psychoanalytic Study of the Child, 61*, 139–144.

Chapter 11

Show me the money

(The "problem" of) the therapist's desire, subjectivity, and relationship to the fee*

Kachina Myers

How did money get left behind on the relational journey from attachment to intersubjectivity (Mitchell, 2000)? While psychoanalysis has taken an undisputedly relational turn, the analyst's subjectivity regarding the money paid him or her remains surprisingly unexamined and undisclosed in the literature. As the analyst's subjectivity gains respectability overall, the analyst's desire for money remains dirty, debased, and disreputable.

In the treatment room, the fee both symbolizes and communicates the analyst's desire, and any struggle over or exploration of money by patient and analyst provides an extraordinarily rich opportunity for competing subjectivities to unfold. Standing in the way of this vital process, however, are analysts' counterresistances. Freud (1913) famously urged analysts to "treat ... money matters with the same matter-of-course frankness [as] ... things relating to sexual life" (p. 131), which suggests that discussing money has been a challenge in our profession from the beginning. I have found that we analysts still resist talking with patients about money—especially our desire for their money.

Pasternack and Treiger (1976) were able to increase the total income of a low-fee psychotherapy clinic 400% just by having therapists and supervisors focus their attention on fees for a period of time. Imagine increasing your income by 400%. Their findings make it seem simple—except, of course, for analysts' inhibitions around self-assertion and their patients' generally negative response to that assertion. Herein lies the dilemma of the analyst's desire: The fee is a real intrusion of the analyst's need into the therapeutic situation. Either the patient gets what she wants or the analyst

* With tremendous gratitude, I acknowledge Judith Kaufman and all the ambitious women in her study group, especially Toby Bloomfield and Patricia Tidwell; Ruth Stein, who gave encouragement all along the way, and Gladys Foxe, who did an extensive revision on an earlier version; Linda Robinson for support and more edits; Kristin Miscall Brown for suggesting a paper like this; Edmund Cyvas for the title; and most of all, my analyst, Wendy R. Walker, for helping me transform my own relationship to money. This chapter originally appeared in *Contemporary Psychoanalysis, 44*(1), 2008, pp. 118–140. Reprinted with permission.

prevails. I propose a possible resolution to this dilemma and describe how to move from an either/or problem to a both/and solution, using Jessica Benjamin's perspectives on intersubjectivity.

My interest is in addressing therapists' resistance to setting fees that are commensurate with their income needs and with their patients' ability to pay. While the literature* overwhelmingly supports the value for patients in paying what they can afford (a few say even to the point of some strain), it is my experience that analysts all too frequently are unable to ask for, or get, their desired fee, even from patients who can afford to pay it. Fear of losing patients, fear of patients' rage, anxiety about having more shame, guilt, and other apparently unbearable affects seem to prevent many analysts from getting their due. While the literature also focuses on the need for flexibility in fee setting, and supports the idea that there are cases where free treatment can be successful, and a work is still needed about analysts who are financially exploitative of their patients to be sure, these are not the problems I hope to address. The focus here is an examination of the way that analysts' inhibitions about ambition and self-concern block therapeutic growth opportunities and how the resolution of that block helps both parties.

After outlining the various conflicts with money and ambition that tend to be exaggerated for analysts in particular, I provide two clinical examples—one in which I avoid a fee conflict and another in which I embrace the conflict. I also address some of the issues that arise when patients refuse to pay. These patients create extraordinary challenges for therapists. I examine the way that focusing on the fee in treatment offers an opportunity for both patient and analyst to develop mutual recognition, a basis for real intimacy. Conversely, I assert that avoidance of the fee in treatment may really be an avoidance of growth for both analyst and patient because, as I suggest, the fee can be used to liberate and strengthen the therapeutic interaction.

For many practitioners, this issue has its roots in the very reason they became psychoanalysts. Many analysts got their start by being compulsive caretakers as children. A lot of us learned early that someone else's needs were "more important" than our own. According to Alice Miller (1983) narcissistic disturbances predominate in the families of psychoanalysts, and, analysts-in-the-making generally felt compelled to meet their parents' emotional needs, even when those needs overrode their own. Our validation as children came from being good at putting our own subjectivity to the side. Caring and sacrifice can seem synonymous when we come from

---

* See Allen (1971); Blanck and Blanck (1974); DiBella (1980); Dimen (1994); Eissler (1974); Fingert (1952); Freud (1913); Liss-Levinson (1990); Loewald (1960); Meyers (1976); Nash and Cavenar (1976); Pasternack and Treiger (1976); Reider (1986); Schonbar (1986); Whitson (n.d.).

families where others' needs could only be satisfied when we split off our own needs to meet theirs.

It may be a truism: Therapists have trouble with desiring. We are only supposed to give. By increasing the fee or asking for a high fee, we may be threatening our own fantasy of what connects our patients to us: that we give. We risk losing that "good" feeling of being the generous helper if we pursue our desire for money from them.

Ambition, on the other hand, is all about assertion of the self. Consequently there is an inherent conflict within the profession between the desire to help selflessly and the desire to succeed and earn money from what we do. In fact we hate to call our work a "business." When patients accuse us of running a business, many of us have been known to wince. But in fact we are running a business: This is how we support ourselves, so why shy away from that? Psychoanalysts are likely to have a strong identification with patients; to become analysts, we have to be patients first. This is not the case in other fields: Medical students are not required to undergo surgery to become surgeons, nor do law students have to withstand being sued. This intense identification with our patients can make it particularly difficult for us to assert our needs, especially when our needs conflict with theirs.

Another anxiety that singles therapists out from other professional groups is a sociological factor: Therapists are more likely than other professionals to surpass the income bracket and class position of their families of origin (Lasky, 1984). Anxiety about abandoning or being abandoned by one's family of origin makes success problematic. There can be a loss of identification and sense of connection with one's roots, not to mention guilt about leaving others behind.

Felix Lorenzo (2000) has spoken about this in relation to the conflict for professionals of Latin heritage. Sharing and communal connection, not individuation, are the core values of their ethnohistorical tradition. Elaine Pinderhughes (1982) has addressed this value conflict in African Americans who often struggle with how to join African values of "collectivity, sharing, affiliation, [and] obedience to authority" with Western values of "individualism, independence [and] autonomy" (p. 109). These two systems can seem at odds with one another. Comas-Diaz and Greene (1994) have detailed the way that women of color who achieve professional success and status frequently feel a great deal of guilt and anxiety about that success. Often these women experience themselves as "impostors" (p. 367) so as to deny their own desire and the ambition that got them where they are. After all, if their success was only luck and they are "faking it," then they do not have to reconcile the fact that they have internalized the dominant value system's emphasis on external and independent achievement. Impostor feelings in successful white women also abound. As I discuss later, for many women there is still a felt conflict between femininity and ambition, as if professional accomplishment were a masculine virtue. In this case, the anxiety of feeling like an impostor can be a defense against the shame of failing to achieve an ideal femininity.

In addition to these broader issues, there are often particular conflicts for new clinicians about fee setting. Newer therapists are especially likely to struggle with guilt feelings about charging for their services because they may have "deep doubts about the relative value of their therapy work" (Pasternack & Treiger, 1976, p. 1064). When someone feels anxious that what they have offered is not good enough, undercharging can work defensively to lower performance pressure on the therapist. Fingert (1952) describes a patient of his, a clinician, who "consistently charged low fees to his own clients, ostensibly to be kind, but during treatment ... revealed his unconscious fantasy that he was not responsible for his results, because his fees were so low" (pp. 103–104).

Experienced therapists struggle with this dilemma as well. George Whitson (n.d., p. 23) wrote that therapists tend not to pursue overdue payment when they feel that there is something "inadequate" in the work they have done with patients. Pursuing nonpayment or increasing the fee brings up anxiety for most analysts because as soon as money is addressed with a patient, the value of the treatment is open for discussion. And, if analysts do manage to allow that discussion, they will eventually hear how much or how little the treatment is worth to the patient. Beware the "kind" therapist who does not want to deal with money, for he or she will also be reluctant to deal with aggression and the clash of subjectivities. Schonbar (1986) quotes Hilde Bruch:

> Nonattention to payment may conceal serious defects in the progress of therapy. [Bruch] describes a psychiatric resident with a "deep interest" and "a warm and protective attitude" toward his patients, who attended sessions regularly. It was eventually discovered that none of them had paid any fees for a year, and that little of what one might call dynamic therapeutic intervention had taken place with any patient. What developed was a cozy mutual [confidence], but without the exploration of any troublesome issues. (p. 42)

This kind of problem reflects the confusion many clinicians have about what their responsibility to the patient actually is. This confusion is often based on analysts' own early childhood especially if, as children, they felt deserving only in proportion to how much they gave to their parents. How much we are helping has nothing to do with the fee, otherwise we would charge differently for each session based on its outcome. As a point of contrast, medical doctors aren't expected to charge differently depending on whether the patient lives or dies.

Women, who make up the majority of the practicing analysts, have their own struggles with ambition and self-concern. While we are all too aware that women still earn less money than men in the workplace (in 2003 women earned 75.5 cents to every dollar that men earned; Hagenbaugh, 2004), Liss-Levinson (1990) cites the troubling Burnside findings that "female psychologists in private practice set their own fees significantly lower than those of their male colleagues, regardless of level of experience or training" (p. 120). Liss-Levinson goes on to assert that the

> extensive body of experimental literature ... suggests that women consistently pay themselves less when allocating resources to themselves. Callahan, Levy, and Meese (1979) asked subjects from first grade through college to perform a specific task, and then to pay themselves for the work they had done using money left for them by the experimenter. At all ages, girls and women paid themselves less than did boys and men. Major, McFarlin, and Gagnon (1984) found that when undergraduates were offered a fixed sum of money for doing "as much work as they thought was fair," women worked longer, accomplished more, and were more accurate in their work than their male counterparts. (pp. 120–121)

How can we understand women's reluctance to allocate money to themselves? Shame has a well-documented effect on women's experience of self-concern and self-assertion. Kaufman (in press) writes:

> Shame is related to a perception of failure to live up to [the] ego ideals or parental ideals ... that determine value and lovability to oneself and others. ... [W]omen's shame about ambition ... is aroused when aspirations and successes in the world conflict with important feminine ideals of attuned, caring, and nurturing intentions. Success itself can be experienced as shameful if it is perceived [as interfering] with ... these ... ideals.

Adrienne Harris (1997) has described women's relationship to ambition as being fraught with the fear that others will be hurt in the wake of their self-assertion. Harris suggests that many women do not make clear distinctions between "being active, being ambitious, being destructive, or being angry" (p. 298). Because women are often received angrily when they are being assertive, women have come to believe they are hurting people and in danger of losing them when they assert themselves. And I would add, when they succeed.

Drawing on Dinnerstein, Harris points out that for the majority of us the person who had the most power over us when we were the most vulnerable, as infants, was female. Therefore, a powerful and assertive female stirs anxiety and envy for both sexes, even as adults. Additionally, and this is particularly relevant to our profession, Harris states: "[W]omen and men can feel [great disappointment] at anything less than total gratification ... when the person in charge is a woman" (p. 315). Once we understand this, we can see how charged the situation in the consulting room becomes for female analysts when facing patients' early yearning and primitive rage.

It is no surprise, then, that a woman's anxiety about the envy of others will be heightened. When any of us, male or female, raise patients' fees we risk igniting our patients' envy. We can also stir our colleagues' envy. But for women the envy that is stirred will be especially powerful because of early transferences to women as mother figures. Furthermore, envy is especially problematic for women because it disrupts our affiliation needs: We do not like to engender envy because we fear we will be abandoned if we do.

Having said all of this about women, however, I postulate that male analysts tend to be "female-identified" as compared with men in other professional groups and struggle with these issues more than most men do. Furthermore, conflicts over fees will most likely be heightened for male therapists as those conflicts come up in clinical practice when patients of both sexes long for a mother figure in the analyst.

Then there is the problem of success anxiety that we analysts are as likely to suffer from as anyone else. This is a problem we and our patients share: We face many losses when we succeed professionally. The most immediate loss is the hope and fantasy that someone will take care of us financially. Once we can financially support ourselves, there's not much reason to believe someone else is going to lift us out of our deprivation.

Cameron and Bryan (1992) describe success as the "Unseen Enemy":

> As practicing money drunks [anyone dysfunctional with money], we have become very good at crisis. Our families give us sympathy. Our friends loan us money, help us move, call us up to see how we're doing, volunteer to buy us coffee. We feel safe, cared about, cared for. With this help and support, we feel competent and confident enough to start again. Starting again, we set the sails, set our course, sail along smoothly until. ... Until we just have to capsize our lives. (p. 193)

I suggest that financial support can feel like love to many of us and that ending the support can feel intolerable. This is a variation on the fear of autonomy and separateness—from our families and from others. By being independent, we must deal with the disappointment that we are the source of our own supply. Being our own source of supply means having agency and offers many new possibilities. There is freedom in it, but we have to be willing to live through the loss first.

To the degree that we are conflicted about being financially self-sustaining, we will be ill equipped to help patients become financially independent.

Understanding our own fears of success can help us address these issues with patients.

Suze Orman (1999), the popular finance guru, wrote a book called *The Courage to Be Rich*. I bought this book as soon as it came out but then, guiltily sneaking out of the bookstore, I hoped that no one would see me with it. I kept it in my bookshelf with the title facing the other way for well over 2 years. I thought the title outrageously presumptuous, naïve, and obnoxious. When I finally allowed myself to look at the book (with the alibi of preparing this paper) I saw Orman's point. Having the courage to face the *feelings* that surround money—frequently fear, shame, and anger—is what allows us to confront and improve our relationship to money.

Because money represents survival to most of us, *fear* about not having enough is commonly attached to the process of making money. Fear can immobilize us and stop us from taking risks. Many therapists are familiar with this in relation to the big jump from a salaried job to private practice. The courage to risk financial instability is essential to having more and, ultimately, gaining financial freedom. *Shame* about wanting more is also debilitating. I did not have the courage to even look at Orman's book when I first bought it because that felt like showing my desire to have money, which is a forbidden desire in my family, as in many others. *Anger* about being deprived and expecting others to make this up to us also stops us from pursuing our desires. When we are resentful, we lie in wait for the help of others, rather than taking responsibility for our own financial well-being.

Lastly, therapists' individual character styles can also influence fee setting and negotiation. Riemann (cited in Lasky, 1984, p. 294) suggested that the compulsive-obsessional therapist is the most thorough in establishing the patient's financial situation to determine the fee, whereas a hysterical personality, equating a higher fee with greater professional worth, sets fees too high to satisfy narcissistic needs. A schizoid therapist may be so detached and aloof about fees that the patient is given no opportunity to discuss them. Depressive therapists leave fee setting to patients; these therapists do not ask about finances and later resent it when they realize a patient could have afforded more.

Having outlined some basic anxieties involved for therapists in pursuing and attaining financial gain, I'd like to discuss the opportunities that develop *for patients* when therapists overcome these inhibitions. Jessica Benjamin (1988, 1995, 1998) has described mutuality, mutual recognition, and intersubjectivity as the place where two subjects meet: the place of subject-to-subject relating, the place where both individuals know their own subjective experience and simultaneously recognize the other's subjective experience, even when these experiences differ. (Subject-to-subject relating is different from the subject-to-object relating of submission and domination and also is different from subject-to-self-object relating as in the early newborn's experience of the mothering one as part of "me.")

When we ask a patient for money, we are putting him or her in the position of having to recognize and acknowledge our separate needs and desires. Analyst and analysand do not always feel the same way, and that hurts; but the pain of separateness is unavoidable. Full recognition entails an understanding that we are different from one another. For the patient, recognition means being able to tolerate this moment of conflict without ending treatment. The patient recognizes that the analyst has her own life and needs. This means that he is able to tolerate not getting what he wants (e.g., free or inexpensive therapy; a purely nurturing figure with no demands of her own) because he recognizes that her needs are also valid. He may continue to hate her needs—hate her for having those needs—but he will acknowledge that she has them. His realization that they do share the desire to know him helps. And his discovery that she is still with him even though they are in conflict is invaluable.

That most patients have to live through this conflict in order for treatment to happen seems obvious; otherwise session times could not be scheduled and agreement might never be reached over the length of the sessions and so on. But I am suggesting that the journey the patient takes to attain recognition and understanding of the therapist's separate needs is a desirable goal of therapy because it is the basis of real intimacy.

Benjamin (1992) advocates for the developmental desirability of mutual recognition. She updates Freud's (1933) classic statement that "where id was, there ego shall be" (p. 80) by recommending, "Where objects were, subjects must be" (p. 44). She writes:

> In infancy, the complementary interaction, in which the parent facilitates a positive change in the infant's states, is often a prelude to intersubjective sharing. The [m]other must often do something to regulate, soothe, and make the self receptive for such exchange. But increasingly the relationship should shift in emphasis from regulation to the true exchange of recognition itself. What we see in domination is a relationship in which complementarity has completely eclipsed mutuality, so that the underlying wish to interact with someone truly outside, with an equivalent center of desire, does not emerge. (1988, p. 73)

The need for recognition is a basic one: We all want to be seen for our true selves. What may be less obvious to patients is the desirability of being able to recognize another, one whose needs may be in conflict with theirs. Recognizing the other's consciousness means seeing that the other's consciousness is outside of our control. Why would that be desirable? First of all, if we are not separate—if we are undifferentiated—then we cannot be seen. Furthermore, the alternative to acknowledging the other's desires is deadness, subjugation, and splitting. Unhappiness at seeing another's separateness is surely better than the deadness that comes from submitting to the other or having the other submit to us. When patients attempt to control the people in their lives, including us, they are deprived of the experience of authenticity and spontaneity emerging from the other. They are deprived of ever truly discovering the other or seeing the other as he or she is. By controlling others, patients may diminish their anxiety but they also forgo the input that could help them grow and actualize. The possibility for recognition of the other while holding on to one's own self-experience is a developmental achievement that lets patients see others as independent agents, thereby allowing them the freedom not to take the actions and feelings of other people personally. (Other people do what they do for their own reasons not always because of something we did, or because of their feelings about us.) It becomes possible to accept others without self-incrimination, and without needing them to change.

In the struggle towards mutuality, however, the analyst must also grapple with the separateness of the patient; again, there can be "good" feelings and "bad" feelings for the analyst in being separate. The independence and freedom of separateness and differentiation can feel affirming as our patients recognize us. But the loss and potential abandonment can be painful. For one thing, the patient is beyond our control and has the power to leave treatment or never begin treatment because of the fee. Consequently, we must acknowledge our own dependence on the patient. One possible (but problematic) way to defend against this dependency is to keep the fee low and to act as if we do not need the patient's money. Another is to detach from our desire and remain unaware of it, thus submitting to the patient. The problem with these strategies is that we end up resenting the patient, and may act on this resentment later. I had a supervisor once who told me that it was better for the *patient* if the patient resented me for his fee than if I resented him (Arthur Gottdiener, personal communication, 1995).

It may be difficult for a patient to believe that her therapist can make her unhappy while still remaining available to her. I have had patients say, "How can you take care of me when you're trying to get my money? Isn't that a conflict of interest?" But it can also be difficult for us to believe that making patients unhappy is in their interest; when we identify with a patient's feeling that to give us more leaves the patient with less, we are likely to deaden our own desire accordingly (Judith Kaufman, personal communication, 2002). To compensate, we may bring fees down, or never increase them. To the degree that we identify with the patient's sense of deprivation—and to the degree that we believe that money will make up for being deprived—we will use a low fee to counter the patient's discomfort rather than using analysis to help the patient understand her feelings, work through them, and mourn what she never got.

This misstep is seductive for a number of reasons. Out of our own unresolved wish that someone will do the same for us, we may hope to make up for what the patient did not get. (We, like our patients, want to be taken care of, to be given to, to have our war wounds recompensed.) Another reason this passive approach is seductive is that it is easier than facing the patient's devastating realization that she is grown-up now and must take care of herself. The time is over when the world will anticipate and offer her what she needs without her participation. The patient must rely on her own resourcefulness and ability to reach out to others. For the therapist, the guilt and anxiety at being the messenger of this terrible news can be daunting.

Then there's the issue of being resented or even hated. It is difficult to be hated as the "depriving" object when we start a confrontation around the fee. Buckley, Karasu, and Charles (1979) revealed that the number one mistake trainees made was working to be liked by their patients. When we examine this need to be liked, we catch glimpses of how it conflicts with our true task, which is to help the patient grow. Our own recognition of the patient's separateness, therefore, can enable us to look at this need to be liked by patients for what it is: our way of feeling secure and connected. But without this realization, we may keep fees low in an effort to hold onto patients. Believing that we are lovable and professionally valuable only if they stay, we might do anything to keep patients.

The problem with this tactic is that we have no freedom and neither does the patient. Our movement is constantly constricted by our fear of loss. Either we become a slave to the patient or else we demand that the patient be a slave to our security needs.

Additionally, when we keep the fee lower than what the patient can pay, the patient can become suspicious of our motives, often rightly. We are letting her know we do not want to tangle with her anger and are making an implicit contract for her to return the favor by being compliant and nonconfrontational (Nash & Cavenar, 1976, p. 1066). Some would even call this blackmail (Lynn Schultz, personal communication, 2004). Whenever we submit to patients' demands we are in danger of consciously or unconsciously expecting payback for our "good" deed. The difference between submission and collaboration, therefore, is crucial: Submission means one person's desire is dismissed; in collaboration, both desires are acknowledged.

By showing patients that *we* have a subjectivity, we offer them the chance to claim their own subjectivity in response. When we show our "hate" in Winnicott's (1947/1958) sense by charging for our time, ending the session, and so on, we give our patients permission to express their hatred of us. This is also what Winnicott (1969/1989) meant when he described the baby discovering the mother only after trying to destroy her. By making an impact on his mother, and by seeing her survival, the baby recognizes the mother anew and is cheered by her presence. Loving means being able to live through hating the other (Khan, cited in Dimen, 1994).

Muriel Dimen (1994) offers a fine example of the close relationship between love and hate in her description of her clients' reaction to her moving her office to "a new and ... upscaled location ... [a] setting ... far more elegant and professional than the old one." She states, "Most of my patients ... were pleased with their new environment. They read it as a sign of surging hope for their therapeutic progress and, not coincidentally, a sign of hardiness in my ability to survive their aggression" (p. 92). She describes a particular interaction around this new location with a patient who had been struggling with feelings of hatred and envy of Dimen for charging her and for having so much power and status:

> While the disparity in our financial, social, and ethnic status had always been apparent [the patient was African-American and Dimen is white] ... the envy, greed, fear, and hate stimulated by these economic differences had become far more accessible in my new surroundings. Until now, [the patient] had denied the contradictory dimension of our strange intimacy. ... My new office, which flagged not only my standing and authority but her own aspirations for the best for herself, now permitted her to move the contradiction between money and love into the center of the relationship, where it produced the hate it always does. ... Her discovery of the paradox ... created this utopian moment in which there began to grow another kind of love, the kind of bond you have with someone only when you have shed blood together. (pp. 94–95)

By experiencing a patient's aggression and surviving it, we also help the patient to see that others in her life can survive hardy self-assertion. Additionally, when analysands have the opportunity to live through our assertions, they may realize that others can live through theirs. If they can survive it, why not everyone else? When we ask for more from patients, they, in turn, are prompted to ask for more from others: bosses, clients, partners, family members. Conversely, if we cannot ask for more from a patient, how can she learn to ask for more for herself?

But what about the patient who refuses to pay? John Gedo (1963) has said, "When a patient in psychotherapy fails to pay his bill he has violated an explicit and agreed upon responsibility" (p. 368). Arnold Allen (1971) responded to Gedo: "[C]onversely, when a therapist ignores or fails to properly deal with the whole area of payment or nonpayment of his patient's bills, he too is violating an explicit and agreed upon responsibility—namely, that of effectively functioning as his patient's therapist" (p. 132).

I learned this lesson early on in my practice when I treated a young college senior who was unable to assert herself within her family. On first meeting Stephanie, I was startled to see someone so deformed by plastic surgery. She let me know that she had had several facial reconstructions, her first at 14, because her grandmother found her ugly. Her grandmother wanted her granddaughter to consider "one last" surgery "to fix up" what had gone wrong in the previous ones. Despite serious infections after each procedure, which required her to take antibiotics chronically, Stephanie came to treatment unsure of whether she wanted to undergo another surgery. Her grandmother would pay for it; that seemed tempting to her.

Everyone in Stephanie's family suffered from this same financial dependency. Her parents were divorced; her father did not work and received an allowance from his mother. Stephanie had never worked. The grandmother paid her college tuition and all her expenses. Stephanie's grandmother was also very controlling: After not being able to reach Stephanie during one 12-hour period, she mailed her a cell phone and demanded that Stephanie call her daily as well as keep her phone on at all times so that her grandmother could have complete access.

Therapy had been the mother's suggestion; she also suggested that Stephanie get her grandmother to pay. Her mother was a special education teacher, now remarried to a fellow teacher. The patient was too fearful of her grandmother's rage to broach the topic of therapy and instead did all she could to hide the treatment. So she began paying for therapy herself, out of her allowance and her trust fund.

Shortly after she began treatment Stephanie became frantic about the financial burden of therapy and wanted to discontinue. I interpreted her anxiety about the cost of therapy as anxiety over the cost to her family connections by being in therapy. Because of treatment she was beginning to question her grandmother's control over her and her grandmother's motivation in wanting her to undergo more surgery. She said she was able to understand that, but still didn't think she could manage the money. Her mother refused to help her financially, and told her that it was not an option for her to ask the patient's stepfather for the money. For mother, father, and patient, money came from other people.

I raised the possibility of Stephanie's working part-time in order to pay for therapy, but that suggestion was so anxiously dismissed by her, accompanied by another threat to leave, that I quickly dismissed it too. I found myself twisting and turning to accommodate complicated insurance arrangements, delayed payment, and "IOUs" in hopes that eventually I would both help this patient and be paid, hers being a family with more than ample financial resources. But I was functioning within the same delusional system as the patient: Someone else will pay.

Although I was helping Stephanie to begin to set limits with her family, I was not standing up to her when she acted just as they did. She wanted someone else to pay and if it wasn't going to be her family, it was going to be me. In fact, she left treatment owing me a sizeable sum of money. She moved back to her grandmother's hometown at the end of the year and I never heard from her again.

I did not protect my own needs with her and I was therefore not a model for her in her quest for self-preservation. I was just as intimidated by her dramatic threats to leave treatment as she was intimidated by her family's dramatic threats to cut her off financially. Even if I had asserted myself with her and lost her as a result, I would have done my job because at the very least she would have had one experience of someone refusing to submit to her family's mode of destructive, controlling behavior.

It was difficult for me to acknowledge my rage at this patient who could pay for anything but therapy—or anything but me. In cutting off my feelings of anger, I blocked my ability to address this issue with her. Blinded by the family's wealth, I imagined that they would pay because they had so much. My fantasy was a way to deny the patient's hostility and my own: No need to get mad—they'll pay me eventually. I was also being concrete: Because they have money, they will pay—as if money is a resource in and of itself, without respect to the interpersonal and intrapsychic dynamics of the people involved.

Whitson (n.d.) makes a convincing argument for the importance of therapists' awareness of their own feelings in relation to the fee and payment: The lower our awareness, the more likely we are to act out or not to act at all. He suggests that we are most likely to avoid our anger at patients. Perhaps it is difficult to look at and confront patients' exploitive tendencies because it requires us to be in contact with our feelings about being exploited. A further problem with money-blindness (Lieberman & Lindner, 1987), he suggests, is that inevitably our patients will know more about our money issues than we do and we won't be able to keep the discussion open.

Payment and nonpayment can mean different things to different patients. They can also mean different things at different times within the same span of treatment. Understanding this shifting meaning helps the therapist know how and when to address the issue of money with a variety of patients.

In some cases, there are patient-therapist dynamics that call for containing (Slochower, 1996; Winnicott, 1986) one's subjectivity around the fee, at least until the patient can tolerate recognizing the analyst's independent self. There are patients for whom the threat of abandonment and loss of the other is a primary concern. A key defense for these patients is the denial of any separateness of the therapist in order to ward off potential feelings of loss. According to Gedo (1963) "[Their] ... distress [is] relieved when they [are] offered a consistent external object in the therapy, but the maintenance of the internalized representation of this object depend[s] on the illusion of symbiosis. When disillusioned by reality, these patients [use] the transitional phenomenon of withholding payment to deny their separateness" (p. 370). The patient's fantasy is that the analyst will not charge, out of love for the patient.

These patients are seeking an opportunity to regress to a kind of dependency that they did not get enough of, if any at all. There is a curative hope that the treatment will be an opportunity to depend on someone entirely, and safely, for the first time. Once the illusion of symbiotic dependency has been achieved (for example the patient believes that I keep her fee low because I am her mother), the disillusionment back to reality must be titrated slowly. And while it is possible to prevent this level of regression, for example by never allowing nonpayment, when the regression is prevented the opportunity to engage these core dependency needs in the patient may also be prevented (Gedo, 1963; Whitson, n.d.).

I have been able to participate with patients on this journey from full dependency to mutual recognition, and many of these patients began treatment with limited financial resources. They experienced themselves as special or valued because the fee was low. When we began, I let them know that as their income improved their fee would increase. This communication was an attempt to accomplish at least two things. First, I conveyed the message that the decreased fee was something I was affected by but was willing to live with; in other words, I agreed to it consciously and willingly. The second goal was the message that I accepted the patient where she was at that moment, but also recognized she had the potential to reach beyond her present capacities (Allen, 1971).

Along the way, as the patient's finances improved, I would check in on what the lowered fee now meant to her. I have also, in some of these cases, allowed a patient to run up a bill, in which case the unpaid balance itself becomes a transitional space. This debt can be interpreted to mean one of several things: The patient is so valuable to me that she is worth the risk and trouble of the nonpayment; the hope that I will "forgive" the debt out of love; or that the balance is binding us together—in that I would not be able to abandon the patient because the unpaid money between us serves as an umbilical cord, and we would have to stay in touch at least until the money was paid back. This arrangement acts like a kind of reverse retainer that the patient uses to hold on to me. At the point that the patient becomes secure in the knowledge that I will not leave, the need for the unpaid bill can then be challenged.

I am alerted that it is time to renegotiate this arrangement when I notice that I resent the unpaid balance. My resentment tells me that the patient is now capable of more. Renegotiation heralds a time of intense and sometimes brutal struggle: At the point that I declare separateness, the patient invariably retaliates. The dependency can seem to patients like a promise and they kick and scream when I change the rules. Furthermore, the sense of "specialness" that the low fee represented is now challenged, which means that the patient's need to be special has to be worked through in a new way. This is a very difficult transition and it's understandable that therapists would want to avoid it, either by not confronting the dependency once it has begun or by never allowing it to develop.

However, renegotiation also heralds great new possibilities for the relationship. In addition to the wounding that is inevitable, there is a good deal of hope communicated implicitly by my belief that the patient is now more competent and able. My recognition of her new capabilities can challenge her to see herself differently. This new perspective also challenges her to shift from an identification with her family to an identification with me as an independent and successful professional.

There is a distinction here between patients who use money as a transitional object and patients who withhold money out of a need to devalue the therapist and the therapy. Patients whose initial intention is to trick the therapist in order to get something for nothing will not be helped by this kind of dependency arrangement. There is a clear diagnostic difference between patients who seek a therapeutic regression and those who seek to swindle the therapist. Patients who begin treatment from the devaluing perspective have another need propelling them: to prove that the therapist is worthless. Theirs is an attempt to hold on to a connection and identification with the patient's family of origin because a therapist deemed worthless need not be taken seriously when challenging the pathological family system (Arthur Gottdiener, personal communication, 1977). In this situation firm limits are necessary or the treatment will be so undervalued by the patient that he will ultimately see no point in staying in it. Furthermore, when the analyst caves in to destructive manipulation, the patient learns that the analyst is helpless against the patient's destructiveness and cannot facilitate a solution (as with my patient Stephanie).

In all of the cases when a financial dependency was constructive, my initial feeling was that of being genuinely appreciated. This impression can be a reliable diagnostic indicator; if the patient's need for the dependency does not feel authentic, then what is probably operating is a kind of sociopathy—just as breast-feeding an infant can feel wonderful but breast-feeding a 13-year-old would feel monstrous. This also describes the difference between two different developmental stages in the same patient: Whereas early on, this arrangement can feel good to the analyst, once it no longer feels that way, it is time for renegotiation because the patient has outgrown it.

Here is a clinical example of a fee conflict that had many positive outcomes, including an excellent return on investment for both the patient and for me. Justine was a young woman beginning a doctoral program in clinical psychology when we started out. She was extremely bright, extraordinarily articulate, progressive and politically correct with a self-righteous streak that both impressed and intimidated me. I felt honored to work with her and hoped I would be able to keep up. When I originally accepted the low fee she proposed, I felt noble; we were fighting the good fight—who needed money? (Actually, I remember a brief internal chafe at her sense of entitlement to the low fee, but I ignored that and instead got swept up in our commitment to the work.) Because she was so hard working, I was inspired to work hard too. She was also very stimulating and lively, and she usually made me feel useful.

With hindsight, I realize that from the beginning she wanted me to take care of her financially. Before me, her father took care of her financially. He was physically absent and emotionally remote, and when she was 9 he moved out and left her with her dangerous and severely borderline mother. But he was responsible and giving with money. His money stood in for affection, caring, and love. Understandably, she felt neglected.

She overspent and her father paid off her debts more than once. Eventually he put his foot down, and she began building a balance with me. She was very angry with him and I was afraid of her anger. Sometimes it seemed to me that her anger made the whole building shake. Meanwhile, secretly, I applauded her father's limit, but remained very gentle with her in every discussion of their struggle. We did a lot of good work in this period on the issue of her debting. We explored her hunger, her deprivation, her resentment, her refusal to mourn, her attempts at self-sufficiency—for example, rather than ask anyone for help, she shopped.

This is what made me notice my own limit: She had paid her father back. She had cut up her credit cards. She had paid back a bank loan. She was paying her back taxes. Actually, I was the only person she was not paying. And her bill was growing, rapidly. I also noticed that she was wearing something new to every session: jewelry, shoes, tights, scarves, handbags, blouses, skirts, pants, boots, hair clips, sunglasses.

I had to work up the courage to confront her.

When I first suggested a payment plan, she seemed devastated. Naturally she would have to cut her session frequency way down, she informed me. How could I put her in this position, she wondered? Didn't I know how much she needed therapy? How could she have missed all the signs of my heartlessness and coldness, not to mention my questionable ethics? How could she have trusted me so foolishly? She planned only to work with poor people, she told me, and she certainly hoped that I wasn't suggesting that she do otherwise—"You know, like starting a private practice or changing jobs." I wondered aloud, "If you can't afford your lifestyle, just exactly what is your objection to bringing in more money?" But she insisted she was not going to change her charitable intentions just so that she could pay me back.

I held firm, but she was not budging either. We struggled with each other in almost every session, three times a week, every week, for months. I kept bringing up her balance and she kept threatening to leave. We were in trouble. I asked her what she wanted me to do. There was a long silence. I struggled very hard to stay with that silence and not jump in to offer her something. Then she began banging her arms against the couch (she was lying down). Soon her arms and legs were going in tandem and she was yelling with her mouth closed. Eventually, she began to sob. The sobbing subsided. More silence. More internal struggle on my part to not do anything. Finally, in a very small and hoarse voice she managed to squeak out: "I want to be special to you. I know you couldn't do this with everyone or you'd go broke, but I've been hoping you could wipe out my balance."

When we discussed this years later, Justine said that I never demonstrated how at sea I was. Instead, I managed to convey complete confidence that we would work things out. My confidence angered her because I seemed immoveable, but it also reassured her that we would go on working together, no matter what. There were many days, she told me, when she could not believe I tolerated her and did not kick her out of treatment. I'm torn about revealing how difficult it was. It was a really long haul. Nevertheless, I have come to see that nothing other than my constant attempts to break through her financial dissociation would have allowed us to get to the truth.

And, in fact, by holding firm, not rescuing her, and not wiping out her debt, something new did happen. We discovered that Justine felt her older brother was more special to her father than she was. Invariably, her brother got into worse trouble (Justine was the good one) and cost their father more money; her father spent money paying for her brother's drug rehab, counseling, rescue missions that necessitated last-minute airplane tickets to faraway places, lavish vacations trying to cheer him up. Additionally, Justine's mother complained bitterly that her ex-husband was financially withholding, and Justine identified with her mother's feelings of abandonment and rejection. Her father seemed exceptionally generous only with her brother.

She wanted to be my exception.

This desire led us to wonder together what made someone special. How could she tell? Could she be special to me even if she paid me back? Had she ruined her chances by telling me how angry she was with me? She had never told her father that she was angry with him. And another thing: What would I do if she let me know how much she wanted from me? Would I be disgusted? Overwhelmed? She believed that her father only appreciated and loved her when she was easy and didn't ask for much.

She was shocked to discover that by telling me how much she hated me she found herself wanting to come in more often. She became aware of her yearning for more of a connection with me. She also began to feel deep sadness over her long-buried desire for her father's love and attention.

Following these realizations, she began to pay me back. Once she was all paid up we had another contentious discussion because it was time to raise her fee. She knew it was coming but that seemed only to increase her resentment. She said she did not want to pay me more money. I told her that just because it was fair to me didn't mean she had to like it. The difference for me was that this time I was not as threatened by her rage and so I was less worried about frustrating her. I was also quicker to ask her what was under the rage.

This round of struggle brought up her anxiety about competing with her mother and with me. She realized that there was a fairly simple way to handle my fee increase: increase her own fees and expand her private practice. (Our first round of fighting had, in fact, ushered in her private practice.) Now her conflict was about having more; she feared her mother's retaliation and criticism. By increasing her financial resources she was separating from her mother. Previously she had been joined to her mother by feelings of helplessness, resentment, and deprivation, and literally by their joint dependence on her father's income. What would connect her to her father if she didn't need his financial rescue ever again? And how would she live through her mother's retribution for separating? Who was she if not her mother's reflection?

We rolled up our sleeves and fought some more. During this period she developed a very lucrative consulting practice that brought her more patients than ever. As her own fees grew she became frightened of my retaliation. When she recognized that I did not retaliate and instead celebrated her success she began to mourn the difference between my reaction and her mother's.

Recently, now quite well established in the field, she beat me to the punch about raising her fee. *She* wanted to increase my fee and expressed a great sense of pride both about wanting to and being able to pay me more. I helped her make a lot more money; surely that is part of her generosity. But I also helped her break a malignant dependency on her father and a destructive identification with her mother. As a result, she can embrace her competence; recognizing and accepting her own resourcefulness makes her feel more abundant and full. The reward for me was obviously financial but the emotional gratification was also intense. We had moved closer: I no longer had to defend my need to be paid and she could see me as a person with needs as well as value.

CONCLUSION

For many analysts and patients alike, the assertion of the fee is a metaphor for the assertion of subjectivity, separateness, and desire. I have suggested that the negotiation of the fee is particularly well suited to working through the paradoxical tension between separateness and connection that always exists between two people who are subjects to one another. Although these conversations are difficult, the potential outcome of a financial confrontation with a patient can be a greater sense of aliveness, increased engagement, and real intimacy. The freedom to talk about something that was previously unspeakable also opens up room to talk about other taboos. When we ask more of patients, they have permission to ask more of us and of their environment. But to accomplish this we have to overcome our own fear of increased engagement. Increased engagement can make us feel vulnerable. The risks are staggering. We risk encountering our patients' separate, alive, and authentic selves, ones that *we* cannot control. We risk abandonment. In fact, we may be abandoned exactly as we were as children—for asserting our needs. Also, we cannot know in advance whether or not a patient will engage in the dialogue and whether or not the conflict will be successfully worked through.

We also have to face our own anxiety about patients demanding more from us or calling attention to our mistakes, from their more liberated place. Hearing new—not necessarily positive—information can disrupt our self-image. Our self-esteem may be badly wounded. We may feel totally shaken to learn that a patient now sees us as greedy or withholding or disappointing in some other way. Furthermore, since we cannot retaliate, it may feel as though the patient has all the ammunition.

Nevertheless, when I am more engaged, less cut off, and not in denial, I am more free—free to do my job and free to address what needs addressing. Actually, when I am free I find I have more to offer. But this kind of freedom has another by-product. By being free to show our separate selves, I believe we offer patients the opportunity to struggle for more integration—in their perception of us and in their perception of themselves. By recognizing us, patients are free to use us more fully and effectively. After all, recognition that is valuable to them can only come from another true subject.

REFERENCES

Allen, A. (1971). The fee as a therapeutic tool. *Psychoanalytic Quarterly*, 40, 132–140.

Benjamin, J. (1988). *The bonds of love: Psychoanalysis, feminism, and the problem of domination*. New York: Pantheon.

Benjamin, J. (1992). Recognition and destruction: An outline of intersubjectivity. In N. Skolnick & S. Warshaw (Eds.), *Relational perspectives in psychoanalysis* (pp. 43–60). Hillsdale, NJ: Analytic Press.

Benjamin, J. (1995). *Like subjects, love objects*. New Haven, CT: Yale University Press.

Benjamin, J. (1998). *Shadow of the other: Intersubjectivity and gender in psychoanalysis*. New York: Routledge.

Blanck, G., & Blanck, R. (1974). *Ego psychology: Theory and practice*. New York: Columbia University Press.

Buckley, P., Karasu, T., & Charles, E. (1979). Common mistakes in psychotherapy. *American Journal of Psychiatry, 136*(12), 1578–1580.

Cameron, J., & Bryan, M. (1992). *Money drunk/money sober*. New York: Ballantine Books.

Comas-Diaz, L., & Greene, B. (1994). Women of color with professional status. In L. Comas-Diaz & B. Greene (Eds.), *Women of color: Integrating ethnic and gender identities in psychotherapy* (pp. 347–388). New York: Guilford.

DiBella, A. (1980). Mastering money issues that complicate treatment: The last taboo. *American Journal of Psychotherapy, 24*(4), 510–524.

Dimen, M. (1994). Money, love, and hate: Contradiction and paradox in psychoanalysis. *Psychoanalytic Dialogues, 4*, 69–100.

Eissler, K. (1974). On some theoretical and technical problems regarding the payment of fees for psychoanalytic treatment. *International Review of Psychoanalysis, 1*, 73–101.

Fingert, H. (1952). Comments of the psychoanalytic significance of the fee. *Bulletin of the Menninger Clinic, 16*(3), 98–104.

Freud, S. (1913). On beginning the treatment (further recommendations on the technique of psycho-analysis). In J. Strachey (Ed. & Trans.), *The standard edition of the complete psychological works of Sigmund Freud* (Vol. 12, pp. 132–144). London: Hogarth Press.

Freud, S. (1933). New introductory lectures. In J. Strachey (Ed. & Trans.), *The standard edition of the complete psychological works of Sigmund Freud* (Vol. 22, pp. 5–183). London: Hogarth Press.

Gedo, J. (1963). A note on non-payment of psychiatric fees. *International Journal of Psychoanalysis, 44*, 368–371.

Hagenbaugh, B. (2004, August 26). Women's pay suffers setback. *USA Today*.

Harris, A. (1997). Aggression, envy and ambition: Circulating tensions in women's psychic life. *Gender & Psychoanalysis, 1*, 291–325.

Kaufman, J. (in press). Shame: A hidden dimension in women's ambition. *Studies in Gender and Sexuality*.

Lasky, E. (1984). Psychoanalysts' and psychotherapists' conflicts about setting fees. *Psychoanalytic Psychology, 4*, 289–300.

Lasky, E. (1999). Psychotherapists' ambivalence about fees: Male-female differences. *Women & Therapy, 22*(3), 5–13.

Lieberman, A., & Lindner, V. (1987). *Unbalanced accounts: Why women are still afraid of money*. New York: Atlantic Monthly Press.

Liss-Levinson, N. (1990). Money matters and the woman analyst: In a different voice. *Psychoanalytic Psychology, 7*(Suppl.), 119–130.

Loewald, H. (1960). On the therapeutic action of psycho-analysis *International Journal of Psychoanalysis, 41*, 16–33.

Lorenzo, F. (2000, May). *Cross-cultural issues in couples work with gays and lesbians*. Association of Lesbian and Gay Affirmative Psychotherapists (ALGAP), Lecture Series 1999/2000, New York City.

Meyers, B. (1976). Attitudes of psychiatric residents toward payment of psychotherapy fees. *American Journal of Psychiatry, 133*, 1460–1462.

Miller, A. (1983). *Drama of the gifted child*. New York: Basic Books.

Mitchell, S. (2000). *Relationality: From attachment to intersubjectivity*. Hillsdale, NJ: Analytic Press.

Nash, J., & Cavenar, J. (1976). Free psychotherapy: An inquiry into resistance. *American Journal of Psychiatry*, *133*, 1066–1069.

Orman, S. (1999). *The courage to be rich: Creating a life of material and spiritual abundance*. New York: Riverhead Books.

Pasternack, S., & Treiger, P. (1976). Psychotherapy fees and residency training. *American Journal of Psychiatry*, *133*(9), 1064–1066.

Pinderhughes, E. (1982). Afro-American families and the victim system. In M. McGoldrick, J. Pearce, & J. Giordano (Eds.), *Ethnicity and family therapy* (pp. 108–122). New York: Guilford.

Reider, A. (1986). The clinical management of the nonpaying patient. In D. Krueger (Ed.), *The last taboo* (pp. 189–201). New York: Brunner Mazel.

Schonbar, R. (1986). The fee as focus of transference and countertransference in treatment. In D. Krueger (Ed.), *The last taboo* (pp. 33–47). New York: Brunner Mazel.

Slochower, J. (1996). *Holding and psychoanalysis: A relational perspective*. Hillsdale, NJ: Analytic Press.

Whitson, G. (n.d.). *Money matters in psychoanalysis: The analyst's coparticipation in the matter of money*. Unpublished manuscript.

Winnicott, D. W. (1958). Hate in the countertransference. In *Through pediatrics to psychoanalysis* (pp. 194–203). New York: Basic Books. (Original work published 1947)

Winnicott, D. W. (1986). *Holding and interpretation*. New York: Grove Press.

Winnicott, D. W. (1989). The use of an object and relating through identifications. In *Playing and reality* (pp. 86–94). New York: Routledge. (Original work published 1969)

Chapter 12

Money and gender

Financial facts and fantasies for female and male therapists

Arielle Farber Shanok

> The issue of money and fees for treatment is one of the most inadequately discussed in the psychotherapy literature.
>
> —Shields (1996, p. 233)

"Sooo, I owe ya 40 bucks, do I?" my usually polite, clean-cut, 33-year-old client, Mr. C., said to me as he slowly reached into his pants pocket, legs spread wide apart, at the end of our fifth therapy session. Our 50-minute session was supposed to end 8 minutes earlier. Before finding his wallet, he declared that he had to use the restroom. Without hesitation, Mr. C. leapt out of his chair and exited the room, closing the door behind him. Mr. C. had paid without noteworthy reluctance after his first four sessions. I found myself sitting across from his briefcase waiting for his return feeling baffled and becoming frustrated.

This chapter addresses both the difficulties and importance of talking about money within clinical training and therapy. Fantasy components of discussing money are distinguished from facts, the reality components, and both are viewed as critical to address. Fantasy here refers to the individual and interpersonal meanings and feelings attached to finances. Facts mean the concrete, practical financial aspects of a situation. The clinical moment described is drawn from my first year of clinical training a decade ago. I describe the case in more detail and draw on more recent clinical examples and my own professional evolution to illustrate the topics covered in this chapter. These topics include the challenges and risks of discussing money, the meanings of money to female and male therapists and clients, as well as ways that addressing money can deepen our work. Current literature is examined with a focus on ways that gender influences both our own and our clients' experiences, expectations, and choices around money. Cultural understandings about money are highlighted in case material. A thorough research review on culture and money is largely beyond the scope of this chapter, but necessary to include in future literature. The chapter concludes with suggestions about how to discuss money in therapy and training.

In this chapter, I make the case that to be effective clinicians who handle money matters well ourselves, with our clients, and with our trainees, we need to grapple with splits that often exist both within ourselves and in our professional fields of practice. We need to integrate our male and female identities around caring, work, and money and recognize that both traditionally male and female approaches offer us something valuable. It is important to fully realize that male and female clinicians can both be caring and earn good money.

WE DO NOT TALK ABOUT MONEY

Money matters are complex, multidimensional, and impact everyone. Although money is a topic of universal significance, some money matters are taboo to discuss even among therapists who are otherwise trained to address highly intimate personal details (Shields, 1996). This is evidenced by the fact that few therapists know the incomes of their close friends. Every mental health professional has to discuss and make decisions about money in their work, yet very few graduate programs provide formal training in the area. In fact, of the many excellent clinical supervisors I had over the course of my training, most of whom had private practices, only one discussed practical money matters with me. (She is Dr. Berger, one of the editors of this book.) For my part, I was curious but did not know how to appropriately ask. Money questions, I feared, would make supervisors feel uneasy and would be viewed as intrusive or make me look greedy. Instead, as Lasky (1999), a clinical psychologist, writes: "We learn about money and money issues in an unspoken way, and the individual meanings are determined by one's life circumstances: the religion, culture, and social class of one's family; the attitudes of one's parents towards money; and the way money actually was handled in the family" (p. 7).

By learning about money in an unspoken way, we also learn not to talk about money. We may also learn not to introspect about it, that is, to allow many money matters to lie unexamined at the outer margin of our awareness. These factors detract from our competency as therapists.

In illustration, a colleague of mine told me that during her training at a top New York clinical program, she was referred by her training director to a therapist who treated trainees at a reduced fee. The therapist was very well regarded in his field and indeed, during the first few sessions, seemed to live up to his reputation. My colleague found his questions and interventions to be consistently "insightful," and she felt "safe" in his presence. Yet, she was perplexed by his failure to raise the topic of payment at all. With some trepidation, she brought it up at the end of the third session. When she did ask, he named a fee that was about 50% of the going rate in the field for a therapist of his stature. She was relieved, and the work continued. However, several sessions later, while discussing another matter, my colleague shared with her therapist that she would be reimbursed for part of her therapy expenses by her insurance company. At the end of that session, the therapist informed her that the fee would be increased by 35% because of the insurance reimbursements. My colleague had the presence of mind to open up her concern with him that the insurance company would not reimburse her for the new amount as it was above the "usual and customary rate." The therapist replied that she should submit his bill, and they would choose the top fee that the insurance company would reimburse. Several days later, the client received two bills in the mail from her therapist for the 2 months that she was treated by him. She paid him in full and submitted the bills to her insurance company. When she did receive the reimbursement check several weeks later, the insurance company covered only 80% of the fee. She therefore expected her therapist to establish the fee at the top amount that the insurance company would reimburse, 15% higher than the first fee he named. She expected that he would credit her the extra money (several hundred dollars) that she had overpaid. While he did establish the fee as he had promised, he declined to credit her any money, saying that they would start with the new fee going forward.

My colleague readily—and heatedly—told me about the negative impact that this journey to a fee had on her. During the initial sessions, not knowing what the fee would be or how it might be discussed increased my colleague's anxiety. She described holding back from attaching to her therapist. She did not know whether she could afford to work with him. Furthermore, she felt that money was not a concern to him, and that he would not be able to understand the daily stress that living on a small stipend caused her. When he abruptly raised the fee that she thought was set, based on information that he had not asked about when he established the fee, she felt angry and distrustful. She explored with him her dynamic issues around feeling taken advantage of, a discussion that she found useful. However, she continued to feel angry that he never acknowledged his own missteps. His failure to credit her the amount she overpaid only fueled her distrust and made her feel like a "sucker" for paying and submitting both bills. Furthermore, as a trainee in the field, the process undermined what could have become for her, under better circumstances, a model for her own fee setting in the future.

WHY WE DO NOT TALK ABOUT MONEY

Money is a vehicle used by everyone to meet, or attempt to meet, needs, wants, and wishes. Money has been called "a concrete representation of energy ... an archetypal symbol of power that signifies much about the person who possesses it and how she or he uses power in relationship to self and others" (Buck, 1999, p. 37). As such, it is a window into one's "primitive passions," potentially revealing greed, envy, competitiveness, and other strong feelings that most people do not like to show or even acknowledge about themselves (Dimen, 1994). One's hourly fee or yearly income can feel like a summation of one's personal value. It can also feel like a revelation of personal characteristics, including, but not limited to, greed, inadequacy, disappointment, need, or narcissism.

Concurrently, as money is measured numerically, it can seem to negate the meaning of anything by reducing the item or service to a number. As Dimen (1994) says, "Money degrades because it makes everything the same" (p. 88). For example, a client might discount a therapist's otherwise potentially mutative caring for her because a session can be numerically equated with the dollar amount of her new bathroom mats. In part for these reasons, strong societal norms exist around money. In many circles, revealing the amount one earns or wishes to earn, or asking how much others earn, can lead to people distancing from the person disclosing facts or interest.

Most therapists choose their professions at least in part because they have a sense of compassion for others, a wish to help, and a desire to see themselves and be seen as altruistic. Furthermore, in training, therapists are taught to leave their own needs, desires, and wishes that are not about helping their clients outside the therapy room. Compounding all of these factors in both therapists and clients, the idea of thoroughly addressing money in session can often be an anxiety-provoking endeavor. That emotional set, however, need not dominate.

In therapy, money can and should be addressed across the continuum from facts to fantasy. On the reality, or fact, end of the spectrum, topics include the following: the fact that a therapist charges a certain fee for services or the fact that sometimes a client cannot afford a certain fee based on income, lack of savings, and other expenses for vital needs. On the opposite end of the spectrum are the vast multitude of individualized intrapsychic and interpersonal meanings that are projected into money. These may include a client's feeling that a therapist's high fee is an aggressive act toward him or her or a client's sense of inability to afford a fee because he or she believes that spending money on him- or herself is a selfish thing to do. According to Herron and Welt (1992), money as a reality is rarely discussed in therapy; money as a fantasy, although not a favorite topic of either therapist or client, is more easily discussed. After all, while few therapists receive training on practical money matters, most learn to help clients explore their wishes and fantasies.

As illustrated by the example about my colleague and her therapist, even if we are otherwise excellent therapists, failure to effectively discuss and make decisions about reality-based aspects of money exacts a high clinical price. By not being clear and up-front about what the fee is, or how it will be decided, or by not acknowledging when we have made mistakes, we risk unnecessarily increasing our clients' anxiety, anger, and distrust around both ourselves and our fields. Worse still, we risk reenacting our clients' and our own issues. Yet, the many meanings of money, and the fact that it is used in most therapy settings, make it not only a reality but also fertile with potential insight into our clients' intrapsychic and interpersonal dynamics.

FEE, FREE, AND INSURANCE SETTINGS

Therapy settings vary widely in how clients pay (or do not pay) and how therapists are compensated. Currently, as assistant director of a university counseling center, I earn a salary and provide services that are free for students. At the same time, I am also in private practice where I make and implement all decisions related to fees and billing. These different roles and settings give me the experience of approaching money in therapy from differing angles. While my private practice requires a more proactive approach to addressing money matters, the topic comes up in different ways in both settings.

Perhaps most complex for therapists is the self-run private practice setting. Here, the therapist has the most control over the size of the fee and cancellation and payment policies. Also, the relationship between client and therapist finances is the most direct: The more the client pays, the more the therapist earns. In other settings, therapists earn salaries or stipends. Sometimes, they earn a set fee for each client appointment regardless of what the client pays. At other times, they may earn a fee related to what the client pays, or perhaps they may not earn any money but instead gain experience and credits toward licensure. Clients pay via insurance, which may or may not include a copay, a set rate out of pocket, or an amount on a sliding scale out of pocket. Some clients do not pay at all. In settings where clients do not pay fees, they may provide other forms of compensation. They may agree to fill out questionnaires in research studies, have a novice therapist in training settings, or may wait for a long time in socialized health care settings.

Thinking and speaking about money in private practice settings is clearly necessary if the therapist is to be paid, while outside private practice, where the relationship between client payment and therapist income is more distant, therapists should remain aware nonetheless of relationships—everywhere on the spectrum from real to imagined. For example, a therapist who earns what he or she considers to be a low salary may feel resentment that a high-earning client only pays a minimal copay. In addition, therapists' thoughts and feelings about their clients and treatments may be impacted by what their clients are paying independent of what they are earning and vice versa. For example, the amount a salaried therapist earns at a clinic will likely influence how he or she sees his or her work, particularly if this therapist views the salary as particularly low or high. A therapist earning low fees may feel that he or she does not need to put much effort into treatments. Alternatively, the therapist may feel more strongly than otherwise that he or she is providing therapy for altruistic reasons. This could result in the clinician having a greater need for expressed appreciation from clients and more resentment if such appreciation is not supplied.

The previously widely held belief that clients need to pay to benefit from therapy has more recently been debunked (Herron & Welt, 1992). While client investment and commitment to the process are clearly important, clients can benefit from free therapy. Similarly, research has revealed that the amount that private practice therapists charge does not make a significant impact on client expectation of therapy outcome or assessment of therapist credibility (Schneider & Watkins, 1990).

A clinical setting in which therapists' and clients' financial needs are most removed from the treatment situation is the one in which a therapist is paid a salary and a client does not pay at all. This situation may seem to free a therapist from having to address finances. However, caution should be exercised here as well. Clients still have feelings about not paying—and, at least for some, the emotions may be even stronger than if they were paying. In addition, therapists have feelings about their salaries and about providing a free service. One client whom I saw in such a setting at a university counseling center thanked me profusely during and at the end of each session. Exploration of the meaning of free treatment to him was enlightening. The discussions revealed that he lacked any sense of being entitled to support and interest in him. Instead, he experienced himself as a burden. These feelings were connected with his being gay and being raised by generous but rigid Italian Roman Catholic parents. Yet, his overconcern with my needs worried me about the genuineness and fullness of what he would allow himself to express in our short-term treatment. For these reasons, I reminded him of the reality that I earned a salary, that the center was partially funded by student fees. In the context that we coconstructed, I was then able to encourage him to tolerate the discomfort of focusing more on his needs than mine.

Given the historical and present-day gender differences in ownership and usage of money, and given money as representing power, potential, and desire, the topic of money is best addressed taking gender into consideration.

WHY FEMALE THERAPISTS EARN LESS, EVEN WHEN SELF-EMPLOYED

Findings from the most recent surveys taken by national social work, psychology, and psychiatry associations revealed that full-time female clinicians earn significantly less on average than full-time male clinicians

(American Psychiatric Association, n.d.; Finno et al., 2010; National Association of Social Workers, 2002). The survey done by the American Psychiatric Association included only practitioners who described private practice as their "primary work setting," while the psychology and social work surveys included clinicians in all clinical settings. Sentell, Pingitore, Scheffler, Schwalm, and Haley (2001) held constant patient demographics, caseloads, practice profiles, and payment sources among a sample of psychologists in California and found that if female psychologists were paid like male psychologists, they would earn, on average, $16,440 more per year. Several potential explanations for this gap were measured, including more domestic obligations for women, choices about work focus and specialization, and differences in levels of training. However, all of these factors combined only explained a small part of the disparity. When ruling out institutional discrimination, by comparing only private practice settings in which fees are self-chosen, female psychologists still set their own fees significantly lower than male colleagues. This was true despite equivalent levels of experience and training (Burnside, 1986). Furthermore, female therapists tended to lower their fees more often and more dramatically than their male counterparts in the study.

Viewed from a social learning theory perspective, we might wonder if men tend to charge more because of their traditionally assigned role around earning money. Their self-esteem is closely connected to their professional and financial achievement. In contrast, the traditional role of women is to be nurturers; their sense of self tends to come in large part from being caring and connected to others. With a female mind-view, financial and professional achievement may actually endanger the possibility of personal connection. Another social learning theory explanation is that women charge less because they see that other women are paid less; women may have internalized the lower value society places on the work of women. This phenomenon of women and men undervaluing women's work and overvaluing men's work has been demonstrated and replicated in multiple studies (Heilman, 2001; Langan et al., 2008).

Liss-Levinson (1990) proposed that female therapists tend to experience themselves as needing money less than male therapists. She provided the explanation that female therapists experience more tension than male therapists between their own monetary needs and those of their clients. As discussed, men are socially rewarded for prioritizing their own needs, while women may risk social penalty in doing so. Significant divergences from these social expectations, such as women therapists charging high fees and not adjusting them in response to clients' needs, may cause discomfort in both therapists and clients. As women therapists tend to see more female clients who, on average, earn less money, even if male therapists were equally responsive to monetary needs of their clients, women would still earn less overall.

Another cultural factor leading women to see themselves as needing less money than men may entail the fact that some heterosexual women do not view themselves as the main provider. Instead, they rest somewhat on the incomes of their husbands or partners. This theory is supported by the finding that women in same-sex couples tended to earn more and report paying for more of their purchases than comparable women in heterosexual relationships (Soloman, Rothblum, & Balsam, 2005). Regarding heterosexual women who are the sole earners in their households, many may embrace the "Prince Charming myth" that someday soon a man will come along and take care of all their financial needs (Liss-Levinson, 1990). A potentially enlightening area for future research lies in the fee practices of lesbian and gay therapists.

Research done by Prince (1993) about gender differences in attitudes about money in general may add a dimension to Liss-Levinson's (1990) findings that female therapists feel they need money less. Prince found that both men and women see money as related to power and esteem. Yet, men were more likely to feel competent in handling money and were more willing to take risks to generate wealth. Women reported feeling higher levels of envy and deprivation related to money as a means of obtaining enjoyable items and experiences. If indeed women feel stuck in their roles as selfless nurturers, setting limits, such as declining a request for a fee reduction, or charging a high fee may feel beyond their reach. We might wonder if women reducing their fees for their clients functions at times as a sublimation of their envy and deprivation. Through this defense, they empower their clients to self-advocate and get a good deal in therapy. The energy of the anger that they feel in not getting what they want may instead be channeled into helping their clients to surpass their own limitations.

The work of women in many societies has traditionally been done without financial compensation. The jobs of raising children and maintaining a household are assumed to be done out of love, with no monetary reward. Both sexes develop expectations of mothers as self-sacrificing and caring. Common transferential reactions may be anger at female therapists for not playing this selfless role or resentment of payment as a reminder that the therapist is not (only) offering therapy out of love. Countertransferential reactions of female therapists may be to downplay their need and desire for money.

Another hypothesis that Liss-Levinson proposed about the differences between male and female therapists' fees relates to early bonds. Most infants initially experience themselves as merged with their mothers, who are imagined not to have needs of their own. As boys grow older, they often have to give up this merged relationship with their mother to identify with their father. The father represents a separate individual with separate needs. A girl's development, however, often evolves without need for this break in relatedness. Because of this ongoing relationship, girls never experience themselves as completely separate. "The feminine sense of self," Liss-Levinson (1990) wrote, "is self in relation to others, while the masculine sense of self involves separation from others" (p. 127). Spelled out, a female therapist would be more aware of the connection between her earnings and her clients' spending on therapy, while a male therapist would tend to see his income in a separate category from his clients' financial situations. While this compelling explanation is certainly relevant in many families, it does not accurately reflect other family structures that exist.

Ella Lasky (1999) interviewed 60 psychotherapists about fee setting and other related parameters in the therapeutic contract. She found that two thirds of those surveyed expressed deep concern about the topic and noted dramatic gender differences in concerns about money and fees. Women were more likely to lower their fees for patients who seemed in need. Lasky, like Liss-Levinson, attributed this to higher empathy among women. The amount that men were paid was also significantly more important to the men than the amount that women were paid was to the women. This finding supports Liss-Levinson's (1990) theory that women tend to deny their desire and need for money, and perhaps that they are resigned to earning less. In another study, Lasky (1985) found that 75% of women charged lower fees than men of the same level of experience in the same geographical location. She offered several potential explanations. Like Liss-Levinson, she suggested that women may undervalue their work or men may overvalue theirs. In addition, she suggested that perhaps to many women, providing high-quality professional services was more important than the income earned for it. She suggested that this reality may be perpetuated because women compare themselves to female colleagues and men to male colleagues.

Lasky (1999) found that women tended to have more difficulty resolving their internal conflicts about money than men. In general, men were more comfortable setting fees, focusing on the amount of income needed to support their families. Women were usually torn between charging high fees and working long hours to generate the income they needed to support themselves and their families. Women articulated struggling between wanting to spend time with friends and families and awareness of the financial needs of their clients.

TIME: ANOTHER IMPORTANT VARIABLE

Another variable must be included in this discussion on money that shockingly has been absent from the money literature: time. Perhaps, time has been implicit; as the popular saying goes "time is money." Although closely related, time is a different dimension than money. Yet, issues about money may surface through time and vice versa. Like money, women in most cultures have not owned their own time until the 20th century in America. Women's time has been dedicated to selflessly serving others. Therefore, to charge money for their time, and to delineate when their time providing services begins and ends, is a relatively new role for women. In the therapeutic context, as with money, a common transferential reaction to a female therapist ending a session might be anger about her break from her traditional role. Likewise, women are more likely to feel reluctant to interrupt a patient to end in a timely fashion. I suspect that if a study were done looking at female versus male leniency about time, the results would probably show that women are more likely than men to have 50- rather than 45-minute sessions and to run over time in emotionally charged sessions. Among staff and trainees in my own current workplace, although the sample is small, a large majority of women hold 50-minute sessions, while a large majority of men choose 45-minute sessions.

Given the gender difference in approaches to fee and the discrepancy between incomes, and given all the suggested explanations for the differences, what should our goals as male and female psychotherapists be? Should women increase their fees and make an effort to value their time and work more highly? Should men try to be more flexible and democratic and perhaps question their own expertise more, like women? The first step is for all of us to begin addressing these questions and the exploration of the topic within ourselves, with our supervisors and supervisees, in our classes, and with our clients.

BACK TO MR. C.

The research reviewed here, together with the time variable, enables a deeper look and better understanding of the dynamics that occurred around money with Mr. C. during my first year of clinical training. In the session following the one described at the beginning of this chapter (about Mr. C.'s rapid departure from the room while paying), with much effort, I brought our attention to the moments surrounding the previous payment and asked about his experience of the encounter. Our conversation gravitated toward the topic of caring. He was able to articulate that he hoped that I cared about him and that paying the fee was a reminder that this was a job for me. In essence, as Liss-Levinson (1990) suggested, Mr. C. wanted me to be working with him because I cared, not because I would get paid. His hatred of his own job may have fueled his discomfort with paying for his appointments: In so doing, he had to realize that my being with him was my job. His traditional family upbringing, in which his mother raised him while his father worked, probably added to his transference toward me as a female nurturer.

My countertransferential experience was to want to fill that nurturing role. I wanted him to know that I genuinely *did* care and wanted to deemphasize the financial aspect of our arrangement. It is easy to see how collusion between therapist and client could occur around the socially uncomfortable topic of money. The fee was a set rate established by the director of the training clinic; therefore, my compensatory collusion occurred around time. I began to notice that I usually allowed sessions to run 5 to 10 minutes over, perhaps to show him that he was special to me. Likewise, he tended to be slow and casual about leaving. Had Mr. C. been working with a male therapist, he may have seen the work more as *work* and less as nurturing and consequently might have had less resistance to both ending and paying. Likewise, a male therapist may have been less inclined to embrace the role of nurturer.

Another reason that I realized I allowed sessions to run late was that Mr. C. was paying the top clinic fee; a part of me felt the need to make sure to give him his money's worth. This dynamic existed even though I was not earning any money from my work at the clinic. Likely, my shaky confidence in the value of my work was related both to being a novice and to some internalized devaluation of the work of women. Further, as Lasky (1985) suggested, providing a high-quality service was (and is) important to me. With supervisory support, I began to observe myself in the last minutes of sessions that I was having difficulty ending; the self-observation helped me realize that the reason why was usually that I did not want to cut Mr. C. (and other clients) off from sharing an experience or an emotion. My needs to feel and be perceived as a compassionate therapist propelled me to focus on Mr. C.'s momentary emotional needs above my needs to eat dinner, do readings for my classes, or attend to any other self-related purpose.

I pushed myself to address the tendency to run late in therapy with Mr. C. This led to an enlightening conversation about his dynamics around time and style of saying good-bye. Indeed, he revealed that he did not like good-byes and tended to drag them out. He related this difficulty with endings to the way he was prolonging his anticipated breakup with his girlfriend of 6 years, the issue for which he initially came to therapy. We discussed the more relaxed attitude about time in his mother's South Asian country of origin compared with his father's European country of origin. His preference for the time culture of his mother's country was connected with his alliance with his mother and anger at his father. As with discussions about money, talking about the meanings of time helped Mr. C. to understand both his predilections and behaviors.

Yet, only exploring meanings of time for Mr. C. was not enough. During this conversation, I took ownership for my own contributions to the sessions running late. While I did not discuss my specific dynamics around money, it was important to acknowledge reality: He had a partner in what had evolved between us. When I realized the extent to which endings were a pervasive issue for Mr. C., I suggested that we share the responsibility of ending sessions and introduced a clock into session that we would both be in charge of monitoring. He agreed, and we did increasingly end sessions on time. Yet, for most of the rest of the year, he often commented sarcastically about the clock, "Good thing we have the clock so we'll be *right* on schedule." Occasionally, he also continued to find ways to drag out "goodbye" and payment. For example, at least twice he said that he did not have enough cash and would have to get some at the cash machine downstairs. Although I told him he could pay the following session, he insisted on returning to pay me. Like paying, the clock was a reminder that my time and role with him were limited to a professional 50 minutes. Would he have felt and acted this way with a male therapist?

Overall, I worked with Mr. C. for 18 months. While much of the treatment focused on topics less relevant to this chapter, his awareness about his difficulty with endings increased, and the actions he took to avoid endings decreased. Termination with Mr. C. occurred by necessity because I finished my time working at the training clinic. In a letter that he sent to me after we ended, he let me know that he had finally broken up with his girlfriend not long after our last session. He ended the letter saying, "I guess I finally learned how to end." I suspect that the mutative therapeutic factors were balancing exploration of the meanings of money and time and concrete modeling of the mutual responsibility we had for maintaining these aspects of the frame. My clinical supervisor helped me with the fantasy-based aspects of the case, but I was on my own in figuring out how to concretely get paid and how to end. In retrospect, I am surprised that it did not occur to me or my supervisor to discuss these necessary concrete tasks. Perhaps they seemed too simplistic or obvious. The clinic expectations that I request payment in the therapy room at the end of each session and that I exit the room at the end of the hour forced me to confront these challenges, which I believe ultimately helped Mr. C.'s development as well as my own.

An important lesson that I learned from the treatment lay in my emotional response to Mr. C.'s pressure to act as a selfless caregiver and his consequent anger when instead I acted as a treatment-providing professional. My initial instinct was to collude with Mr. C. in pretending that the treatment was being done predominantly out of caring. Likely most female and many male therapists can relate to this pull, as it protects us from recognizing that we are doing therapy mainly to fulfill our own needs (including the need to feel helpful). Concurrently, I felt angry when Mr. C. used his money as a form of power to take control of when the session ended. While anger can be uncomfortable when we feel it toward a person we are supposed to be helping, my anger strengthened my resolve and lit up my courage to override my discomfort in bringing up the topics. I learned that protecting my needs by maintaining professional boundaries could, in fact, serve the treatment.

MY OWN EVOLUTION

Many of my recollections of Mr. C.'s treatment remain vivid because I explored the case in a paper I wrote about money during my first year of clinical training. The paper was an attempt to learn about this taboo topic and to process my own complex feelings about having clients pay to meet with me. In the paper, I wrote the following reflections and predictions:

> Gender, time and money and how the three dance together will be continuously awkward for me in my professional life. True to my traditional gender role, I am uncomfortable assuming authority, yet am ambitious, sensitive to being treated with condescension and furious when confronted by gender inequalities. I am fearful of hurting others' feelings, of being abrupt or making unrealistic demands, yet simultaneously aware of the sweat, debt and labor I am spending now so that one day I can delineate my time and fee, should I choose a private practice. Awareness of my own unique associations, anxieties and biases surrounding time and money, and those common to my gender, is vital preparation to be able to openly explore issues that arise in therapy. I accept, though I do not think I will ever enjoy, the awkward gender, time, money dance (Shanok, 2002).

Ten years later, while I have evolved and mastered areas that would have been difficult to imagine when I wrote this, aspects of my predictions still ring true. My current position, as an assistant director of a clinic, where I earn a salary and provide services that are free for clients, is a comfortable place to be. In this setting my need to earn money, and the amount that I earn, are separate from my clients' financial needs. I am not saddled with the task of charging them or discussing payment policies beyond "our services are free and available for matriculated students" or even of reminding them to stop by the front office to pay. Yet, the forces of money are still very much alive, and I realize that I am a more effective therapist if I listen for and address them with curiosity.

One of several reasons that I chose to start a private practice in addition to my full-time job was to confront my fears of managing the business side of a practice. While exploring the fantasy aspects of money to me was enlightening, I recognized that insight alone would not liberate me from my financial stuck places. Choosing a fee that was around the "going rate," as opposed to a low fee, was effortful for me. While I comforted myself with facts—I attended excellent training programs, had received good grades and evaluations and thus was well qualified—and though I felt that I was good at providing therapy, the going rate felt exorbitant and the act of charging it, daunting. Stating my fee to clients without qualifying my statement by quickly offering a sliding scale initially required anxiety tolerance. Bringing to mind strong female mentors who had modeled for me helped. Knowing that I would feel resentful if I was charging less than I was qualified to earn also helped. My self-prescribed exposure therapy has been effective, and I have gradually grown more comfortable managing the business side of my practice. Understanding that addressing money effectively in treatment is an ever-evolving process of learning, unlearning, trying out, staying a difficult course, and admitting mistakes can help us to have patience with our anxieties rather than foreclosing on these important and revealing aspects of therapy.

RECOMMENDATIONS FOR TRAINING

Training clinics should have clear policies and procedures, spelled out in their handbooks, about payment. In this way, clinics can model a direct and transparent approach to reality-based aspects of money. Trainees should be responsible for communicating payment information to their clients either prior to or at the first meeting. If a clinic has a sliding scale, the trainee should at least understand the method used to obtain the decided-on fee. If possible, the trainee should calculate the fee together with the clinic director or another supervisor. Ideally, trainees should be responsible for collecting fees from clients in order to get the hands-on practice.

It is not recommended that trainees determine the fee on their own. As trainees are usually paid little or nothing by training clinics, and any payment that they might receive is not connected to their clients' fee, the dynamics around payment are quite different from most other settings. In many cases, the trainee will be motivated to join the client in advocating for the lowest fee possible. Reasons for doing so may include not feeling that their work is worth much yet, particularly early in training. Trainees usually also feel more connected to their clients, who are human beings, than to the diffuse body of the clinic. It is not uncommon for trainees to feel resentful toward the clinic or larger education system. This may fuel them even more to bond with their clients as fellow underdogs in the system.

Payment-related issues should be discussed regularly in supervision, similar to issues around attendance and time boundaries. Raising the topic is the responsibility of both the trainee and the supervisor. Supervisors should normalize the discomfort that everyone can feel around financial interactions and discussions. Talking about payment issues in fact-based and fantasy ways should be modeled and encouraged by supervisors.

Trainees should learn both to explore meanings and motivations of clients' behaviors around payment and to set limits when appropriate. Cultural factors related to money and time for both clients and trainees should be addressed.

A conversation about money in supervision might begin with the supervisee describing the moments before, during, and after payment for a session. Client body language and perceived emotions as well as trainee emotions around the moments of payment will often provide useful information. Meanings of payment to both client and therapist in the context of the therapy should be explored. Client compliance or lack thereof with the frame should be made explicit. Supervisors should be notified when clients begin to run up balances. Supervisors might suggest phrases or model ways that they use to obtain payment and end sessions. Role plays might be useful.

All clinical training programs should offer at least one course addressing financial matters to trainees as they are beginning to do clinical work. The instructor should normalize the difficulty of discussing money issues and should be familiar with the policies and procedures of the training clinics in which the students are training. Course materials should illuminate reasons that addressing money is difficult; should review individual, cultural, and gender-related meanings of money; and should include case examples. Course assignments should encourage students to explore their own individual, cultural, and gender-related meanings that they attach to money and consider how these might have an impact on their clinical work. Ideally, such a class would be offered in a small practicum or seminar format in which class members take turns discussing relevant case materials.

RECOMMENDATIONS FOR PRIVATE PRACTICE

When establishing fee policies for our practices, we have many options to consider. Should I choose a set rate or sliding scale? If I choose a set rate, how much should I charge? If I choose a sliding scale, what should my range be? What information do I need to decide where on the scale a client fits? How often should I request to be paid? What forms of payment should I accept? Should these transactions be handled in person by me, by administrative staff, by mail, or online? Should I accept insurance? If so, which panels should I join? Even if I do not accept insurance, how much insurance paperwork am I willing to fill out so that clients with PPO (preferred provider organization) plans can be reimbursed? Each of these choices has implications.

Given our discomfort with money, distancing ourselves from the payment component of our practices will feel more comfortable to many of us.

For example, once-monthly bills sent by mail may feel emotionally easier than in-session weekly payment. However, the sooner and more direct payment is, the more information a therapist will have about the client. For example, if a client tends to be late with payment, this will be revealed and can be addressed sooner if payment is expected sooner. Discussions about money owed to the therapist will be easier for most therapists when the amount owed is lower. This also reduces the therapist's chances of incurring significant losses. Flexibility around one's policies may be useful with some clients and even enhance some treatments as long as the reasons for departure from one's usual procedures are understood and discussed.

Procedures and policies around money and time issues should be spelled out early in treatment. Herron and Welt (1992) strongly recommended that a client be informed about what he or she will pay for the first session even before arriving. Communicating clearly about the fee is simpler for therapists who have a set fee and less so but equally important for therapists who vary their rates. If the fee is established after the first few sessions, based on a client's financial circumstances, this should be explained. A common worry about being too transparent about how a fee is established is that clients may take advantage by not being fully honest about their financial situations. Yet, if clients are going to hide their financial means, they will likely do so no matter how much they know about how their therapist sets rates. In any case, the recommendation here is not that one's exact formula be explained (if one even has such a formula), but that the client knows how the process will progress. Referring back to the earlier example of my colleague, my colleague's therapist might have said to her, "During the next few sessions, we will be getting to know each other. In about three sessions, when I have a clearer sense of the concerns that bring you to therapy, the expected course of treatment, and your financial situation, we'll establish a fee." In addition to helping the client know what to expect, by modeling talking about the process, most clients will feel more ease in asking questions and talking about the topic as well. This will increase trust in the therapeutic alliance and decrease misunderstanding.

In my practice, I charge a set rate but am willing to reduce that rate for about a quarter of my caseload. One client whom I had treated for eight sessions of therapy at a university counseling center a year prior called me after graduation asking to be seen in my practice. Over the phone, I told her my fee. With disappointment in her voice, she told me her work and debt situations, and that she could not afford to see me. Knowing that she had a history of abuse that she learned to survive by attending closely to others' needs at the expense of her own, I was concerned that if I reduced my fee for her she would feel overly beholden to me. This could interfere with her using therapy fully and staying in therapy long enough to work through these issues. I told her that I would be willing to reduce my fee, but suggested that she think about how much she could afford to pay and that

I would think about how much I could afford to reduce my fee. The goal I proposed in determining these numbers was that neither of us feel resentful if we were to set the rate at the amount we chose. If the number that I chose was above the number that she chose, then I would help her find an affordable referral. My aim in negotiating the fee this way was to give myself time to think through my own needs, give her space to do the same, and assure her that I was attending to my needs so that she could focus on attending to hers. She called me again a few days later, and we were able to agree on the fee.

Therapists should understand their own meanings, attitudes, and habits around money and have clarity on their financial situations. Some questions that may be useful to ask ourselves as well as our clients about money include the following: What did you learn about money from each of your parents? What did you learn from other important family members? What moments in your childhood taught you about money, and what did you learn? How do those lessons influence you today? Are they appropriate to your current financial situation? When you monitor your choices about spending on a daily basis, what do you notice? For example, when choosing what to eat at a restaurant, where does cost factor in? What would it mean to order something very expensive? What would it mean to avoid ordering something expensive that you like? Considering questions like these in therapy can help you identify ways that you act and feel around money that are not optimal for your current financial and lifestyle circumstances. The next step is to adapt your behaviors and feelings to match your present reality—easier said than done, as our clients often remind us.

Recognizing when our own issues with money are interfering in our practices is important. Inability to establish consistent fee policies and avoidance of communicating clearly about fee policies with clients are both red flags. An ongoing failure to address odd payment behavior or significant breaches in the payment agreement by a client is another indicator that help may be needed. Obtaining a consultation or supervision from a therapist known to be competent in managing money-related issues is recommended. One should choose a supervisor with whom one can reveal what might feel like very personal information about one's experiences, attitudes, and beliefs about money.

CONCLUSION

A century ago, Freud (1913) wrote: "It seems more respectable and ethically less objectionable to acknowledge one's actual claims and needs rather than, as is still the practice among physicians, to act the part of the disinterested philanthropist" (p. 13). A hundred years later, we still need to be reminded. While many issues that were taboo in 1913 are now easily discussed, money remains almost as impenetrable as ever. We therapists pride ourselves on being able to deeply explore a vast range of difficult material and therefore may feel shame at the discomfort we have in addressing this everyday topic. Let's face it—discussing both fact and fantasy aspects of money may never be easy for most therapists and supervisors but should not be avoided. The more we do it, the more we learn and the easier it becomes.

Perhaps the mental health fields themselves suffer from gender identity splitting, between nurturance and empathy, and the need and expectation of professionals to earn their livings. If these two aspects of our jobs continue to be seen as contradictory and mutually exclusive, the topic of money will remain taboo in our helping professions. The motivations to nurture and have our basic needs met need not actually be antithetical. They are both necessary in the challenging work we do with our clients. These two ends of the traditional gender spectrum are dialectic, not mutually exclusive. Our capacity to see the connection between feeding others and ourselves will help each of us to become more flexible in our work. As we draw from a broader range of the gender spectrum in personal, training, and practice settings, I believe that our clinical fields of practice can only grow in their abilities to address the topic of money more openly and fully.

REFERENCES

American Psychiatric Association. (n.d.). *Gross income by gender among active respondents with a primary work setting of private practice.* Retrieved October 30, 2010, from http://www.psych.org/Resources/InterestGroups/ Women/HistoricalStatisticsonWomeninPsychiatry/Statisticsfromthe1980s/ GrossIncomebyGenderAmongActiveRepsondentswithaPrimaryWorkSetting ofPrivatePractice.aspx
Buck, S. (1999). The function of the frame and the role of fee in the therapeutic situation. *Women and Therapy, 22,* 37–50.
Burnside, M. (1986). Fee practices of male and female therapists. In D. Krueger (Ed.), *The last taboo.* New York: Brunner/Mazel, 48–54.
Dimen, M. (1994). Money, love, and hate: Contradiction and paradox in psychoanalysis. *Psychoanalytic Dialogues, 4,* 69–100.
Finno, A. A., Michalski, D., Hart, B., Wicherski, M., & Kohut, J. L. (2010). *Salaries in psychology 2009: Report of the 2009 APA salary summary.* Retrieved April 4, 2011 (http://www.apa.org/workforce/publications/09–salaries/report.pdf).
Freud, S. (1913). On beginning the treatment (further recommendations on the technique of psychoanalysis). In J. Strachey (Ed. & Trans.), *The standard edition of the complete psychological works of Sigmund Freud* (Vol. 12, pp. 123–144). London: Hogarth Press.
Heilman, M. E. (2001). Description and prescription: How gender stereotypes prevent women's ascent up the organizational ladder. *Social Issues, 57,* 657–674.

Herron, W. G., & Welt, S. R. (1992). *Money matters: The fee in psychotherapy and psychoanalysis.* New York: Guilford.

Langan, A. M., Shuker, D. M., Cullen, W. R., Penney, D., Preziosi, R. F., & Wheater, C. P. (2008). Relationships between student characteristics and self-, peer and tutor evaluations of oral presentations. *Assessment and Evaluation in Higher Education, 33,* 179–190.

Lasky, E. (1985). Psychotherapists' ambivalence about fees. In L. B. Rosewater & L. E. A. Walker (Eds.), *Handbook of feminist therapy: Women's issues in psychotherapy.* New York: Springer, 86–94.

Lasky, E. (1999). Psychotherapists' ambivalence about fees: Male-female differences. *Women and Therapy, 22,* 5–13.

Liss-Levinson, N. (1990). Money matters and the woman analyst: In a different voice. *Psychoanalytic Psychology, 7,* 119–130.

National Association of Social Workers. (2002). Social work income 2. *Practice Research Network, 1*(6). Retrieved October 25, 2010, from http://www.socialworkers.org/naswprn/surveyone/income2.pdf

Prince, M. (1993). Women, men and money styles. *Journal of Economic Psychology, 14,* 175–182.

Schneider, L. J., & Watkins, E. (1990). Perceptions of therapists as a function of professional fees and treatment modalities. *Journal of Clinical Psychology, 46,* 923–927.

Sentell, T., Pingitore, D., Scheffler, R., Schwalm, D., & Haley, M. (2001). Gender differences in practice patterns and income among psychologists in professional practice. *Professional Psychology: Research and Practice, 32,* 607–617.

Shanok, A. F. (2002). Gender, time and money: An awkward dance. Unpublished manuscript.

Shields, J. D. (1996). Hostage of the fee: Meanings of money, countertransference and the beginning therapist. *Psychoanalytic Psychotherapy, 10,* 233–250.

Soloman, S. E., Rothblum, E. D., & Balsam, K. F. (2005). Money, housework, sex, and conflict: Same-sex couples in civil unions, those not in civil unions, and heterosexual married siblings. *Sex Roles, 52,* 561–575.

Chapter 13

Dollars and sense
Cognitive biases and personal investing

Dan Grech

In 2010, I explored cutting-edge research into behavioral economics, behavioral finance, and neuroeconomics in a year-long series for the *Nightly Business Report* on PBS. Each of the 12 episodes looked at different cognitive biases, or common errors in investor judgment, and broke these biases down to explore their psychological and neurological bases.

This chapter, like the public television series, talks about money in a different way from the other, more psychoanalytically oriented, chapters in this volume. It is intended to offer a nonprofessional's view and a ground-level perspective of the emerging fields of neuroeconomics and behavioral finance. I lay out in simple terms how the fields developed, I share some of their most powerful insights, and I offer a framework for understanding what discoveries are going to come next.

To understand the revolution of behavioral economics, I must start first with Economics 101, the economics we learned in college, the economics of supply-and-demand curves. This standard model of economics is derived from certain basic assumptions, the most important of which is the assumption that people behave in ways to maximize their net worth. In other words, people look out for themselves and try to maximize their pleasure or their profit. Makes sense, seems logical, and this idea has dominated the field of economics. A second idea at the core of standard economics is that the market is an aggregation of rational actors who as a whole act efficiently. This is the efficient market theory.

Well, it became obvious over time that this economic model of rational actors and efficient markets had certain deficiencies. So, in the 1970s, two psychologists, Daniel Kahneman and Amos Tversky, began a series of seminal studies that took a psychological approach to matters in economies. One of their foundational discoveries came to be known as the theory of loss aversion. Loss aversion boils down to this basic idea: People dislike losing more than they like winning. For example, the pain experienced by someone who has $10 million, loses 8 million of those dollars, and is left with $2 million is greater than the happiness of someone who is simply handed $2 million. Standard economics would suggest both people have

$2 million; they should be equally happy. Loss aversion teaches us that they are not equally happy: The pain of loss is greater than the joy from the gift.

Kahneman and Tversky found that people will do quite a lot to avoid the pain of loss, including making decisions that actually work against their own self-interest. So much for the rational actor maximizing his or her net worth. The discovery of loss aversion paved the way for the field that came to be known as behavioral economics, which would look not at how people should behave but how they actually behave. For their insights, Kahneman and Tversky earned a Nobel Prize in Economics.

Since the 1970s, economists and psychologists have together been discovering how these biases and emotions affect the decisions we make as individuals and how the ways in which we are not rational and not efficient have an impact on the overall economy. The specific subgenre of behavioral economics that specifically looks at investment decisions is called behavioral finance. Then there is the emerging field of neuroeconomics. Neuroeconomics is a fancy term for brain scans of people making investment decisions to identify the loci in the brain for cognitive biases and emotions and to understand better the pathways through which these biases and emotions have an impact on our decisions. Neuroeconomics aims to use mental imaging and scanning to offer insights into why we act the way we act, why we have the biases that we have.

So, let us return to the example of loss aversion, the idea that people get more pain from losing than pleasure in winning. Brain scientists will stick someone in a magnetic resonance imaging (MRI) machine, and they will look at the person's brain while he or she is making a calculus of whether to do something. And scientists have learned that the reason, or one of the reasons, that people do not like loss is because when they experience a loss they experience pain—literal pain. Investment loss is felt in the exact part of the brain that actual physical pain is felt. You can say that to lose money is literally painful. This discovery offers new insight and a new perspective on why we act in the way that we do.

Now, is it irrational for us to feel pain with loss? No, it is hardwired into us. Loss aversion is not in any sense a choice. It is a permanent element of our psychological inheritance. All you can do is be aware of your natural tendency toward loss aversion, to mitigate and guard against it leading you to make bad decisions.

Contemporary behavioral economics suggests there are basically two ways in which we as investors mess up. The more obvious one is when we are too driven by emotions, specifically fear and greed. We saw great examples of greed followed by fear over the past decade, and it is not hard to see how feeling greedy can cloud our judgment. The second way we mess up is through a set of cognitive biases that factor into ways in which we make investment decisions. Think of a cognitive bias as essentially a flawed mental shortcut. As you know, humans are often smarter than computers, even though we do not have the computational ability of computers. That is because our intelligence is intuitive. Over the millennia we have created shortcuts to get to decisions better and faster. These shortcuts allow us to beat computers at chess. But sometimes the shortcuts short-circuit.

Before diving deeper, it is important to clear up one common misconception: For a person to act against his own self-interest because of a cognitive bias is not dimwitted, hasty, or even necessarily irrational. Most seemingly irrational economic behavior is not in fact irrational at all. It is merely a maladaption. Cognitive biases are derived from survival strategies inherited from our ancestors. These strategies have really good reasons for being there, and they more often than not serve us well. It is just that sometimes they steer us wrong.

With that framework, I wanted to talk about what insights behavioral economics can offer for the current economic crisis, known as the Great Recession. First, while the efficient market theory is intended to be a powerful explainer of market fluctuations, behavioral economics is by no means intended to be fully explanatory. In other words, you cannot explain the economic crisis through behavioral economics alone. But, you can talk about elements of the crisis that illustrate behavioral economics and cognitive biases in action.

A nice place to start a discussion of the current economic crisis is in terms of story and narrative. Take our prior major economic bubble, the late 1990s tech bubble. The tech bubble had a narrative associated with it, something along the lines of the following: We are right now in a new paradigm where the old rules of P/E (price-to-earning) ratios and P&L (profit-and-loss) statements no longer apply. Valuations of tech companies can suddenly skyrocket and still be accurate reflections of their value in the Internet economy.

Obviously, there is some truth to that narrative. We are indeed in a new paradigm. Many companies that emerged in the bubble years, such as Amazon and Google, have completely transformed the way we experience the world. But that narrative of a new paradigm where the old investment rules do not apply is what enabled and inflated the tech bubble.

Now, take the late 2000s housing bubble. One narrative at work was that home ownership is a part of the American dream. Subprime lending offered that dream to a larger swath of Americans than ever before, lower-income Americans who never before could own their homes. To be a part of the real estate boom, to buy (literally and figuratively) into the American dream of home ownership, was something an investor could feel good about. Never mind that there were good reasons that banks in the past were reluctant to take a chance on risky subprime borrowers. Another narrative at work during the housing bubble was that homes are a safe investment because housing prices always go up. Both of these narratives—that home ownership is part of the American dream and that homes are a safe investment—have a long history in our country, from Lyndon Johnson on. These are powerful stories that are told and retold in the media and around the dinner table, and they are part of the way in which these economic bubbles are formed.

Think back to 2003 and 2004, and it is likely that versions of these narratives were running through your head as you bought your inflated-priced apartment in the Upper East Side. Or more likely, you heard about a distant acquaintance making a killing on a real estate purchase, and that led you to say, "Oh, you know what, this new paradigm is actually true. Now's a great time to buy a home." You heard all these stories of people doing just what you were doing, and you had all of this ready evidence to support your theory that housing prices would continue to skyrocket, so it was a great time to buy a house. And you ignored any counterevidence that maybe your skyrocketing value theory did not make total sense. That is called confirmation bias. We tend to just look for or acknowledge evidence that confirms what we already believe to be true. Confirmation bias leads to bubbles because people are often blind to the evidence that contradicts their convictions. A rational actor would coolly evaluate all evidence, regardless of which "truth" we are rooting for, regardless of emotion. Turns out it is not that easy to absorb evidence that goes against our beliefs.

You can see other cognitive biases at work in the housing market. One of the most fundamental is the money illusion. The money illusion is the idea that people have a really tough time taking into account inflation when they think about value. Anyone who has ever purchased a house remembers the purchase price. But as the years pass, you do not adjust that price in your head to take into account inflation. When you look at the current market value of your home, you compare it to the price years ago at which you bought it. And you say, "Look, the market value is higher than the purchase price. I've made money on my house. It's been a great investment." Well, if you take into account inflation, that is not necessarily true. Historically, housing is not as surefire an investment as it has often presented to be. Over the long run, studies have shown that you are better off plowing your investment dollar into stock market index funds.

A specific example of the money illusion at play in the current housing bust is the allure of adjustable rate mortgages, those low teaser interest rates that increase, often dramatically, after a certain period of time. Because of the money illusion, people have trouble taking into account what happens when cheap teaser rates adjust upward. It is cognitively difficult for us to factor an adjustable rate mortgage into the long-term value of our home. The money illusion was at work when people got suckered into dubious mortgages they could not afford.

In the housing market, you will also find the anchoring bias. When you have a number in your mind—say, the price at which your neighbor just sold his home—that becomes the way that you measure value. That number acts like a mental anchor, and you use that number to gauge the value of things. Anchoring is a mental shortcut that allows you to sift through an avalanche of data and come to quick conclusions. But sometimes, this mental shortcut steers you in the wrong way. For instance, people tend to anchor the value of their home using the highest price at which a similar home was sold. For a long time, years even, after a housing market reaches its peak and values drop, sellers will hold on to their homes in hopes of finding a buyer willing to pay that outdated, unrealistic, pie-in-the-sky anchor price. This anchoring bias is particularly dangerous during a housing downturn, when holding on to a property means it loses value by the day. Finally giving up the anchor price becomes more painful by the day—and we know how painful monetary losses can be.

Another important bias is the availability bias. This bias is when people predict the likelihood of an event based purely on how easily an example can be brought to mind, by how available that example is. The availability bias, as applied to the housing market, is all the ready examples of people making fortunes speculating on the housing market because those examples were covered in the media or talked about during cocktail conversations. The availability bias might lead you to think that flipping houses is as easy as flipping burgers. A textbook example of availability bias is the lottery. After a lottery drawing, how many media reports do you see of the dejected multitude that did not win? None. You just see the one who wins, beaming on TV, holding a huge check. Crime is another great example of availability bias, one that also can have an impact on housing prices. Local news highlighting crime in your city makes you feel less safe than you should because media coverage makes you think crime is more prevalent than it really is. That can drive down the value of homes in neighborhoods perceived to be crime ridden—not by police stats, but by public perception, by mental availability.

Herding, the tendency to follow a crowd until you all fall off a cliff, is a cognitive bias that exaggerates both the upswing and downswing of a bubble. Simple logic would tell us that we should buy when the market is low (and there are bargains to be had) and sell when the market is high (and everything is overpriced). But we are not that cool, calm, collected rational actor from economic theory. Our tendency to follow the herd will often lead us to buy when the market is rising (causing prices to overinflate into a bubble) and sell when the market is falling (leading to a freefall in prices and a crash).

Hindsight is yet another bias. There is a tendency for you to Monday morning quarterback any situation. You will say in retrospect: It was obvious there was a housing bubble; I knew it all along, I just never stood up and said something about it. Well, that is the hindsight bias talking. In fact, you bought that overpriced condo, and now you are in foreclosure.

Relationships, so powerful in psychoanalysis, also play a role in investing. There is the relationship people have with their investment advisor, whose steep fees often run to the financial detriment of the investor. Or there is the relationship people have with the company where they work, leading them to buy stock in their own company and hold it. Employees tend to hang on to their company's stock because they have an affective relationship, a fondness for where they work. It is about emotion. But it is also risky. To further invest in a company you are already so deeply invested in—the company, after all, is paying your salary and guaranteeing your livelihood—is a dubious investment decision to say the least. It is far better to diversify your holdings.

So, we have these biases, these ingrained mental pathways, these cognitive shortcuts that have an impact on and imperil our investment decisions. How can we avoid making these mistakes? The advice boils down to two things. One is being knowledgeable about your tendency to make these errors. That makes you more likely to recognize a cognitive bias and avoid it. The second way is to put in place a system that does not allow you to change your behavior because of movements in the market. Creating this system means establishing certain heuristics, or rules, about how you invest your money. One such system is dollar-cost averaging, which means investing equal amounts of money regularly over specific time periods (say, $250 a month into your Roth IRA account).

An alternative to this second approach is to hire a really good adviser who makes all your investment decisions for you. But watch your advisor closely; he or she is slave to the same biases you are. And your advisor's self-interest may run counter to your own. Advisors are often paid a commission to peddle certain investment vehicles that may—or may not—be in your best financial interest. Behavioral economists digging into investment advisors recently made this startling discovery: Overconfident advisers tend to be more trusted. Overconfidence, which in and of itself is incredibly risky when investing, creates advisors that are more persuasive. That leads people to follow their dubious advice.

Public policy has gotten wind of the findings of behavioral economics, and economist Richard Thaler has helped popularize an approach known as libertarian paternalism. At the center of this theory is the concept of choice architecture. The idea is that the way in which you set up choices for people influences to a great extent the decisions they eventually make. Take 401(k) retirement plans. In the past, people had to sign up for a 401(k) plan. Now most companies force you to opt out of a 401(k) plan. That simple choice architecture—opt out instead of sign up—dramatically changes the percentage of people who participate in their retirement plan. For a variety of reasons, people tend to stick with the option that they are given, so by simply tweaking the choice architecture, you can make profound changes in the way people invest their money. Another great example of choice architecture is when you renew your driver's license, you are asked if you want to be an organ donor. This simple act of tying the choice to be an organ donor with the process of getting a driver's license has increased by many times the number of organ donors.

The Obama administration is influenced heavily by choice architecture. Richard Thaler coauthored the book *Nudge* with Obama administration regulatory czar Cass Sunstein, and the way the administration structures much of its regulatory policy is influenced by libertarian paternalism.

Neuroeconomists in recent years have identified the bases in our brain chemistry for many of these biases. First, here is a terribly oversimplistic primer on the brain: Imagine the brain is like an old house with additions tacked on over the years. You have the reptilian brain, the fight-or-flight versus phew-I'm-safe part of your brain. Then, you have some additions to give you the functionality of the brain of a mammalian ape. And then tacked on the front is the latest and greatest addition, brain 3.0, the prefrontal cortex, which is where higher reasoning happens. The prefrontal cortex is fighting against the reptilian brain for control. Your brain is literally at war with itself, and you can see this in brain scans. It is a battle between the reptilian emotional centers and the human cognitive rational centers. Which side is going to win? Often in this tug of war, a person comes to the rational decision. But sometimes, the emotional or nonrational parts of the brain overwhelm other parts of the brain so you do not make the best decisions. That is where the cognitive biases come in.

Take the money illusion. Neuroscientists have actually located the part of the brain that processes value and the specific region where the money illusion appears to crop up. In brain scans, you can actually identify which brains are not making the cognitive leap to take inflation into account.

A powerful example of the insight that brain science can lend behavioral economics comes out of a study conducted at Emory University on herding. Remember, herding is the idea that people tend to follow the crowd. The pop evolutionary explanation of herding is that there is safety in numbers, so over the millennia we have come to rely on others for cues in terms of how to act. If we see others running from something, we are going to run away as well. Well, perhaps because of that evolutionary conditioning, or perhaps because of the way the brain constructs reality, herding behavior has a powerful locus in the brain. What those Emory scientists found is when people around us have a certain perception of reality, that influences what our brain sees. Other people's perceptions can actually influence the image registered by our eyes. Think of the eyes as a projector onto the back of the brain. So, that image projected onto the back of the brain actually changes through the statements and actions of the people around you.

The Emory researchers discovered this startling fact by taking two geometric shapes and placing them side by side. The viewer then had to decide if the shapes were identical but rotated a bit or were slightly different. It is a relatively easy computational problem. It should only take a second or two to distinguish whether the shapes are the same or different. In isolation, people are very good at figuring this out: 95% of the time they will get it right. But, when you add two people to the room who are voting in the wrong direction, it is likely that you will also get it wrong. And you will get it wrong not because they have influenced you, but because their presence literally changes the way you see the shapes inside your brain. You literally perceive something different from what is on the screen. This is a really powerful finding because it shows that herding is not simply a bias. You are actually responding correctly to the incorrect information that you are seeing. This bit of brain science lends a powerful understanding of why herding is such a seductive, universal, and unavoidable behavior. Herding is clearly not simply irrational. More broadly speaking, brain science is offering new insights into why we do what we do, how cognitive biases crop up, and why they are so hard to avoid.

The promise of neuroeconomists is enormous and alluring. We are just scratching the surface of the insights that it can lend to our behavior. The search is on to find a basis in the brain for every behavior, bias, or emotion. But rather than wax poetic about the possibilities, I conclude with a word of caution. After surveying the research, there is reason to be skeptical about how many answers neuroeconomics can really provide. So far, and perhaps forever, the promise of neuroeconomics will far outstrip the findings. The stack of past-due bills reaches into the sky. My sense is even as the quality of brain scans improves, neuroeconomics will not be able to answer all of the questions the field wants to answer. The brain is just too complex, too nuanced, too human: Good old classic economics, flawed as it is, seems to be here to stay.

REFERENCES

Berns, G. (2008). *Iconoclast: A neuroscientist reveals how to think differently.* Watertown, MA: Harvard Business School Press.

Thaler, R. H., & Sunstein, C. R. (2008). *Nudge: Improving decisions about health, wealth, and happiness.* Ann Arbor, MI: Caravan Books.

Index

A

Abandonment
  family of origin, 145, 151
  parents fear of, 41
Abuses involving money, 11
Acknowledging therapist
  needs, patients, 150
Adjustments in life, 64
Adult children, *see also* Children
  dominating parents, 41
  envy of wealthy parents, 45
  expectations of parents, 40–41
  maturity, 41–42
  overgratification from
    parents, 42–43
  prolonged dependency, 41–43, 137
Affluenza, 37
African Americans, 145
Ahab, King, 56
Alienation, 108–110
Alienation in Perversions, 109–110
Ambitions
  assertion of self, 145
  projected onto patients, 17, 19
Analysts
  amassing wealth, limitations, 40
  anxiety about money, 2, 99–100
  being a patient, 145
  compulsive caretakers as
    children, 144
  denial of greed, 16–17
  desiring, trouble with, 145
  fear of becoming impoverished,
    8–9, 29
  hiding inferiority and
    adequacy feelings, 17–19
  inadequacy feelings, 18

  patients projecting onto, 37
  refusal to disclose fee, 1
  relating to patient's world, 39
  treatment of, 55–56
  wealth in the mind of, 31–32
"Analyst to the great," 31
Analytic schadenfreude, 31
Anchoring bias, 188–189
Anger issues, avoidance, 15
Anonymous stance, 45, 50
Antimaterialism, 31, 41
Appearance focus, 37, 51
Assessing financial situations
  method of determining, 11
  unresolved problems,
    impact on fees, 6–7
Attendance, training
  recommendations, 178,
    see also Missed sessions
Autonomy, 41, 130
Availability bias, 189

B

Bad luck, blaming, 38
"Bad them," projected onto
  patients, 17
Balance, wiping out, 157–160
Behavior, lack of consequences, 39
Behavioral economics, 190–191
Berger, Brenda, *xv–xviii,* 59–73
Biblical commandments, 56
Big bang theory, 119
Billing procedures, 10, *see*
    also Payments
Billionaires, 55
Blackmailing, 135, 152

out of love, 155–156
vignette, 79–82
wiping out balance
vignette, 157–160
Friends
children's interest in, 133–134
referrals, 16
sharing therapy with, 135–136

G

G., R. (famous analyst), 57
Gay therapists, 172
Gekko, Gordon, 41
Gender and money
earnings of self-
employed, 170–173
fundamentals, 165–166
reasons for money talk
taboo, 167–169
taboo, money discussion, 166–167
time, 173–174
Gender roles
challenged, 41
spouses of wealthy, 27–28
General-purpose money, 115–117
Get-rich-quickism, 72
Glick, Robert Alan, 21–33
Gluttony, 45
Goethe, 114
Golden prison, 33
Golden years, psychoanalysis, 106
GoldVish, 62
Goodbyes, 165, 174–177, 179
"Good me," projected onto
patients, 17
Good omnipotence, 71
Governess example, 1263
Grandiosity
contributing factor, subprime real
estate market crash, xvi
dilemmas, self-made wealth, 28
fantasies as protection, 25
Gratitude from wealthy, 31
Great Recession
impact on clinicians, xvi
impact on patients, xv
Grech, Dan, 185–192
Greed
in age of affluence, 43–45
fees for wealthy, 37–38
Gekko, Gordon, 41

introjection, 46
response to, 105
Seven Deadly Sins, xvi, 39
"Greed" decade, 103
"Greening of America," 41
Guilt
central preoccupation, 38
and fears, 29–30
lack of, sociopath trait, 57
traditional guilty man, 38

H

Hate, love and, paradox, 117–119,
122–124, 153
Haves/have-nots
gap between, 35, 103
identification of, 37
Herding, 51, 189, 191–192
Hindsight bias, 189
Hirsh, Irwin, 13–19
Holding onto patients, 7–8, 14
Hospital and clinic settings, 2, 75
Housing bubble, 187–188
Hurting others, little apology over, 39
Hypocrisy, 18
Hysterical misery, 105
Hysterical therapists, 149

I

Illness, expensive, 108
Image, family pressure to
maintain, 5
Immortality fantasies, 25, 73
Impoliteness, 24
Impostor feelings, 145–146
Impoverishment, fear of, 8–9, 29
Income, loss of, 14
Independence, 16
Individuality, not limited by, 114
Individuation, 41
Inflation, taking into account, 188
Inherited wealth, 24–25
Inner work, doing only so much, 65
Interesting patients, 16
Intergenerational transmission,
meaning of wealth, 23–24
Intersubjectivity, 144
Introjection
greed, 46
understanding the patient, 96